S. E. A. L. S. III

SELF-ESTEEM AND LIFE SKILLS: 3rd in a series

reproducible activity-based handouts created for teachers and counselors

A sampler collection of . . .

Coping Skills	Independent Living/Transition Skills	Relationships
Expressive Therapy	Interpersonal Skills	Self-Awareness
Fear	Leisure	Self-Esteem
Goal Setting	Making Changes	Spirituality
Grief	Positive outlook	Stress Management
Humor	Recovery	Supports

Authors: Kathy L. Korb-Khalsa, OTR/L and Estelle A. Leutenberg

Illustrated By: Amy Leutenberg Brodsky, MSSA, LISW

WELLNESS REPRODUCTIONS & PUBLISHING, LLC
A Guidance Channel Company

D1225642

THANK YOU!

To Amy Leutenberg Brodsky . . .

our Wellness Reproductions and Publishing artist, whose creativity and skill as an illustrator, and experience with adolescents, gave the SEALS III book unique, humorous, and meaningful artwork, and whose insights from her clinical work offered guidance on the content as well. Amy Leutenberg Brodsky, Licensed Social Worker, received her Masters of Science in Social Administration from the Mandel School of Applied Social Sciences, Case Western Reserve University. Her art training was received at Kent State University where she achieved a BFA in Studio Art. She continues to pursue her career as an artist, as well as facilitating wellness with members of the community in crisis.

To our supportive WELLNESS Team:

Joan Allison, Wendy Carlton, Maria Hamilton, Ferne Hutchison, Judy Lynch, Christine Longley, Caroline Neillie, Robert Neillie, Tonya Prince, Cecily Ramsey, Lucy Ritzic, OTR/L, Richard Szafarski and Lavonda Talbert.

To Shayna, Arielle and Mason . . .

for being the right age at the right time as we compiled this book and for openly sharing their life experiences and thoughts with us.

Mom and Bubby

To SD and Jay . . .

for being understanding of our time and coffee and tea needs as we write, yet, another book!

Kathy and Estelle

WELLNESS REPRODUCTIONS AND PUBLISHING, LLC, A Guidance Channel Company, is an innovative company which began in 1988. As developers of creative therapeutic and educational products, we have a strong commitment to the mental health and educational professions. Our rapidly growing business began by authoring and self-publishing the book LIFE MANAGEMENT SKILLS I. We have extended our product line to include group presentation posters, therapeutic board games, various EMOTIONS© identification products, the LIFE MANAGEMENT SKILLS and SEALS book series and cards, the Poster Series, skill building cards, and educational products about serious mental illness. Our books are created with feedback from our customers. Please refer to the last page of this book, our "FEEDBACK" page, and let us hear from YOU! This book was created with feedback from our customers and adapted for middle school through high school from LIFE MANAGEMENT SKILLS V and VI. It was preceded by SEALS+PLUS, adapted from LIFE MANAGEMENT SKILLS I and II, and SEALS II adapted from LIFE MANAGEMENT SKILLS III and IV, all available from the vendor where you purchased this book.

We dedicate SEALS III to our
Aunt and Great Aunt Bessie Leutenberg
who, at age 95, continues to inspire us with her
independent living skills, positive outlook and great sense of humor
... as well as her total acceptance and unconditional love!

Special thanks to the following therapists, counselors and educators, whose submissions of activity handouts for Life Management Skills V and VI were selected and adapted for SEALS III.

The Facilitator's Information Sheet on the back of each handout has a box identifying the submitters and the adaptors.

Deena Baenen, COTA/L, LSW*

Elana S. Blachman, OT

Trish Breedlove, OTR/L*

Erika Clements, O.T. Reg (Ont), Sip. Add.*

Nancy Day, O.T. Reg

Marta Felber, M.Ed.

Joanne Garofalo, COTA/L

Rick Germann, MA, LPC

Martin B. Golub, CTRS

Mary Lou Hamilton, MS, RN

Janell Horton, MSW

Allen Klein, MS, CSP

K. Oscar Larson, OT, MA*

Doris Lewis, CTRS

Barbara Lundberg, OTR/L

Mark S. Macko, LMHC, CRC

Bettie E. Michelson, MS*

Sandi Miller, RRT

Kerry Moles, CSW

Esterlee A. Molyneux, MS, SSW

Maggie Moriarty, M.S., COTA/L*

Nan Muder, COTA/L

Sandra Netto, MSW

Susan Olko, COTA/L

Roberta Jean Ott, COTA, TASW

Glenda Pritchett, Ed.S., LPC

Joan Rascati, ADL's Program Mgr.

Lori Rosenberg, MS, CTRS, RTCR*

Mandy, K. Russman, OTS

Debbie Sacerich, LSW

Nina Beth Sellner, M.Ed.

Rev. Donald Shields, BRE., MTS

Elaine Hyla Slea, M.Ed.*

Laura Stergar, SWA

Emily R. Thier, OTS

Mary Kaye Tilden-Walker, LSW

Shirley K. Trout, M.Ed.

Allison Unda, LMSW

Michele Vitelli, BA*

Betty Welch, MS, Ph.D.

Jennifer Whitten, MA, A.T.R.-BC

Robin Wildbur, OTR

Marla Yoder-Tiedt, MSW, LISW

* Contributed Handout(s) in SEALS II

Thank you to the following professionals who adapted pages from Life Management Skills V and VI (that were originally written for adults) to pages suitable for youth from middle school through high school. Their input was invaluable!

Bonny Reed-Bell, OTR/L

Jennifer Campo, COTA

Sheila Freeman, MSW, CSW

Ann M. Fresoli, MA, CAC

Lisa Kvas, Advisor

Susan Miller, OTR/L

Sandra Negley, MTRS, CTRS

Elaine Hyla Slea, M.Ed.

Julie Stoelzel, MSW, LICSW

Robin Teoli, PhD

INTRODUCTION

The inspiration for the LIFE MANAGEMENT SKILLS SERIES originated from an ongoing practical need observed within a mental health setting. Handouts had been typically used in treatment as a launching pad for activities, an organizational tool, a visual aid, a tangible reminder of information presented and as a method for building rapport. However, available handouts often did not meet necessary, high-quality standards in content desired, format, appearance, and organization - and lacked copyright permission for reproduction.

We have attempted to meet these standards by offering this collection of handouts which are highly reproducible, organized in 18 logical units, designed for specific well-defined purposes, and activity-based, allowing for extensive student involvement. The graphic representations are intentionally different from handout to handout in typestyle, art and design, to increase visual appeal, provide variety, clarify meaning and initiate and stimulate class discussions.

SEALS III is a selection of 80 activity handouts from LIFE MANAGEMENT SKILLS books V & VI. It was preceded by SEALS+PLUS, a selection of 75 activity handouts from LIFE MANAGEMENT SKILLS books I & II and SEALS II, 80 handouts from LIFE MANAGEMENT SKILLS books III and IV. They have all been adapted for use with middle school through high school-aged students. Illustrations, language and content have been focused to be age-appropriate and meet the concerns and needs of this population.

The book has been designed to offer reproducible handouts on the front of each page and nonreproducible facilitator's information on the reverse side. The Teacher/Facilitator's Information Sheet (reverse of each handout) includes the following sections: Purpose, General Comments, and Possible Activities; Activity A designed for the middle school student, Activity B for the high school student.

Supplemental pages include two pages of role-plays and a glossary of the challenging terms on the fronts of the handouts.

We specifically chose spiral binding to allow for easier and accurate reproduction, an especially white paper for clear, sharp copies and a heavier paper stock for its durability and opacity. If adaptations to any of the handouts are desired due to sensitivity of content or desire to individualize group needs, it is recommended to make one copy of the handout, include the additions or omissions which will meet your specific needs, and then use this copy as the original.

We hope you find these handouts fun, innovative and informative. Try to incorporate students' input in planning and presenting SEALS sessions, to promote variety, facilitate learning, and individualize sessions. We wish you much success with your educational endeavors and hope we can be of assistance again in the future. Remember . . . creative handouts will hopefully generate creative activities and contribute to a greater sense of WELLNESS!

Wellness Reproductions and Publishing, LLC

Kathy L. Korb-Khalsa   *Estelle A. Leutenberg*

EDITORS' NOTE: When you read 'in conjunction with', on some of the Facilitator's Information Sheets, under III. POSSIBLE ACTIVITIES:, we are referring to pages from the two previous SEALS books: SEALS+PLUS and SEALS II as well as the pages within SEALS III. The suggested activity pages may support and enhance your session. These books are available from the same vendor where you purchased this SEALS III book.

TABLE OF CONTENTS - by Topic

See Supplemental Pages following page 80 - Apartment Hunting Crossword, Real-Life Situations (Role Plays) and Glossary.

TABLE OF CONTENTS - by Handout

Page numbers are on the Facilitator's Information Sheet, located on the reverse side of each handout.

COPING COMPONENTS

attitudes, patterns, goals, activities, strength, trust

PARTS OF A TREE

PARTS OF A TREE	PURPOSE
1. The roots	anchor
2. The bark	protection
3. The trunk	support
4. The branches	balance
5. The leaves	lifegiving energy
6. The fruit	reward

YOUR PERSONAL COPING "TREE"

COPING COMPONENTS
Use Above List

PURPOSE

1. Your anchor _____ (What is keeping you "grounded?")

2. Your protection _____ (Your defense mechanisms: what works, what doesn't, what needs to be "shed"?)

3. Your support _____ (Who gives you help/caring, encouragement?)

4. Your balance _____ (How do you take care of yourself?)

5. Your source of energy _____ (What keeps you going, gives you hope, lifts your spirit?)

6. Your reward _____ (What do you want for yourself?)

coping tree

coping tree

I. PURPOSE:

To expand coping skills' repertoire by identifying specific coping components.

II. GENERAL COMMENTS:

A familiar and universal form of a tree can be used as a metaphor. There are basically six parts of a tree; the root, bark, trunk, branches, leaves and fruit. Each part can be compared to six corresponding coping components; attitudes, patterns, goals, activities, trust and inner strength.

III. POSSIBLE ACTIVITIES: It is recommended that this page be used in conjunction with COPING COSTS AND BENEFITS, page 2.

A. 1. Draw a large, simple image of a tree (as outlined in the handout) including representative roots, trunk, branches, etc., on a wipe-off board or flip chart.
   2. Provide impetus for discussion by asking students to review information that they already know about trees. Possible answers might include: largest plant, home for animals, gives food to other animals and humans, provides shade, fuel, oxygen. Our world would be incomplete without them.
   3. Instruct the class to be specific in identifying each part of the tree along with the functions of a tree in terms of how important and inter-related each part is. Instruct the class to explain what would happen to the tree if any part of it were missing, not working or was damaged.
   4. Distribute handouts. Instruct students to label parts of tree in diagram, reviewing functions of each part.
   5. Explain to the class that for this exercise, each part of the tree has a corresponding relation to a different coping skill.
   6. Ask students to match the six questions regarding their personal coping trees with the six words in the box labeled "Coping Components." Instruct students to write the corresponding term on blank paper.
      a. Which term from the box is your anchor that keeps you in one place emotionally? Possible response: Attitude (beliefs, thoughts about self)
      b. Which term from the box represents what you use for protection when attitudes, thoughts, beliefs are being challenged or questioned? Possible response: Patterns (defense mechanisms/coping strategies)
      c. Which term from the box represents who can you count on for support? Possible response: trust (support system)
      d. Which term from the box represents how you take care of yourself in terms of managing your time/reducing undue stress? Possible response: activities
      e. Which term from the box represents your energy source, what keeps you going, what gives you hope? Possible responses: Inner strength. (Self-awareness)
      f. Which term from the box represents your reason/payoff, what you want for your life? Possible response: goals, (desires)
   7. Generate a discussion on the inter-relation of each coping skill or the value and importance of expanding coping skills.
   8. Process by asking students to complete an inventory of their personal coping tree by answering questions in last section labeled "Purpose."
   9. Suggested supplementary activity: Book talk using The Giving Tree by Shel Silverstein.

B. 1. Draw a large, simple image of a tree (as outlined in the handout) including representative roots, trunk, bark, branches, etc., on a wipe-off board or flip chart.
   2. Supplement with focus on separate coping skills utilizing SEALS+PLUS, SEALS II, and SEALS III handouts.

Attitude	- "Positive Mental Attitude"	SEALS II	- page 14
Support	- "No One is an Is-land"	SEALS+PLUS	- page 63
Protection	- "Coping Costs and Benefits"	SEALS III	- page 2
Balance	- "Balance Your Life"	SEALS+PLUS	- page 69
Activities	- "Leisure Scavenger Hunt"	SEALS II	- page 27
Inner Strength	- "Inner Voice"	SEALS II	- page 79

   3. Process with discussion of importance and challenges of specific coping skill development.

Activity handout and facilitator's information originally submitted for Life Management Skills V by Mark S. Macko, LMHC, CRC, Sarasota, FL. Mark is a program therapist and chief clinician at a mature adult counseling center of a hospital.
He has a part time private practice with emphasis on depression, grief and aging issues.
Mark writes songs and poems, plays 12-string guitar and is a former graphic artist.

Adapted for SEALS III from LMS V by Elaine Hyla Slea, M.Ed., Euclid, OH,
adaptor of *SEALS+PLUS (Self-Esteem and Life Skills)* and *SEALS II.*

COPING: COST$-AND-BENEFITS

Most adults know what it means to be "stressed out". It usually means that they have too much to cope with in their lives and feel overwhelmed. Kids get stressed out too, but may have a more difficult time recognizing what they feel and why they feel overwhelmed. People often try to feel better about themselves and their situations by using defense mechanisms or coping strategies. Some can be healthier than others.

Look over the list of coping strategies and behaviors below. Put a check mark (✔) in the box when you identify ways that you deal with events in your life.

COPING STRATEGIES & BEHAVIORS

☐ When you avoid an emotional issue by doing something unhealthy (not eating, bingeing, spending spree) you are **ACTING OUT.**

☐ Helping others instead of dealing with your issues is called **ALTRUISM.**

☐ Imagining how others might react if you do something is using a behavior called **ANTICIPATION.**

☐ Pretending that nothing is wrong or exaggerating the issue are examples of **DENIAL & DISTORTION.**

☐ "Spacing out" or daydreaming is using **DISSOCIATION.**

☐ Breaking the tension with something funny is called using **HUMOR.**

☐ Using physical problems to ignore emotional problems, is being a **HYPOCHONDRIAC.**

☐ Following someone else's behavior as a model is using **IDENTIFICATION.**

☐ Wanting to know the facts and logic to avoid unpleasant emotions is called trying to **INTELLECTUALIZE.**

☐ Avoidance of being with other people to hide problems is part of **ISOLATION.**

☐ Being **PASSIVE AGGRESSIVE** means getting your own way by intentionally not doing anything.

☐ Thinking that someone else has the problem is using **PROJECTION.**

☐ Reverting back to old habits is a form of **REGRESSION.**

☐ Holding back emotions during certain situations is **SUPPRESSION.**

INSIGHT BOX

COPING STRATEGY		BENEFITS	COSTS
EXAMPLE	TYPE		
Tantrums	regression	attention, got your way, old familiar behavior	won't always work you'll be called a "baby"
"There's nothing wrong"			
"Can I go see the nurse?"			
Dyeing your hair a bright color before a family dinner you didn't want to attend			
"Just leave me alone"			
"Did you ever hear the joke about . . ."			
Eating a whole bag of cookies			

Awareness is oftentimes the first step in making healthy changes.
Investigate your coping strategies.

COPING:
COSTS-AND-BENEFITS

I.   PURPOSE:

To increase understanding of defense mechanisms/coping strategies.
To investigate potential costs and benefits of these avoidance mechanisms.

II.   GENERAL COMMENTS:

A variety of methods are used to cope with situations in our lives. Each strategy or behavior has costs and benefits. Some of the costs and benefits may be short term, and others long term. People learn coping strategies and behaviors at different times during the course of a lifetime. Certain strategies may have desired results that are productive for some time period.

Often when someone is in a crisis, s/he is attempting to use a coping strategy or behavior with which s/he is familiar, but which does not work in that situation. This individual may need to become aware that the costs now outweigh the benefit of that strategy and to consider alternatives. It is important therefore to review how behavior is being used as a coping strategy, and what alternative strategies are needed in current or future crises.

III.   POSSIBLE ACTIVITIES:

A. 1. Instruct class to provide examples of 'excuses' that they have heard or observed in school when a student might be avoiding the completion of an assignment. For example, "He had my book", "I forgot", "My computer crashed." Introduce topic.

2. Distribute handouts.

3. Discuss the concepts of defense mechanisms as coping strategies and behaviors, and define the terms on the list, giving examples and encouraging note-taking in the blanks for future reference.

4. Divide class into pairs and assign each pair a number from 1 to 14. This number then corresponds to the list of coping strategies on the front of the handouts.

5. Give 5-10 minutes for each pair to prepare a brief 'infomercial' selling the costs and benefits of the assigned defense mechanism. Each pair is going to give a presentation for the class. Instruct the pairs that their objective is to persuade the class that their strategy is the best way to deal with life. One member of the pair will give the 'sales pitch' for the benefits of this strategy; and the other member will give the pitch for the costs. (This is intended to raise questions, especially when defending more immature strategies or behaviors.) Promote an atmosphere of wit, sarcasm and silliness to get their points across.

6. Listen to all pairs' presentations. Instruct audience to write down or list specifics from each presentation, which were outstanding or raised questions.

7. Discuss how persuasive each pair was.

8. Process with a discussion of the risks of getting talked into, or falling into the habit of using a coping strategy without considering and evaluating the risks.

B. 1. Before session, collect back issues of newspapers, scissors, tape or paste, blank paper. Select only the local, national or world news sections.

2. Distribute handouts.

3. Discuss the concepts of defense mechanisms as coping strategies and behaviors, define the terms on the list.

4. Divide the class into subgroups of 2 students.

5. Distribute the newspapers, scissors, blank paper and paste to each pair. Assign each pair one of the coping strategies from the list on front of handout. Instruct students to read the news articles (the self-help or advice columns are recommended) and to locate an article, which illustrates the use of their assigned coping strategy.

6. Instruct each pair to cut out the article. After gluing it onto the blank paper, each pair is instructed to identify and label information contained in the article emphasizing crisis, described persons involved, which strategy was used, circumstances, results, costs and benefits.

7. Instruct each pair to brainstorm for alternative behaviors to the crisis and to prepare for a presentation to the class.

8. Listen to all pairs' presentations, listing strategies and alternative behaviors on board.

9. Process by leading class through a reexamination of the discussion topic, stimulating awareness of coping strategies.

Activity handout and facilitator's information originally submitted for Life Management Skills V by
K. Oscar Larson, OTR/L, MA, Alexandria, VA.
Oscar contributed to SEALS II and is a supportive colleague of Wellness Reproductions & Publishing, Inc.

Adapted for SEALS III from LMS V by Elaine Hyla Slea, M.Ed., Euclid, OH,
adaptor of *SEALS+PLUS (Self-Esteem and Life Skills)* and *SEALS II.*

FIRST+AID
FOR LIFE

emotionally

When I am hurt, I need . . .

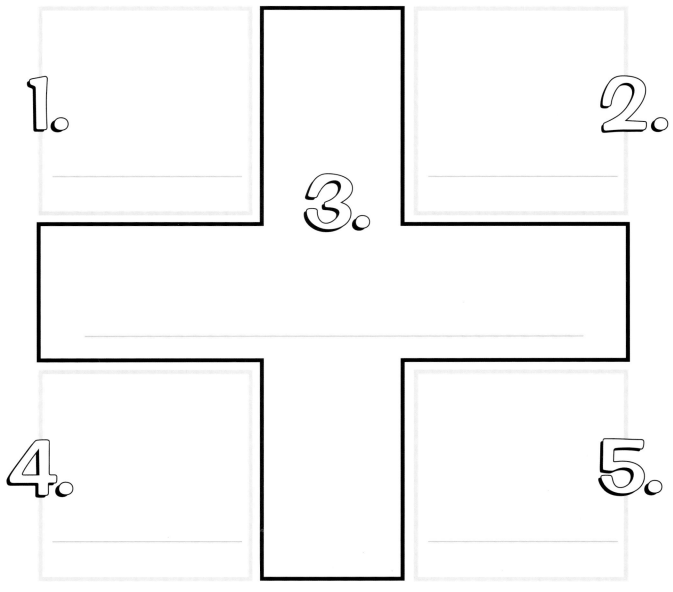

1.

2.

3.

4.

5.

. . . to heal.

FOR LIFE

I. PURPOSE:

To identify differences between physical and emotional pain as well as alternative ways of healing.

II. GENERAL COMMENTS:

Young people often have difficulty recognizing and expressing emotional pain. An enjoyable and supportive activity, done in a safe environment, can help to identify and validate the pain as well as the different ways of healing.

III. POSSIBLE ACTIVITIES:

A. 1. Facilitate discussion on the topic of first aid. Direct discussion to include conventional versus alternative remedies. Conventional medicine looks at health as an absence of disease and will use tests, medications, surgery and radiation as key tools for dealing with physical problems. Alternative medicine tends to view health as a balance of body systems, emotional, physical, mental, etc. Instruct students to list benefits of knowing first aid methods.

2. Instruct class to compare treatments of a headache using conventional and alternative methods and importance of having different methods available.
Possible responses might include:
Conventional — over the counter medications, etc.
Alternative — hot baths, aromatherapy, massage, music therapy, herbs, Biofeedback, nutrition & diet, etc.

3. Facilitate discussion of definition and importance of physical and emotional pain.

4. Use this example of emotional pain, disappointment when not selected to participate in a school activity (cheerleading, drama, school dance, honor society, athletic team, etc.)

5. Write the following on the board:
When I am disappointed, I need…

1. _____ 2. _____ 3. _____ 4. _____ 5. _____
   (Who)   *(What)*   *(Where)*   *(Why)*   *(How)*

…to heal.

6. Using brainstorming, instruct the class to fill in the blanks to A.5. on the board, using conventional and alternative methods.

7. Distribute handouts, paralleling a physical pain requiring first aid to emotional pain and methods available for relief.

8. Instruct students to use handouts to create a personal emotional first-aid plan, using outline similar to one listed on board, if needed.

9. Process by asking students to share something new that was learned from activity.

B. 1. At beginning of session, request that students be aware of the personal nature of topic for session.

2. Instruct class to discuss purpose of chimes and warning lights in a car. Discuss probable causes for alarms being activated along with benefits of listening vs. consequences of ignoring these automotive systems.

3. Facilitate discussion comparing physical and emotional pain to automotive warning system.

4. Share, as able, examples of what has occurred to students that has caused emotional pain.

5. Hold up a handout and ask for a volunteer. Instruct this student to identify five ways of personal healing and write them down on the blanks. Then ask, "Is there anyone in this class, or in your support system that would be willing to see that any of these needs are met?" Put his/her name down if applicable by the corresponding number(s).

6. Continue until all students have a completed handout.

7. Process the variety of healing methods mentioned, and how some can be met by being aware of what one needs, and having the courage to ask. Instruct students to share this handout with people who need to see it and/or place it where it can be reviewed, at a later time.

Activity handout and facilitator's information originally submitted for Life Management Skills V
by Mary Kaye Tilden-Walker, LSW, Cuyahoga Falls, OH. Mary Kaye has been in her present position
as a social worker for 12 years and absolutely loves doing group work!

Adapted for SEALS III from LMS V by Elaine Hyla Slea, M.Ed., Euclid, OH,
adaptor of *SEALS+PLUS (Self-Esteem and Life Skills)* and *SEALS II.*

Getting a Handle on WORRYING

Make a list of things you worry about, large and small. Be sure to include personal, relationship, family, community, school, world and general life worries.

_____

_____

_____

_____

Select one worry and send it "through the system."
Start here.

Is this _really_ important to me? → **YES** → **Do I have control of this?** → **YES** → **Do I exercise the control I have in this area? If so, there is nothing more to worry about. If not, why? How can I begin to use my control?**

↓ **NO**

List reasons for wasting time worrying about this. What does it do for me?

Do I have control of this? ↓ **NO**

Can I gain control of this? → **YES** → **How? Identify specific steps or goals for gaining more control.**

↓ **NO**

Re-evaluate. Is there anything I can do to change or gain control of this? → **YES** →

↓ **NO**

How can I soothe myself and surrender my worrying? After all, my worrying will not change the problem!

What can I do when I find myself worrying about this again?

_____

_____

_____

_____

_____

_____

Getting a Handle on WORRYING

I. PURPOSE:

To increase the ability to cope with worries.

II. GENERAL COMMENTS:

Often people lack awareness of how many things they worry about, and the emotional and physical toll such worrying takes. It is important to evaluate worries, both in terms of their relative importance, and in terms of the amount of control we have over the worrisome situation. Adolescence can be a worrisome period due to social, family and academic pressures. Learning to dispense with the worries that aren't really important, deal effectively with those that are in our control and surrender those that we cannot change, are important coping skills.

III. POSSIBLE ACTIVITIES:

A. 1. Before class session, reproduce front of handout on overhead transparency or flip chart.

2. Obtain print copies (available from library, local bookstores or via Internet) or obtain a video of 'Top Ten' lists from "Late Night with David Letterman."

3. Ask students if they are familiar with David Letterman's 'Top Ten' lists. Invite them to share (with a reminder of appropriate classroom subject matter) examples and purpose of his work. Share two or three of your own favorites either in print or on video.

4. Conduct discussion on what makes these lists amusing. Possible responses might include: short, concise statements, humor, sarcasm, exaggeration, understatement, elements of truth, current event, meaningfulness, appeal to audience.

5. Instruct students that they will be creating and sharing their own 'Top Ten Things to Worry About.' Ask for a sample item to be written on board, e.g., "Imagine the worst that could happen by telling my friend who I want to go out with." Rewrite the sample as a class, encouraging students to use the guidelines in A.4., encouraging creativity, humor and exaggeration but with good taste. Possible new sample might read "Best friend blabs over PA system who I have a crush on." As soon as activity is understood, divide class into 10 small groups to write one item for the list.

6. Select a spokesperson from each group to share with the class, writing each list item on board or overhead, then ranking list in importance from 1-10, #1 being most important. With emphasis on information in GENERAL COMMENTS, discuss results and process benefits of this part of class activity.

7. Refocus classes' attention on topic of getting a handle on worrying. Discuss the effects of worry and the benefits of the ability to manage stress effectively. Introduce the concept of evaluating the worries in terms of importance and control. Distribute handouts.

8. Ask for a class member to 'volunteer' a worry from the list on board to put through the flowchart system, and do this together as a class. Encourage class members to comment on whether or not the individual has control or not and whether or not the person is exercising control or if s/he gains it.

9. Ask the class for feedback about how the worry could be surrendered or how the person might soothe his/herself if control cannot be gained.

10. Instruct class to complete top of handout, select one worry from their personal worry list and put it through the flowchart system.

11. Discuss results and process benefits of this activity.

B. 1. Begin class activity by instructing class to create an analogy of a smoke alarm to worry. Discuss possible purposes, effects and benefits of both. Ask class to discuss effects/consequences when either item is malfunctioning. Introduce topic by distributing handouts and ask class members to complete the "worry lists".

2. Discuss the effects of worry and the ability to manage stress effectively. Introduce the concept of evaluating the worries in terms of importance and control.

3. Reproduce front of handout on overhead transparency or flipchart.

4. Using overhead transparency or flipchart, demonstrate how flowchart system works using a hypothetical situation or worry; e.g., expressing concern to your friends when asked to drive to an evening event just as a severe weather advisory is announced.

5. Allow 5-10 minutes for class members to complete the handouts.

6. Divide class into pairs or triads to discuss responses and to provide each other with feedback.

7. Reconvene as a class and discuss results. Attempt to determine similarities or trends of this class's worries (boys' worries vs. girls', relationship, financial, personal, etc.) Ask class to compare how worries might have changed over the past years. Process by discussing the value of this flowchart system for future use. Emphasize that stress management is about handling everyday worries and how this can affect one's overall health.

8. Suggested follow-up activity might be to read a selection daily from Richard Carlson's "Don't Sweat the Small Stuff...And It's All Small Stuff" as a prompt for journaling.

Activity handout and facilitator's information originally submitted for Life Management Skills V by Robin Wildbur, OTR, Royal Oak, MI. Robin has been in mental health practice over 20 years — and counting!

Adapted for SEALS III from LMS V by Elaine Hyla Slea, M.Ed., Euclid, OH, adaptor of SEALS+PLUS (Self-Esteem and Life Skills) and SEALS II.

IT'S YOUR CHOICE!

When your life is getting difficult, you have a CHOICE how to handle it:

YOU CAN HANDLE IT POSITIVELY	YOU CAN HANDLE IT NEGATIVELY	HOW MIGHT YOU HANDLE IT
1 ▶ talk to someone who listens well and will give you support	▶ hurt yourself	▶ _____
2 ▶ stay away from people who put you down	▶ hang around with people who put you down	▶ _____
3 ▶ change your surroundings to meet your needs	▶ isolate yourself	▶ _____
4 ▶ talk to yourself in a positive and nurturing way	▶ be aggressive and get yourself in trouble	▶ _____
5 ▶ give yourself a special treat that you enjoy (movie, visit a friend, etc.)	▶ never do things you enjoy, stay at home ALONE	▶ _____
6 ▶ take up a hobby you are good at so you can feel successful	▶ set yourself up to fail by trying things that are too difficult	▶ _____
7 ▶ seek spiritual support	▶ spend LOTS OF TIME thinking negatively	▶ _____
8 ▶ remember that you do have within you, the strength, knowledge and courage to change	▶ relish the feeling of powerlessness	▶ _____
9 ▶ take care of your body: get enough sleep and exercise, make healthy decisions	▶ overindulge, never take time for your body, or to relax or to care for yourself	▶ _____
10 ▶ watch a TV show that is happy and uplifting	▶ watch TV and read books that are sad and upsetting	▶ _____
11 ▶ practice relaxation techniques	▶ let yourself REACT to whatever happens without stopping to cope	▶ _____
12 ▶ use the information and coping techniques learned to help you handle the stressful parts of life	▶ forget about coping skills and keep repeating the same problems over and over	▶ _____
13 ▶ _____	▶ _____	▶ _____
14 ▶ _____	▶ _____	▶ _____

IT'S YOUR CHOICE!

I. PURPOSE:

To facilitate healthy choices and coping skills when life's situations become difficult.

II. GENERAL COMMENTS:

Recognizing choices can be a very difficult process. When faced with stressful situations many people immediately react by using previously learned coping behaviors. Despite being familiar and comfortable, and perhaps automatic, these learned behaviors often enable unhealthy choices. This almost all of the time makes them feel worse and can make the situation worse. It is important to realize that it is our 'choice' how we react to situations and stress. The information contained in this handout will define terms involved in making choices, describe steps involved in the process and offer a model for recognizing and making positive choices.

III. POSSIBLE ACTIVITIES: This handout can be used in conjunction with COPING COSTS AND BENEFITS (page 2).

A. 1. Before session, bring or make a decorative glass 'snow-ball' to class. A simple 'snow-ball' can be made by putting glitter in an empty glass jar, filling it with water, leaving room for "shaking" and sealing the lid tightly shut with glue or caulk. For further visual clue, glue a small 'scene' cut from a magazine on the outside of the jar.

2. As an introductory activity, ask the class to compare the activity in 'snow-ball' to the process of recognizing choices in their lives. Possible responses might be: we can't control the weather but we can control the way we prepare or respond to the weather, we can choose if our lives are tranquil or tumultuous just like we can control the snow in the 'snow-ball'.

3. Discuss the meaning of the word 'choice' and how this applies to our reactions to various situations. Ask class to offer synonyms to the word 'choice' by instructing students to use a dictionary or thesaurus. Possible responses might be: free will, opportunity, selection, option and decision.

4. Distribute handouts and read together as a class.

5. Review handouts for a second time, allowing class to self-reflect and to write in the "what you do" section, what their 'choices' might be.

6. Instruct class to circle all the various 'positives' or 'negatives' they usually use. If necessary, refer to *Coping Costs and Benefits* handout for review.

7. Ask class to state aloud which coping strategies they would like to keep, which they would like to eliminate and which they would like to start implementing.

8. Return to analogy of the 'snow-ball'. Ask class to observe the results of shaking the 'snow-ball'. Inquire what happened to the glitter and how the action of the glitter can be compared to discussion topic. Possible responses might be: After shaking the 'snow-ball' and waiting, calm returns. All situations in life are temporary, we can choose to make them 'calm' or we can make them 'confusing', etc.

9. Process activity by helping class to make plans to recognize and implement productive choices in the future.

B. 1. Instruct students to bring pens and two different color highlighters to next class session in order to complete the proceeding discussion activity.

2. At beginning of session, distribute handouts and explain the concept of 'choice'.

3. Ask class to read each choice and to write in the third column what they typically do and/or to elaborate, if different from the 'positive choice' or the 'negative choice'.

4. Instruct class to highlight the 'positive choices' that each student is proud of, and to highlight, in a different color the 'negative choices' that each is ready to work on.

5. Commend class on all 'positive choices' and on the willingness to work on the 'negative choices'.

6. Ask class to reflect back on a recent situation where, if they had chosen a different reaction, a more favorable outcome might have occurred, e.g.,

YOU . . . POSITIVELY	OR NEGATIVELY	WHAT I DO
take up a hobby you are good at so you can feel successful	set yourself up to fail by trying things that are too difficult	look at my hobby materials on a shelf, overindulge & feel guilty and sad.

7. Instruct each student to choose one 'choice' that can realistically be addressed in the next several days or weeks.

8. Process by encouraging personal healthy 'choices' and by giving the support necessary to make these 'choices'.

9. Follow-up activity might be a reading of the poems "Choices" by Nikki Giovanni and/or "The Road Not Taken" by Robert Frost. Discussion might include: the choices each speaker makes, the feelings of each speaker, which speaker is happier and the results of their choices.

Activity handout and facilitator's information originally submitted for Life Management Skills V
by Debbie Sacerich, LSW, Wickliffe, OH and Laura Stergar, SWA, South Euclid, OH.
Debbie Sacerich, LSW and Laura Stergar, SWA, work as class counselors in a Partial Hospitalization Program. Outside of work, Laura loves to read and play volleyball. Debbie instructs and competes in a new sport, Dog Agility, with her dog "Buddy".

Adapted for SEALS III from LMS V by Elaine Hyla Slea, M.Ed., Euclid, OH,
adaptor of *SEALS+PLUS (Self-Esteem and Life Skills)* and *SEALS II.*

musical coping

front

In day-to-day life we are challenged by numerous stressors.

Listening to and enjoying various types of music is one possible method of coping with these stressors.

affirmations

back

When stressors arise, listen to music, state your affirmations and take productive action to decrease your stress.

I. PURPOSE:

To introduce the concept of using music as a coping skill.

II. GENERAL COMMENTS:

Everyone experiences stress in one way or another. It is possible to use music and affirmations as one method of coping with stress.

III. POSSIBLE ACTIVITIES:

A. 1. Before session, photocopy handout using a variety of colors if possible.

2. Ask the class to recall if they are able, the events portrayed in the movie and stageplay, "Footloose". Ask students to recall or explain to those who didn't see the movie, the results of students not being able to dance or listen to their preferred styles of music. Instruct students to imagine what life would be like in these circumstances and to discuss.

3. Ask class to brainstorm other examples of the power and influence of music. Which emotions or feelings are triggered by motion picture soundtracks, e.g., "Psycho" or "The Twilight Zone"?

4. Explain the concept of how music can also be a creative way of managing stress.

5. Contrast introductory topic with discussion on how different types of music can . . .
a. relax, soothe, energize, etc.
b. be used with affirmations to strengthen, empower, revitalize, etc.

6. Distribute handouts, giving class members the choice of the color of handout.

7. Instruct class to complete the top half or the 'Front' of their personal Compact Disc covers by drawing symbols of how music is, or can be, fulfilling. This can answer the questions . . . "When listening to your favorite type of music, how do you feel?" or "What is a favorite musical memory?"

8. Instruct class to complete the bottom half or 'Back' of their personal Compact Disc covers by writing one to three affirmations that might be valuable to reflect on while listening to the music. For example: "I can make healthy choices.", "I can relax.", "Every day in every way, I am getting better and better."

9. Allow class to share the finished products.

10. Process and discuss how the class can creatively use music during stressful situations..

B. 1. Discuss the variety of types of music that the class is familiar with (jazz, rock, soul, religious, country, orchestral, classical, easy listening, nature themes, choral, rap, new age etc). Ask class to identify which music is especially helpful during stressful periods. Conversely, what music angers, disturbs or offends students?

2. Distribute handouts.

3. Explain the activity of developing personal Compact Disc covers to reinforce the concepts outlined in the GENERAL COMMENTS.

4. Instruct class members to portray something personal about the way that music has affected them or can affect them, on the front side of their personal CD cover. Develop a list of questions that the front can answer, or use these as samples:
"What are some memories or images that you associate with a certain song or piece of music? What was happening in your life which made this song so special?"
"What type of music motivates or moves you?"
"What is your favorite type of music, favorite song or lyric? What kind of feelings do you associate with it?"

5. Allow 20-30 minutes for the personal CD front covers to be designed.

6. Ask each student to share his or her personal CD front cover.

7. Ask class to give each other feedback as to what personal affirmations may be worth reflecting on, when listening to music. For example, Student A gives details about her CD cover which includes that she likes relaxing music including nature music; she feels that she can leave her problems behind her when she hears that music. Suggested affirmations may include: "I can find a peace of mind," "I will let my body and mind relax," "I will stay in tune with nature during stressful times."

8. Ask each student to choose three favorite affirmations from the class' suggestions and write these on the 'Back' or bottom half of handout.

9. Process by asking students to summarize the activity and possible benefits of musical coping.

Activity handout and facilitator's information originally submitted for Life Management Skills V
by Emily R. Thier, OTS, Dyersville, IA and Mandy K. Russman, OTS, Long Grove, IA, occupational therapy students in
Davenport, IA. "Special thanks to our professor, Christine Malaski, MS, OTR/L for encouraging us to submit Musical Coping."

Adapted for SEALS III from LMS V by Elaine Hyla Slea, M.Ed., Euclid, OH,
adaptor of *SEALS+PLUS (Self-Esteem and Life Skills)* and *SEALS II.*

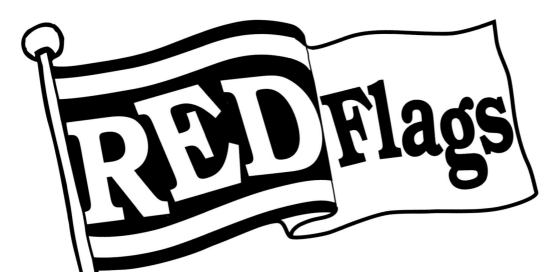

REDFlags

are signals to alert me that I am losing control.

For example:
- ↬ thinking suicidal thoughts,
- ↬ not taking care of my body,
- ↬ an "I don't care" feeling,
- ↬ not as interested in being with my friends or family,
- ↬ not taking my medications,
- ↬ not caring about school, work, other responsibilities,
- ↬ weird/confused thinking.

Other

1. _____
2. _____
3. _____

In this flag, write in your own

1. _____
2. _____
3. _____

If I experience any of the above I will . . .

1. _____
2. _____
3. _____

I.   **PURPOSE:**

To facilitate learning by identifying when one is out of control, overly committed, in a crisis or in need of support.

II. **GENERAL COMMENTS:**

A self-monitoring system may assist in preventing a crisis or melt down and help in maintaining wellness. Becoming aware of and identifying 'red flags' gives a sense of control in an oftentimes over-committed, pressured life style.

III. **POSSIBLE ACTIVITIES:**

A. 1. Introduce the topic of 'red flags.' Offer a stop sign as a comparison - a halting signal to look around.

2. Distribute handouts and pencils.

3. Instruct students to complete.

4. Review and discuss responses.

B. 1. Draw a 'red flag' outline on a flipchart. (RED Flags)

2. Introduce the topic of 'red flags' by listing early warning symptoms of the flu: feeling hot then cold, very tired, slight stomachaches, etc. Ask for class input and write in the 'red flag' outline.

3. Draw a second 'red flag' on flipchart. Discuss emotional 'red flags' when one feels pressured or out of control. Write symptoms in the 'red flag' outline.

4. Distribute handouts, pencils and red colored pencils/markers.

5. Allow ten minutes for completion; students may color 'red flags' in red for emphasis.

6. Draw a third blank 'red flag' outline large enough for all students' input. Ask each student to write in his/her own 'red flag' signals in collective red flag. Discuss common and unique entries.

7. Discuss what participants will do when experiencing red flags. Support ideas, making sure that information is complete, e.g., if student writes, "Call a friend", have them identify a specific friend and their phone number.

8. Process by asking student, "Where is the best place to put completed handout?"

Activity handout and facilitator's information submitted by Marla Yoder-Tiedt, MSW, LISW and Sandi MIller, RRT, both employed at a psychiatric hospital in Columbus, OH, with 15 years and 22 years in the mental health field respectively.

Adapted for SEALS III from LMS VI by Sandra Negley, MTRS, CTRS, Salt Lake City, UT,
author of *Crossing the Bridge, A Journey in Self-Esteem, Relationships and Life Balance.*

Focus on the POSITIVE

◀ **Things I like**

People I like ▶

◀ **Things I look forward to**

Things I like about myself ▶

I. PURPOSE:

To provide a creative, non-verbal outlet for expressing and exploring positive qualities, attributes and thoughts.

II. GENERAL COMMENTS:

Negativity often prevails in thoughts, conversations and actions. Positive thoughts and attitudes may need to be fostered and nurtured within each of us. Providing an avenue for non-verbal exploration of positive qualities can be helpful.

III. POSSIBLE ACTIVITIES: This handout may be used in conjunction with POSITIVE FOCUS (Life Management Skills III - page 11).

A. 1. Distribute handouts and art materials. Have a variety of art materials available such as colored pencils, markers and oil pastels.

   2. Instruct students to use lines, shapes and colors to illustrate the areas on the handout. Lists may also be used.

   3. Assure students that lines, shapes and colors could end up looking like something (representational) or could end up looking abstract.

   4. Discuss students' responses to this activity.

   5. Process benefits of looking at one's positive images as well as the images of others.

B. 1. Discuss how negativity may be perpetuated in today's society by the media. Ask the class, "Does misery really love company?"

   2. Explain that positive energy is needed to become a well-balanced and healthy individual.

   3. Distribute handouts and art materials. Have a variety of art materials available such as colored pencils, markers and oil pastels.

   4. Give class ten to fifteen minutes to complete handouts. Encourage students to work individually and to separate themselves so that each person has ample space to work. If class chooses to listen to music, play a relaxing CD.

   5. Assure students that lines, shapes and colors could end up looking like something (representational) or could end up looking abstract.

   6. Process by asking participants to discuss, "Which was the most difficult box?" "The easiest box?" Facilitate discussion on positive effect noticed from focusing on the positive.

Activity handout and facilitator's information originally submitted for Life Management Skills VI by Jennifer Whitten, MA, A.T.R.-BC, Oberlin, OH. Jennifer is a registered and board certified art therapist. She has been working with incarcerated psychiatric patients for the past four years.

Adapted for SEALS III from LMS VI by Sandra Negley, MTRS, CTRS, Salt Lake City, UT, author of *Crossing the Bridge, A Journey in Self-Esteem, Relationships and Life Balance*.

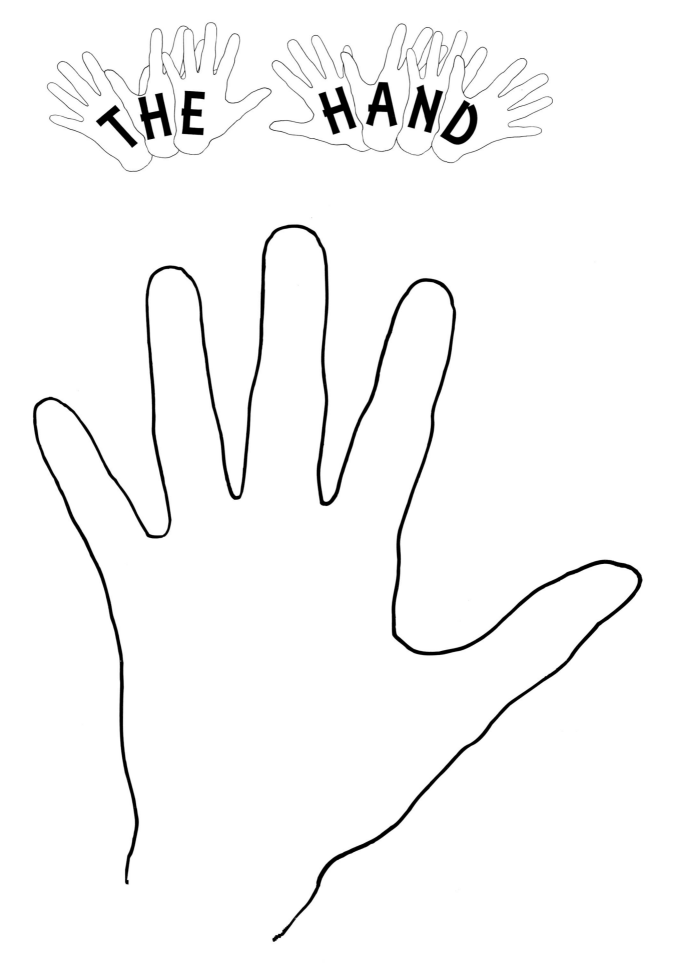

THE HAND

THE HAND

I. PURPOSE:

To provide a creative outlet for expressing and exploring oneself, developing personal insight.

II. GENERAL COMMENTS:

Using a universal concept such as the hand may elicit all kinds of feelings visually, creatively and/or symbolically. Non-verbal exploration of self may provide an avenue for insight.

III. POSSIBLE ACTIVITIES:

A. 1. Distribute handouts, art materials and writing materials. Have a variety of art materials available such as colored pencils, markers and oil pastels.

2. Choose one or more of the following concepts to explore with the class:

INSIDE OF THE HAND	OUTSIDE OF THE HAND
What you have	What you want
What you control	What is not in your control
Things you can change	Things you cannot change
Things you like about yourself	Things you like about others
How you respond to stress	Things that stress you out

3. Instruct the class to complete the handout by either drawing or making lists on the inside of the hand outline or the outside of the hand outline.

4. Encourage each student to share his/her art with class.

5. Discuss any personal insights gained from activity.

B. 1. Write the word 'insight' on the board.

2. Elicit definition from class or use/modify the following: the act or power of seeing into oneself.

3. Explain to class that typically it is far more helpful, exciting and powerful to discover insights on one's own rather than be 'told' insights.

4. Distribute handouts, explaining to students that one way to develop insights is through non-verbal means.

5. Place art materials in the center of the tables, with ample space in between participants. Have a variety of art materials available such as colored pencils, markers and oil pastels.

6. Give students the choice of the following possibilities to illustrate:

INSIDE OF THE HAND	OUTSIDE OF THE HAND
What you have	What you want
What you control	What is not in your control
Things you can change	Things you cannot change
Things you like about yourself	Things you like about others
How you respond to stress	Things that stress you out

7. Ask students to volunteer and share what they portrayed inside of the hand and outside of the hand. Discuss possible insights gained.

Activity handout and facilitator's information originally submitted for Life Management Skills VI by Jennifer Whitten, MA, A.T.R.-BC, Oberlin, OH. Jennifer is a registered and board certified art therapist. She has been working with incarcerated psychiatric patients for the past four years.

Adapted for SEALS III from LMS VI by Sandra Negley, MTRS, CTRS, Salt Lake City, UT, author of *Crossing the Bridge, A Journey in Self-Esteem, Relationships and Life Balance*.

What a MOOD changer!

Music is a helpful tool to use in personal growth.

Music can create a change in mood. It can turn us from being sad to happy, from being bored to being energetic, from being tense to being relaxed.

Name two songs which make you feel sad.
(for example - songs about broken relationships).

1. _____

2. _____

Name two songs that give you energy.
(for example - rock, fast-paced music, movie themes).

1. _____

2. _____

Name two songs which help you to relax, to dream.
(for example - soft rock, classical music, instrumentals).

1. _____

2. _____

List music which gives you pride and faith.
(for example - spiritual, patriotic, ethnic)

1. _____

2. _____

I. PURPOSE:

To introduce music as a therapeutic, expressive activity.

II. GENERAL COMMENTS:

Music can be used as a means of self-expression, pleasure and stress management. A person can learn to change or gain control over one's mood — using a radio, audiotape, CD or even the human voice! Music can lift the spirits and make the day ahead more purposeful, productive and fun.

III. POSSIBLE ACTIVITIES:

A. 1. Discuss different types of music and what are some of the student's favorite types of music. Prepare ahead of time in order to play short examples of a variety of music.

2. Discuss with students their emotional responses, when listening to their favorite music. On flip chart or white board list responses, e.g., gets mind off problems, helps me get to sleep, puts me in a good mood.

3. Distribute pencils and handouts. Allow class 5-10 minutes to complete.

4. Divide class into small groups of 3-4 members. Ask each member of the group to share their responses on the completed handouts and then, to brainstorm a list of their favorite songs and the mood those songs help to create. (It is important to address how some music can create negative or destructive emotions.)

5. Discuss the importance of "doing what works." Encourage class members to use music for healthy purposes; relaxation, leisure, and fun.

6. Problem solve how to go about acquiring music for personal use, e.g., buy, borrow tapes to hear from friends/library, get new and used CD's at music stores, thrift shops, garage sales, Internet.

B. 1. Discuss with the class what makes an activity therapeutic, or good for personal growth.

2. Choose a music selection that the class can relate to (age appropriate), e.g., currently on the pop charts, old or familiar music, or introduce something new. After listening to part or all of the musical selection, ask class to share what mood that particular excerpt seemed to create in them.

3. Distribute handouts and pens. With the class, complete one section at a time, asking for volunteers to share their answers.

4. Discuss plans of how and when the students could use music, as a daily/weekly/as needed way of changing moods and reducing stress.

5. Provide each student with a list of community resources where music can be obtained.

- Libraries
- Music stores - new/used
- Thrift stores
- Radio station

Include addresses, open hours and phone numbers of these sources. Discuss how to obtain catalogues, Internet information, etc., to supplement the local list.

Activity handout and facilitator's information originally submitted for Life Management Skills VI by Roberta Jean Ott, COTA, Allentown, PA. Roberta is a former elementary school teacher. She has worked at a state hospital for several years and is employed part-time at a local nursing home.

Adapted for SEALS III from LMS VI by Sandra Negley, MTRS, CTRS, Salt Lake City, UT, author of *Crossing the Bridge, A Journey in Self-Esteem, Relationships and Life Balance.*

Nurturing Myself

...as a Poet
...as a Person

Writing poetry is one way of making sense out of the world. It has power. For in poetry is release, healing and an affirmation of life.

Listen for directions, then write your responses here:

1. _____
2. _____
3. _____
4. _____
5. _____
6. _____
7. _____
8. _____
9. _____
10. _____
11. _____
12. _____

1. _____
2. _____
3. _____
4. _____
5. _____
6. _____
7. _____
8. _____
9. _____
10. _____
11. _____
12. _____

Oftentimes the poet is the first, last and only person to read the poet's words.
The poet is the only one to hear the message contained in the lines of the poem.
The message begins, but doesn't end at least for the poet.
As a result, poetry, like journalizing, helps to reflect a person's past experiences
but also can influence a person for the rest of his/her life.

I. PURPOSE:

To increase an individual's self-expression.

II. GENERAL COMMENTS:

Shelley once said, "Poetry strengthens the moral value of man as exercise strengthens a limb." Self-awareness and understanding through poetry writing can provide an essential part of character development. Poetry is a powerful tool of insight and change. Poetry can be a source of comfort during loss, provide healing, facilitate transformation, reconciliation and a continuing experience of 'mindfulness'. Poetry can be a means to allow adolescents to express feelings and thoughts they sometimes can't verbalize. This can also serve as a helpful means of education and communication to family and friends.

III. POSSIBLE ACTIVITIES:

A. 1. Before class session, make a copy of handout, write the following 'Autobio' poem questions on the spaces numbered 1-12 on the left side of the handout:

1 - Your first name 2 - Four traits that describe you 3 - Sibling of _____ 4 - Son or daughter of _____
5 - Lover of (three people, ideas, activities, etc.) 6 - Who feels (three emotions) 7 - Who needs (three things)
8 - Who gives (three things) 9 - Who fears (three things) 10 - Who would like to see _____
11 - Resident of _____ 12 - Last name only.

Make photocopies of edited handout for each student.

2. Discuss the importance of self-discovery, awareness and expression. Open a discussion about the impact that denial or lack of growth has on disrupting emotional experiences and relationships.

3. Ask students to generate a list of 'feeling' type words that adolescents are most likely to experience, e.g., depression, anxiety, exhilaration, etc.

4. Request that students identify typical fears associated with adolescence, e.g., rejection, poor grades, lack of popularity, peer pressure, change, etc. These lists may be used to assist students with writing autobiopoems.

5. Distribute handouts and instruct students to complete by reading the directions on the left and writing the responses on the right. Explain this poetry will be a collection of words based on experiences and beliefs.

6. Ask students, who are willing, to share poems aloud.

7. Focus discussion on the ways in particular that poetry would be useful in helping people verbalize thoughts, beliefs or feelings that are otherwise difficult to express.

B. 1. Before class session, make a copy of handout and write the following 'Found' poem questions on the spaces numbered 1-12 on the left side of the handout:

1 - Describe a recent conflict, loss or event (yours, a family member's or friend's)
2 - When you first learned of it 3 - Behaviors, people, words associated with event 4 - How you feel
5 - Your concerns 6 - Desired outcome 7 - Two things that have been helpful or might help cope with situation
8 - Three ways you would like to feel or three things you would like to do
9 - What image invokes memories or symbolizes the conflict? 10 - How the persons involved are bound together by this image 11 - If the conflict were a person what would it have to say?
12 - Your response or lesson learned or to be learned.

Make photocopies of edited handouts as needed for class.

2. Discuss the importance of self-discovery and awareness. Open a discussion about the impact that denial or lack of growth has on disrupting emotional experiences and relationships.

3. Ask students to brainstorm a list of events that can generate anxiety or be a source of concern for adolescents, e.g., Valentine's Day, graduation, prom, etc.

4. Ask students to then list behaviors/thoughts/beliefs/emotions associated with these concerns.

5. Distribute handouts. Instruct students to complete by reading the directions on the left and writing the responses on the right, using above information as a guideline, if necessary. Explain this poetry will be a collection of words based on experiences and beliefs.

6. Ask students, who are willing, to share poems aloud. Focus discussion on the ways in particular that poetry would be useful in helping people verbalize thoughts, beliefs or feelings that are otherwise difficult to express feelings.

7. Collect handouts to create a poetry collection (with permission of students) that may be used as:

a. a book to be shared with future classes.
b. a book to be shared with families during parent/teacher conferences or school open house.
c. submissions for a school newspaper or internet home page.
d. materials for a bulletin board entitled 'Nurturing Ourselves As Poets and Persons'.

Activity handout and facilitator's information originally submitted for Life Management Skills V by Barbara Lundberg, OTR/L, Sandra Netto, MSW, and Betty Welch, PhD, all employed at a Geropsychiatric Partial Hospitalization Program in Manchester, NH. Betty and Sandra specialize in geriatric mental health. Barbara has over 20 years experience in community mental health.

Adapted for SEALS III from LMS V by Elaine Hyla Slea, M.Ed., Euclid, OH,
adaptor of *SEALS+PLUS (Self-Esteem and Life Skills)* and *SEALS II.*

Your Own **PICTURE** of Health

I. PURPOSE:

To identify one's positive attributes and learn to create positive affirmations.

II. GENERAL COMMENTS:

People often have difficulty expressing their positive attributes as well as identifying positive affirmations. A creative process might assist in the goal/purpose.

III. POSSIBLE ACTIVITIES:

A. 1. Facilitate discussion on positive attributes. Ask students, "What does having positive attributes do for you? Do for others?", "How does one feel emotionally if one has positive attributes?"

2. Distribute handouts with pencils, colored pencils and markers.

3. Encourage students to take the blank handout and fill in the extremities of the figure with their own personal attributes. Brainstorm a list of positive attributes on the board for prompts or offer examples of already completed handouts if needed.

4. Direct students to color the background of their star so it will represent their unique self.

5. Process by asking each student to share with the class their 'picture of health' star and discuss what those attributes mean for their self-confidence.

B. 1. Facilitate discussion on positive affirmations, positive outlook, self-esteem, etc.

2. Distribute handouts, colored markers and pencils.

3. Instruct the students to design the star, with colors, so it represents themselves.

4. Instruct students to write in as many affirmations, especially those that will be helpful to them, around the star. Brainstorm on the board for additional suggestions:
   For example: I am motivated.
   I am capable.
   I am flexible.
   I am hopeful.
   I am dependable.
   I am reliable.
   I am responsible.

5. Instruct students to put the positive attributes that have been told to them recently or in the past, in the extremities. If a student has not experienced positive affirmations recently, then allow class, or the leader only, to share positive qualities with each student. For example, "Susan, you are kind."

6. Display all completed works for others to see in gallery style. Allow each student to describe his/her star to the class.

7. Process by asking students for feedback of this activity. Discuss the lifelong process of obtaining, maintaining and nurturing a high self-esteem and the value of doing so.

Activity handout and facilitator's information originally submitted for Life Management Skills VI by Susan Olko, COTA/L, Suffield, CT. Susan has experience in an inpatient mental health setting, physical rehabilitation and is a group specialist designing and facilitating groups in a behavioral health out-patient sector.

Adapted for SEALS III from LMS VI by Sandra Negley, MTRS, CTRS, Salt Lake City, UT, author of *Crossing the Bridge, A Journey in Self-Esteem, Relationships and Life Balance*.

Are you stuck in the CYCLE of fear?

New or threatening or challenging situation

Normal fear/anxiety reaction:
- release of adrenaline & glucose into bloodstream
- helps prepare us by giving extra energy, increased alertness and learning powers
- may feel shaky with increased breathing and heart rate

Lack of experience and knowledge:
- ignorance breeds more fear
- fear is increased

Avoidance:
- refusal to face situation
- followed by feeling of relief

Distorted Interpretation:
- perceive that feelings of fear are unacceptable and can't be tolerated
  - fear of fear develops
  - make faulty decision that situation must be avoided so feeling of fear will go away

QUESTIONS TO CONSIDER:

1. What am I avoiding because of my fear?

2. What other factors may be adding to my fear?

3. What small step could I take to work through my fear?

Are you stuck in the CYCLE of fear?

I. PURPOSE:

To identify the various factors contributing to the 'Cycle of Fear.'

To increase awareness of the dynamics involved in unhealthy, non-productive fear.

II. GENERAL COMMENTS:

Individuals with mental health difficulties can have many overblown and paralyzing fears (e.g., shopping, answering the telephone, coming to class, meeting new people, etc.). Maladaptive avoidance strategies are oftentimes developed by individuals in a misguided attempt to manage fear. It can be helpful to look more closely at this unhealthy 'Cycle of Fear.'

III. POSSIBLE ACTIVITIES:

A. 1. Ask the following question: "What words do you associate with fear?" List students' responses on flipchart.

2. Distribute handouts and pens.

3. Review the 'Cycle of Fear' discussing each step starting at the top with 'New or Threatening or Challenging Situation.'

4. Facilitate discussion, encouraging students to share own experiences with being stuck in the fear cycle.

5. Provide time for students to complete the questions at the bottom of the handout.

6. Encourage students to share answers to question #3. Conclude class by asking students to commit to trying their 'small step' in the near future.

B. 1. Introduce concept of unhealthy fear. Ask students, "What is unhealthy fear? Are all fears unhealthy? What are the problems associated with having unhealthy fear?"

2. Distribute handouts and pencils.

3. Review steps involved in the 'Cycle of Fear.' Offer relevant examples to the class.

4. Divide class into pairs. Instruct each pair to verbally share responses to the three questions on handout. Create a supportive, safe atmosphere of open sharing. Provide an opportunity for pairs to give feedback about the responses.

5. Reconvene and poll the class to see if there are any commonalties. Is there more than one person who is fearful of parties? Heights? Water? Tests? Is there more than one person whose small step includes getting professional help? Telling a friend?

6. Process by asking each group member to identify one insight gained from this activity.

Activity handout and facilitator's information originally submitted for Life Management Skills VI by Nancy Day, O.T. Reg., Markham, Ontario, Canada. Nancy is an Occupational Therapist working in the mental health field, within the hospital sector. Her primary role as a group psychotherapist provides daily opportunity to design and facilitate group treatment. She believes it is a privilege to work in this capacity and witness the 'magic' that occurs as individuals connect with one another and share in each other's growth.

Adapted for SEALS III from LMS VI by Sandra Negley, MTRS, CTRS, Salt Lake City, UT,
author of *Crossing the Bridge, A Journey in Self-Esteem, Relationships and Life Balance.*

can help to work through FEAR

Can I do it?
Of course I can
Using what I've learned
Realizing I can
And reaching within myself
Growing so
Every time, yes, I can

What are some powerful, fearless words?

COURAGE	**BRAVERY**	_____
SPIRIT	**SUPPORT**	_____
STRENGTH	_____	_____

Choose a word from the list in the box above or make up your own. Print each letter of your word inside the stars below. Now, write a short and encouraging poem or rap or if you would prefer draw something that is encouraging to work through your fear. For the poem or rap use each letter of the word to start each line of your poem or rap (like in the above example: courage).

☆ _____
☆ _____
☆ _____
☆ _____
☆ _____
☆ _____
☆ _____
☆ _____
☆ _____
☆ _____

TIPS: • Write your poem/rap or draw from the heart.
• Don't worry about trying to sound clever or talented.
• It doesn't have to rhyme (many great poems/raps don't) or look perfect.
• Be creative and be yourself!

I. PURPOSE:

To introduce creative expression as a coping strategy and specifically to cope with fear.

To experience the process of creating a poem / rap / drawing to deal with fear or anxiety.

II. GENERAL COMMENTS:

Many students have difficulty with fears and anxiety. Creative expression is used in this exercise as a way of reaching within for inner strength. Students may need lots of gentle encouragement to free themselves of self-critical judgements about their own creativity. Options for expression include poetry, rapping, or drawing.

III. POSSIBLE ACTIVITIES:

A. 1. Distribute handouts and pencils.

   2. Ask for a volunteer from the class to read aloud the poem on the handout entitled "Courage." Encourage students to share their thoughts about the poem.

   3. Refer to question on the handout, "What are some powerful, fearless words?" Write responses on the chalkboard.

   4. Instruct students to create a poem / rap / drawing following the directions on the handout.

   5. Provide an opportunity for those who choose to share their poem / rap / drawing with the class.

   6. Facilitate discussion on the experience of writing the poem / rap / drawing to handle fear.

   7. Ask for ideas on how this exercise can be applied to situations in which they may be experiencing fear or to handle other problems.

B. 1. Ask students to comment on past experiences with creative expression (poetry / drawing).

   2. Introduce concept of creativity with poem / rap / drawing being used as a recovery tool or coping strategy.

   3. Distribute handouts and pencils. Have them read "Courage" poem to themselves. Provide time to comment about it.

   4. Review instructions on the handout and provide time for students to write a poem / rap / drawing emphasizing the 'TIPS' at bottom of handout.

   5. Divide into subgroups and ask students to share their poem / rap / drawing with each other as well as to discuss the difficulty or ease of the experience.

   6. Reconvene and ask subgroups to report back to the class with feedback about the exercise.

   7. Discuss how creativity may be useful to cope with fear or other stress in the future.

Activity handout and facilitator's information originally submitted for Life Management Skills VI by Nancy Day, O.T. Reg., Markham, Ontario, Canada. Nancy is an Occupational Therapist working in the mental health field, within the hospital sector. Her primary role as a group psychotherapist provides daily opportunity to design and facilitate group treatment. She believes it is a privilege to work in this capacity and witness the 'magic' that occurs as individuals connect with one another and share in each other's growth.

Adapted for SEALS III from LMS VI by Ann M. Fresoli, MA, CAC, Bethlehem, PA
who works in an outpatient and school counseling program.

Working through FEAR

Too much fear can be . . .

PARALYZING Stagnating draining panicky

ISOLATING *Defeating* **emptiness** roller coaster

_____ _____ _____ _____

STRATEGIES I HAVE USED IN THE PAST TO WORK THROUGH MY FEAR . . .

POSSIBLE COPING STRATEGIES TO TRY . . .

____ Accept that some fear is normal

____ Learn to tolerate fear feelings

____ Mental rehearsal of feared situation

____ Ask for encouragement from a friend

____ Use positive "I can do it" thoughts

____ Just do it

____ See yourself accomplishing positive results

____ Focus on successes

____ Don't try to fight fear 'perfectly'

____ Notice and be happy about small steps

____ Keep trying, don't give up

____ Discuss fears with supportive person

____ Deep breathing

____ Read quotations from famous people

____ Don't try for perfection

____ Be willing to try

____ Use the buddy system

____ Reward yourself afterward

I. PURPOSE:

To identify the negative impact of being excessively fearful.

II. GENERAL COMMENTS:

Individuals may experience excessive fear that is bringing unwanted feelings and outcomes. It is important to acknowledge and verbalize the feelings and the impact that excessive fear has in one's life. Since individuals may not have learned how to manage fear in a constructive manner, it is necessary to provide assistance in learning alternative and more effective coping strategies to combat fears.

III. POSSIBLE ACTIVITIES:

A. 1. Write "A recent situation when I used my courage…" on flipchart.

2. Ask each student to complete the sentence, reminding him or her that even small steps can require a lot of courage.

3. Facilitate a brief discussion on specifically how participants used their courage in those situations, e.g., asked a friend to accompany me to the 'dreaded' crowded school registration.

4. Distribute handouts and pens.

5. Review how too much fear can affect us, asking class members to add to list from own experiences in the top third section of the handout.

6. Provide ten minutes for students to complete remainder of handout.

7. Reconvene and allow for sharing of which strategies students plan to try in the near future.

B. 1. Write on flipchart: F -
                          E -
                          A -
                          R -

2. Invite participants to suggest ways of coping with fears, using each letter of the word fear, e.g., F - face it
   E - empty your mind of negative thoughts
   A - ask for help
   R - rehearse feared situations.

3. Ask class the question - "How does too much fear affect us?" Jot down responses on flipchart.

4. Distribute handouts and pens.

5. Compare responses on flipchart to those on the handout.

6. Provide ten minutes for class members to complete the handout.

7. Divide students into subgroups of three or four, and encourage them to share responses with each other.

8. Reconvene and ask students for feedback on the coping strategies listed on handout. Discuss using examples already prepared on handout or effective strategies suggested from the group. Offer experiences such as simulations, readings or demonstrations to integrate.

9. Process by asking a class member to summarize what was presented in class. Ask each student to identify a favorite strategy that s/he is going to use in the future and/or any role-models who have overcome fears successfully.

Activity handout and facilitator's information originally submitted for Life Management Skills VI by
Nancy Day, O.T. Reg., Markham, Ontario, Canada. Nancy is an Occupational Therapist working in the mental health field,
within the hospital sector. Her primary role as a group psychotherapist provides daily opportunity to design
and facilitate group treatment. She believes it is a privilege to work in this capacity and witness the "magic" that occurs
as individuals connect with one another and share in each other's growth.

Adapted for SEALS III from LMS VI by Sandra Negley, MTRS, CTRS, Salt Lake City, UT,
author of *Crossing the Bridge, A Journey in Self-Esteem, Relationships and Life Balance.*

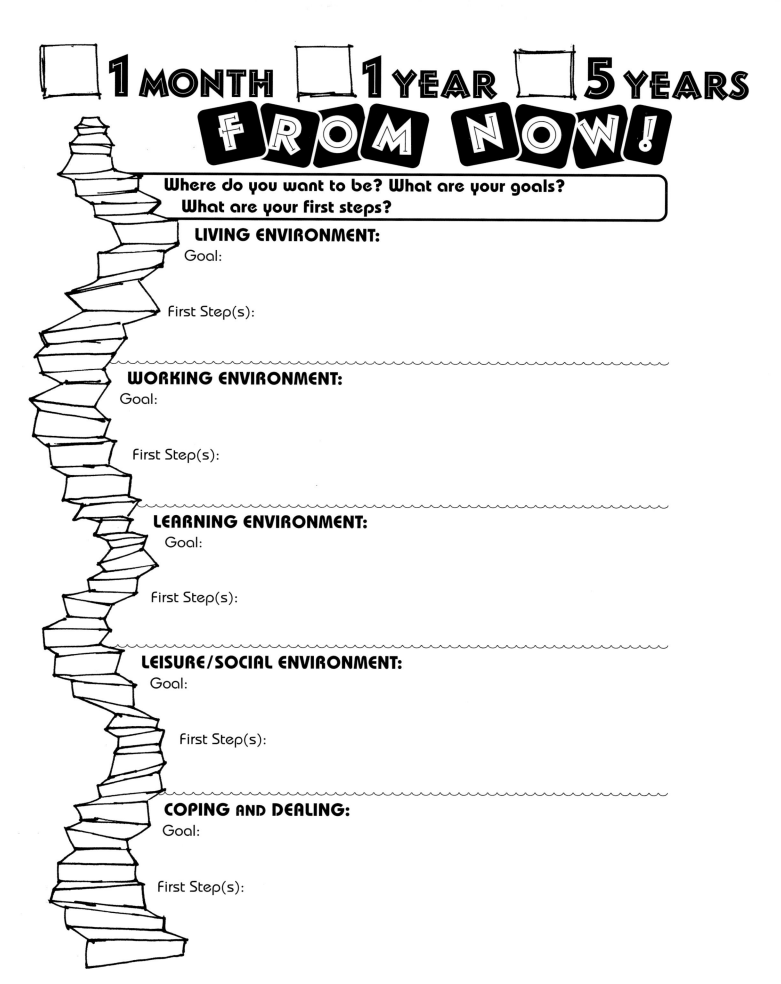

☐ 1 MONTH ☐ 1 YEAR ☐ 5 YEARS

FROM NOW!

Where do you want to be? What are your goals? What are your first steps?

LIVING ENVIRONMENT:

Goal:

First Step(s):

WORKING ENVIRONMENT:

Goal:

First Step(s):

LEARNING ENVIRONMENT:

Goal:

First Step(s):

LEISURE/SOCIAL ENVIRONMENT:

Goal:

First Step(s):

COPING AND DEALING:

Goal:

First Step(s):

I. PURPOSE:

To establish life goals and identify the next steps necessary to reach those goals.

To identify major life areas.

II. GENERAL COMMENTS:

To know that there is a future and the promise of a brighter tomorrow may be difficult for some people to realize. Encouraging people to begin to think about their lives in major life areas may offer a realistic way of examining where one would like to be in the future and how to begin to get there.

III. POSSIBLE ACTIVITIES: This handout may be used in conjunction with GOAL SETTING section (SEALS + PLUS - pages 29-33) and GO FOR THE GOAL Deck of Cards.

A. 1. Ask the class to assess their feelings about the future; what do they see as their challenges, uncertainties and opportunities. Emphasize that many students may share similar feelings regarding the future.

2. Encourage each student to write five words or phrases that would best describe a positive future. Share and compile the list for the entire class. Promote discussion concerning feelings and attitudes that may assist them in their approach to the future.

3. Introduce the five areas listed on the handout: LIVING ENVIRONMENT, WORKING ENVIRONMENT, LEARNING ENVIRONMENT, LEISURE/SOCIAL ENVIRONMENT AND COPING AND DEALING. Ask the group to define each of these areas, (e.g., the Living Environment would include residential options such as apartment, parents' home, living with a friend, etc.) as well as how to make the Living Environment more satisfactory to each individual (living in a dormitory, different area of town, having nicer furniture, having more personal mementos in one's Living Environment). Process through each of the four environments, stressing all of the possible options. Encourage discussion, support and the sharing of the ideas. Using a dry erase board, list all the ideas under each environment.

4. Discuss the role of COPING AND DEALING in establishing and achieving future goals. Encourage the class to come up with a list of things they would like to be able to cope and deal with better.

5. Distribute handouts, assigning completion by the next class. Offer the choice of focusing on and developing short-term goals (one month, one year) or long-term (five years) and to check the choice at the top of the page.

B. 1. Distribute handouts with pencils. Review concepts outlined in GENERAL COMMENTS.

2. Offer the choice of focusing on and developing short-term goals (one month, one year) or long-term (five years) and to check the choice at the top of the page.

3. Go through each of the four environments and COPING AND DEALING and have the class come up with their goals and step(s). Offer assistance as needed for goal and step writing.

4. Facilitate open and supportive environment as each student shares goals and steps. Have class provide feedback and suggestions on the viability of the goals and steps each student presented.

5. Assist students in prioritizing a direction. Pose the question, "Is it better to begin with the smallest of steps or the most important goal?"

6. Discuss accountability and goal setting. Develop an evaluation with the class, to assist them in working toward their goals.

Activity handout and facilitator's information originally submitted for Life Management Skills VI by Martin B. Golub, CTRS, Rochester, NY. Marty would like to dedicate this page to his wonderful parents, Aaron and Arlene Golub of Skokie, Illinois. Their legacy is their devotion to each other, their family and their friends. On February 25, 2001 they will be married 50 years. Mazel Tov! (congratulations)

Adapted for SEALS III from LMS VI by Sandra Negley, MTRS, CTRS, Salt Lake City, UT,
author of *Crossing the Bridge, A Journey in Self-Esteem, Relationships and Life Balance.*

PHYSICAL HEALTH • NUTRITION • SPIRITUALITY • FAMILY

JOB • ANGER • TIME • FUN • EMOTIONAL HEALTH • SUPPORT

"In life, as in football, you won't go far unless you know where the goalposts are."
- Arnold H. Glasgow -

Daily goals are essential to our self-esteem and sense of productivity.
Look at the suggested words in the goalpost or add your own,
and write some goals you might want to incorporate in your life!

• EXERCISE • HOBBY • CHARITY • LEISURE • TRAVEL • FINANCIAL • HUMOR • •

1 Today, I will _____

_____

_____

_____

2 Today, I will _____

_____

_____

_____

WEIGHT GAIN/LOSS

DEPEND-ABILITY

GRUDGES

SELF-CARE

STRESS

EDUCATION

3 Today, I will _____

_____

_____

_____

4 Today, I will _____

_____

_____

_____

I. **PURPOSE:**

To introduce the idea of goal setting.

To increase goal utilization as a daily life skill.

II. **GENERAL COMMENTS:**

Goal setting is frequently thought of in long-term standards - one month, one year, ten years, etc. It is also possible to think of goals for the present day. Small, daily accomplishments may include brushing one's teeth, making a phone call, cleaning one's room, putting away the dishes, having a conversation or working ten minutes on a project. Breaking down large issues or directions into daily goals is a skill that many people may benefit from and is an excellent way to measure progress!

III. **POSSIBLE ACTIVITIES:** This handout may be used in conjunction with GO FOR THE GOAL Deck of Cards.

A. 1. Draw goalpost sketch on board or flipchart, as seen on handout.

2. Present concept of daily goals comparing them to longer-term goals.

3. Write the group's responses to the following questions on board/flipchart:
    "What might be a quarterback's goal the day of the game?"
    "What might be a mother's goal on her child's first day of kindergarten?"
    "What might be a teacher's goal when s/he first meets a student?"
    "What might be a student's goal when starting High School?"

4. Discuss that daily goals give a sense of purpose and direction.

5. Distribute pens and handouts.

6. Read quote aloud, asking class for meaning.

7. Offer class five minutes to write a personal goal for this day. Suggest or expand on topics/categories listed in goalpost area for ideas, if needed.

8. Ask each participant to share most important goal aloud.

9. Process by asking students to state how daily goals may assist each member personally.

B. 1. Photocopy seven handouts per student and staple together. Distribute handout packet and pencil to each student.

2. Explain concept of thinking in daily terms when making goals; it is possible to feel overwhelmed when thinking about goals too far into the future.

3. Review handout aloud, giving students ten minutes to complete.

4. Write the following questions on flipchart:
    "Is this goal realistic? (Can you really accomplish this today?)"
    "Why is this goal important to you?"

5. Divide class into pairs, instructing them to review the written goals on the handouts by asking each other the questions on the flipchart.

6. Reconvene into larger group.

7. Share results. Were goals realistic? Did partners have insight into why goals were important?

8. Explain that the remaining six handouts are to be completed daily, in the next week, as homework.

Adapted for SEALS III from LMS VI by Sandra Negley, MTRS, CTRS, Salt Lake City, UT,
author of *Crossing the Bridge, A Journey in Self-Esteem, Relationships and Life Balance.*

PLAN

What I will do to accomplish my goal.

OBSTACLE

What is preventing me from reaching my goal?

GOAL

MEASURABLE

REALISTIC

G⊙AL / OBSTACLE / PLAN

I. PURPOSE:

To provide a structured opportunity to establish goals, recognize and identify potential obstacles and establish a plan that would encourage making changes.

II. GENERAL COMMENTS:

While it is relatively easy to set goals, most people don't realize their objectives because they haven't planned adequate steps to achieve them. It is valuable to anticipate what factor(s) or condition(s) might interfere with, or prevent, goal attainment. In doing so, it is possible to increase the probability of successfully making significant changes.

III. POSSIBLE ACTIVITIES:

A. 1. Discuss similarities between a road map, a blueprint and a cookbook. (All give instructions, set a plan, or design for success.) Ask class to discuss what information is provided, when are they needed and for how long. Instruct class to relate topic of discussion to handout topic.

   2. Distribute handouts reviewing definitions of key words if necessary. Instruct students to:
      a. Identify one realistic, measurable goal.
      b. Anticipate obstacles - what might interfere with one's ability to attain the identified goal?
      c. Given those obstacles, identify a multi-step plan, which would address each obstacle.

   3. Use the following example, or elicit example from students to demonstrate process.

      GOAL: To save enough money to purchase a desired new electronic device (hand-held game, portable CD player, etc.).

      OBSTACLES:
          1. Too long to wait
          2. Low motivation
          3. Hope someone else will buy it for me
          4. My own negative thoughts about saving money
          5. Might go on sale soon and I still might not be able to afford it.

      PLAN: 1. Acknowledge-need patience
          2. Ask for help from family, friends
          3. Take a risk-be prepared to wait
          4. Stop negative thoughts
          5. Think positive deliberately - I CAN DO IT.

   4. Instruct students to complete handouts.

   5. Provide an opportunity for each student to read aloud his/her GOAL/OBSTACLE/PLAN. Encourage students to listen to the goal (assessing if it is realistic and stated in measurable terms), offering feedback and support as appropriate.

   6. Direct each student to keep the handout in a visible place (refrigerator, mirror, locker, etc.) to serve as a visual reminder to self.

B. 1. Review key words in goal identification, using the following examples: realistic - within your reach; that which can actually be accomplished; specific / measurable - states how one will know if the goal is actually attained; how the goal can be measured.

   2. Discuss the variety of goals that can be set in relation to one's wellness - assertive goals to manage stress, physical goals to take care of one's body, spiritual goals to tend to one's inner self, personal growth goals to foster self-esteem and leisure goals to establish a balanced lifestyle.

   3. Instruct students to identify one goal for self and all possible obstacles.

   4. Collect papers and redistribute so that each student receives one other than his / her own.

   5. Instruct class to review the goal and obstacle(s) and offer a possible plan that would address the identified obstacles, thereby leading to goal attainment.

   6. Provide an opportunity for each student to read aloud the goal and obstacle they were given and the plan that was subsequently identified.

   7. Encourage feedback and suggestions from the class.

   8. Process by asking students if it was helpful to hear suggestions, thoughts or ideas of what to do in order to accomplish the goal.

   9. At the conclusion of the session, leave the handouts on the table, encouraging the original authors to claim their work. Encourage students to use as a visual reminder towards goal attainment.

Activity handout and facilitator's information originally submitted for Life Management Skills V by Maggie Moriarty, M.S., COTA/L, Rocky Hill, CT. Maggie has been a practicing clinician in the behavioral health field over the past 20 years, creating and leading a variety of treatment students. She is also an assistant professor of Occupational Therapy at a community college.

Adapted for SEALS III from LMS V by Elaine Hyla Slea, M.Ed., Euclid, OH,
adaptor of *SEALS+PLUS (Self-Esteem and Life Skills)* and *SEALS II*.

Mission Statement

for the _____ Group
which includes (list individual members):

_____   _____

_____   _____

_____   _____

Our Mission is:

This Mission Statement to be revisited on _____ in the year _____.

A mission statement needs to be specific enough that
it provides a foundation for decisions, yet general enough
that it allows for nurturing individual talents and
personal growth by every person within the group.

Mission Statement

I. PURPOSE:

To write a statement that will guide groups through good and challenging times.

II. GENERAL COMMENTS:

Regardless of the size of a group, a Mission Statement answers the question, "Why do we exist?" This statement then serves as a foundation upon which all decisions within the group are based. Adolescents have frequent contact with groups in school, family and work throughout the community, all of which could benefit greatly from a Mission Statement. This statement can serve as a 'flight plan' taking into account the principles the group values. Combining these values with mutual dreams and expectations groups can move toward their goals with vision, purpose and support. The Mission Statement will need to be revisited as group members mature and individual strengths become clearer. Wording should be studied from all points of view to allow guidance without repressive restriction of every person's growth and development.

III. POSSIBLE ACTIVITIES:

A. 1. Present class with the following question: "What determines a safe airplane ride?" Responses need to include the components of a flight plan: training, weather, radar, air traffic controllers, maintenance of equipment, runways, etc.
   2. Relate a 'Mission Statement' to a 'flight plan' for an airplane ride. Discuss reasons a pilot must always be in constant communication with others. "S/he must modify the flight plan due to unexpected changes to ensure the safety of her/his passengers." Discuss PURPOSE of activity and explain GENERAL COMMENTS as stated above.
   3. Divide class into sub-groups of 4-5 students. Ask them to imagine as if they were the governing body of a school organization, e.g., student council, leadership committee, peer mediation, etc. Distribute handouts. Instruct students to use the reverse side and make a grid as follows:

Inventory Group Strengths & Weaknesses	Group Goals
Outline/Rough Draft of Mission Statement	Fine Tune Mission Statement

   4. Instruct students to complete the grid by supplying the following information:
      • INVENTORY: List members of sub-group, including strengths and areas for improvement, etc.
      • GOALS: Make a list of the qualities you would like your group to be known for, e.g., honest, hard working, reliable, fun loving, etc.
      • OUTLINE/ROUGH DRAFT OF MISSION STATEMENT: Instruct sub-groups to brainstorm ideas for Mission Statement. Review information contained in GENERAL COMMENTS as a guideline if necessary.
      • FINE TUNE MISSION STATEMENT: Instruct sub-groups to write the Mission Statement in their own words, using terms that will make it personal and easily recognizable to the sub-group and the rest of the class.
   5. After several minutes ask sub-groups to share. Elicit feedback from class, listing ideas for everyone to see.
   6. As a culminating class activity, using information from above, create a group Mission Statement, instructing students to write final draft on 'certificate' area on handout.
   7. Facilitate discussion of benefits of a Mission Statement and specifically a Group Mission Statement.
   8. Distribute extra copies of handouts. Recommend that students discuss this handout with their family, prior to the next session, for possible revision and adoption as individual Family Mission Statements.
B. 1. Before session locate several examples of organization Mission Statements and obtain copies to share with class as relevant examples.
   2. Introduce topic, PURPOSE and GENERAL COMMENTS.
   3. Ask students if they are familiar with business, hospital or organization Mission Statements. Share examples and then distribute handouts.
   4. Explain that to develop a Mission Statement requires time, energy and knowledge as well as a vision. Follow directions as explained in section A.3. above.
   5. Offer the following activity to gain insight into family members: Instruct class to use section of grid titled, "INVENTORY." To do this, write each family member's name, listed one on top of the other, along the left-hand side of the sheet. Across the top, list as many types of activities and qualities as you can think of that describe each individual in your family. The list might include such things as: plays musical instrument, works on motors, attends concerts, decorates personal space, sings, reads, is involved with others, spends time alone, enjoys quiet activities, likes cultural activities, charitable in nature, environmentally involved, etc. For each person, move to the next box on the grid and identify that person's GOAL, as you understand it to be.
   6. Review the suggestions for Mission Statements as described in GENERAL COMMENTS ABOVE.
   7. Ask each student to write an OUTLINE or ROUGH DRAFT of the MISSION STATEMENT and share it with the group. Offer challenging questions to refine the statements to ensure that the Mission Statement will provide guidance during adversity, as well as during favorable times. "What if some family member rebels and becomes addicted to a substance or deviant behavior?" "What if asked or forced to change one's career?" "What if some member of the family challenges the moral fiber of the family?" "How are spiritual differences supported or challenged by the Family Mission Statement?" Write results on "FINE TUNE" section of the grid.
   8. Instruct students to write final draft of Family Mission Statement on the certificate side of the handout. Encourage group members to display it prominently in the home. Advise group members to mark calendars for the month and year, when you will revisit the Family Mission Statement, and revise as necessary.

Activity handout and facilitator's information originally submitted for Life Management Skills V by Shirley K. Trout, M.Ed., Waverly, NE. Shirley is Parent Education Director of the Nebraska Council to Prevent Alcohol and Drug Abuse and author of parenting books, including Light Dances: Illuminating Families with Laughter and Love. She challenges all parents to envision their homes as havens for humor.

Adapted for SEALS III from LMS V by Elaine Hyla Slea, M.Ed., Euclid, OH, adaptor of *SEALS+PLUS (Self-Esteem and Life Skills)* and *SEALS II.*

Progress Note

for: _____
Your name

Today's date: _____

GOAL: _____

_____

_____

_____

_____

_____
Signature

My teachers and parents would probably:

☐ Agree with me.

☐ Disagree with me. They would say:

_____

_____

_____

_____

_____

Progress Note

I. PURPOSE:

To increase personal awareness of goals for school success and/or parent/guardian relationships.

To introduce a process to evaluate progress in reaching those goals.

To increase awareness of others' perceptions of progress.

II. GENERAL COMMENTS:

On many occasions counselors, teachers, parents/guardians, coaches, etc. discuss the progress or lack of, regarding grades, behavior, communication skills and responsibilities of a student. However, more often than not, the student is not present at the meeting, thus, not fully being represented in the discussion. When this occurs not only do the adults miss hearing the student's perspective, students miss hearing and understanding the adults' perspective.

Collaboration such as this could greatly enhance the overall success of the student. It may also empower the student to understand the process in which they need to engage, in order to make changes. Collaboration may also assist the parent/educator to understand the student's level of insight into their behavior and the reasons for their choices.

III. POSSIBLE ACTIVITIES:

A. 1. Discuss with class the need for identifying behaviors/actions that one may wish to change in order to improve their overall quality of life.

2. As a class brainstorm behaviors/actions the students themselves would like to change (get better grades, get home at curfew, stop drinking, etc.) Write the suggestions on a flip chart or white board.

3. Discuss with class that the first step in change is identifying the behavior to change and then setting a goal to make that change. Once a goal has been set one needs to monitor progress. Introduce the concept of documentation of progress and share with class how counselors or teachers note progress in treatment/school.

4. Discuss with class the importance of having their perspective represented in progress while also listening to others' perspective.

5. Distribute handouts and pens.

6. Give students a few minutes to identify a behavior they wish to change. Beside 'GOAL' have students then write an action step, a goal on the handout.

7. Invite students to share their goal with the class. Allow time for students to exchange feedback.

8. As a homework assignment ask each student to work on his or her goal until the next class. Prior to class have students' complete progress note.

9. Process benefits of this activity and suggest, if appropriate, for students to share notes with school counselor, teacher and/or parents.

B. 1. Bring to class a movie, which characterizes a person who identifies a behavior s/he wishes to change. Prior to class write on a flipchart or white board several goals the character in the movie identifies for themselves.

2. Distribute two handouts to each student.

3. Instruct students to select one of the goals suggested and write it on their handout next to 'Goal.'

4. Midway through the movie, stop and ask students to write a progress note as if they were the character identified in the movie. Ask them to also fill in the area below as they perceive others in the movie view the characters' progress toward his/her goal. Repeat the process at the end of the movie. Facilitate class discussion on what the students noted in movie.

5. Discuss with class the importance of setting goals and documenting progress. Also discuss how important it is for them to be involved in setting their own goals and having a voice in their choices or progress of their goals.

6. Instruct class members to now identify a goal they would like to make for themselves or a behavior or action they would like to change.

7. Divide the class into pairs and facilitate mutual sharing of goals. Support and encourage honesty and insights.

8. Discuss the individuals' feelings if parents/teachers/coaches 'disagree' on progress. Do individuals feel that this could or does impede their progress toward their goals? What suggestions would the class make?

9. Ask each student to complete a progress note at the end of each day, bringing completed progress notes to the next class as follow-up.

Activity handout and facilitator's information submitted by Betty Welch, Ph.D., Manchester, NH.
Betty is the program coordinator at a Geropsychiatric Partial Hospitalization Program.

**Adapted for SEALS III from LMS VI by Sandra Negley, MTRS, CTRS, Salt Lake City, UT,
author of *Crossing the Bridge, A Journey in Self-Esteem, Relationships and Life Balance.***

the GUILT (after loss)
Merry~Go~Round

Everyone experiences loss at some time in their lives.

List your personal losses below, which have involved a(n):

Family Member _____   School _____

Friend _____   Pet _____

Dream or Goal _____   Financial _____

Relationship _____   Social Event _____

Physical/Health Situation _____   Other _____

Most people have feelings of guilt after a significant loss, and it can feel like a Merry-Go-Round that KEEPS ON GOING.

Choose one loss about which you feel guilt, and write it here:

_____

Think of that loss and finish as many of the sentences below as you can. (It is OK to repeat endings.)

(1) I wish _____.

(2) If only _____.

(3) I could have _____.

(4) Why didn't _____.

(5) I needed to _____.

(6) I should have _____.

(7) If I could do it over, I _____.

The Guilt Merry-Go-Round is fueled by thinking self-defeating thoughts and by self-defeating terms.

In order to get off the Merry~Go~Round, we need to let go.

the GUILT (after loss)
Merry~Go~Round

I. PURPOSE:

To deal with feelings of guilt (after a loss) by:
1) identifying personal losses
2) acknowledging the universality of guilt after loss
3) expressing feelings of guilt
4) letting go of these feelings.

II. GENERAL COMMENTS:

It is natural to have feelings of guilt after a loss. When these feelings of self-blame are repeated again and again, they reinforce themselves and may become deeper ingrained. These feelings can keep a person stuck in a 'guilt trip' that seems to have no end. In order to let go, it is important to have feelings acknowledged, accepted and valued. It is important to rewrite the 'inner dialogues' along with sharing openly and honestly with others.

III. POSSIBLE ACTIVITIES:

A. 1. Discuss the universal feelings of guilt after a loss.

2. Distribute the handouts and pencils and refer to the illustrated analogy of the merry-go-round.

3. Allow 2-3 minutes for students to complete the top section.

4. Read aloud the "Most people have..." statement.

5. Ask each student to choose one loss and to write it on the handout.

6. Give student 10 minutes to finish the incomplete sentences.

7. Ask each students to realistically consider the question "How much of this guilt am I really due?" Encourage class support during this discussion.

8. Discuss the destructive nature of self-defeating inner dialogue. Instruct class to brainstorm alternatives to replace the defeating sentences with terms of self-empowerment.

9. Process activity by discussing the importance of this healing part of the grief process.

B. 1. Before session, bring a wastebasket to class. Cut several sheets of blank paper into 2"x11" inch strips, making enough for a demonstration and one for each student.

2. Distribute the handouts.

3. Give class 15 minutes to complete the handouts.

4. Facilitate the experience of letting guilt go, using the following exercise:
   a. The leader states the four steps below and demonstrates by writing a guilt of his/her own on a strip of paper, pausing after each step, and then crumbles the strip of paper and drops it in the waste basket.
      1. "The guilt I feel is _____."
      2. "I did the best I could at that time."
      3. "I forgive myself."
      4. "I now let the guilt go."
   b. Each class member then writes down a guilt on a strip of paper. Each in turn says:
      1. "The guilt I feel is _____."
      2. "I did the best I could at that time."
      3. "I forgive myself."
      4. "I now let the guilt go."

5. Process activity by reviewing symbolism in the steps used in letting guilt go.

6. ALTERNATIVE SUGGESTION: attach strips of paper with guilt statements written on them to a helium balloon. Lead class outside (weather permitting) and release guilt by releasing the balloon. Discuss symbolism of activity.

Activity handout and facilitator's information originally submitted for Life Management Skills V by Marta Felber, M.Ed., West Fork, AR. Marta's M.Ed. is in Counseling. She used her experience from more than 30 years in helping professions, to heal herself after her husband's death. Felber lives in a Yankee Barn home on an Ozark mountaintop in Northwest Arkansas. She continues in her counseling role, with a focus on grief and loss and is the author of Grief Expressed: When a Mate Dies.

Adapted for SEALS III from LMS V by Elaine Hyla Slea, M.Ed., Euclid, OH,
adaptor of *SEALS+PLUS (Self-Esteem and Life Skills)* and *SEALS II.*

HEALING from a Loss

Healing

Loss

HEALING from a Loss

I. PURPOSE:

To increase awareness of feelings regarding a loss and the feelings associated with the expression of healing.

To identify healthy sources of comfort in the healing process following a loss.

II. GENERAL COMMENTS:

Loss is an intrinsic part of life. A person cannot be totally isolated from the pain caused by grief and loss. The natural world, as well as the media, provides exposure to the experience of loss. Although adolescents' reactions to loss may resemble adults', many adolescents show denial by a lack of emotional display. Demeanor and reactions in the classroom can do much to help an adolescent cope with this issue. When a loss occurs, maintaining awareness of the situation, demonstrating care and concern while encouraging honest communication can facilitate a healthy grieving process.

III. POSSIBLE ACTIVITIES:

A. 1. Before session, copy handout, cut in half, separating the 'loss' from the 'healing' section. Re-copy handout with the 'loss' section on the front and the 'healing' section on the reverse. When folded, handout should resemble a greeting card.

2. Introduce the topic of grief and the fact that it is universal. Explain that grief results from the pain of loss - a death, disappointments, disruptions in the family, altered friendships, unfulfilled dreams, end of childhood freedom, not chosen to participate in school events or activities, etc.

3. Elicit further examples from class.

4. Introduce the topic of the importance of communication during the grieving process following a loss. Focus discussion on purpose of greeting cards.

5. Distribute handouts instructing students to fold the handout in half.

6. Instruct class to think of an incident from their own lives associated with the words 'grief' or 'loss.' Instruct students to create their own 'sympathy' cards by drawing an image of the loss on the front of the handout and to accompany the drawing with appropriate words describing the loss.

7. Direct students to open the 'card.' Repeat steps described in A.6. changing focus to healing images and words.

8. Invite students to share as able by asking "What are your reactions to your own art work?" Emphasize the PROCESS and not the PRODUCT, discouraging comparisons of quality differences between students.

9. Process by exploring emotions that emerge in the expression of loss and healing (denial, depression, hope, strength, wisdom, etc.).

B. 1. Ask class to define grief and loss and the healing process in their own words providing input as needed.

2. Explain that oftentimes people get 'stuck' and may need guidance to get through this feeling, but this can come from within.

3. Distribute handouts.

4. Instruct the class to write on the 'loss' side of handouts an obituary about themselves or a loved one using the suggested format below:

    _____ _____ died yesterday from _____.
       (name)   (age)

    S/he is survived by _____.

    S/he will be remembered for _____.

    S/he was working on becoming _____.

    S/he always wanted, but never got to _____.

    The world will experience a loss because _____.

5. Invite each student to share his/her work as able.

6. Ask class to describe emotional reactions to activity. Identify patterns or themes. Guide discussion to the benefits/objectives of activity. Focus on impact of activity upon students' abilities to recognize opportunities for their lives yet ahead.

7. Instruct students to complete healing section by creating survival plans. Offer choice of the following: healing hints and strategies, personal sources of comfort, advice for healing that a loved one would offer, or a realistic plan for the future to which one can look forward. Invite each student to share as able.

8. Process activity by encouraging other healing and creative opportunities stemming from this grief work such as poetry, journalizing, artwork, collages, music, etc.

Activity handout and facilitator's information originally submitted for Life Management Skills V by Mary Lou Hamilton, MS, RN, Wilmington, DE. Mary Lou has worked in educational settings for most of her career as well as a clinical nurse specialist and program developer in psychiatric settings. As a nurse-educator she utilizes expressive art techniques with journalizing activities.

Adapted for SEALS III from LMS V by Elaine Hyla Slea, M.Ed., Euclid, OH, adaptor of *SEALS+PLUS (Self-Esteem and Life Skills)* and *SEALS II*.

STEPS OF GRIEF

AFTER A LOSS

We Go Through Steps of Grief After A Loss

Everyone grieves yet every person grieves differently. There is **no exact plan** for grieving, yet many people who have lost someone or something significant in their lives experience **similar emotions** or steps of grief.

Some of the steps might be: **SHOCK** ➤ **NUMBNESS** ➤ **DENIAL** ➤ **ANGER** ➤ **FEAR** ➤ **GUILT** ➤

DEPRESSION ➤ **SHAME** ➤ **LONELINESS** ➤ **BLAME** ➤ **RELIEF, ETC.**

OTHERS _____

➤ Think about one of your losses and write it here: _____

➤ From the list above, recognize five of the most familiar "steps" and write one, in any order, on each of the next steps.

➤ Stay on each "step" to think, feel and make notes.

➤ Continue up the stairway to **"acceptance"**.

➤ Start with "shock" on the stairway.

➤ Make notes about your experience.
- What did you do?
- What did you think?
- What did you say?

➤ Are you finished with this step?

➤ Are you ready for another "step"? **OK! Let's move on!**

ACCEPTANCE

SHOCK

➤ KEEP IN MIND THAT . . .

➤ Not all persons experience these steps after a loss.

➤ Steps may be repeated.

➤ No step needs to last indefinitely.

➤ Your steps may not be in this order.

➤ All steps are normal.

STEPS OF GRIEF AFTER A LOSS

I. PURPOSE:

To become aware of steps of grief.

To identify personal steps of grief and experience feelings, past and present, at each stage.

II. GENERAL COMMENTS:

All of us wish to live in safe and comfortable circumstances. Try as we may, events do occur and take us by surprise impacting our lives. Most people go through minor changes of circumstance everyday: dead battery, a wrong number, loss of a pet, overdrawn bank account, etc. Catastrophic losses involving natural or man-made disasters, accidents, assaults, violence, abuse or death are outside of our daily routines, normal experiences and comfort level. People can be found dealing with trauma reactions to these situations as well as intense feelings of grief.

Most people do go through steps of grief after either type of loss. Experiences at different steps may vary greatly, causing an individual to feel 'weird', 'different', and in some cases, as if s/he is 'going crazy.' Identifying these steps and/or feelings, sharing with others and knowing others have experienced them also, can help individuals to understand their own personal journeys through grief and feel supported in this process.

III. POSSIBLE ACTIVITIES:

A. 1. Prior to class, use handout to create overhead transparency or copy steps on board or flip chart.

2. Review concepts as outlined in the PURPOSE and GENERAL COMMENTS.

3. Based on students' personal life experiences, ask students to provide definitions for each step, citing possible purposes, behaviors, beliefs, self-talk, etc., identified with each step. List on overhead, board or flip chart.

4. Provide an example of a loss familiar to age group. Facilitate discussion of steps involved in recovery from this loss.

5. Share responses in a supportive atmosphere.

6. Instruct the class to share perceptions of how each step effects emotional growth: which step was… most helpful, most painful, easiest to recognize, most difficult, etc.

7. Ask class to add possible steps to the list: sorrow, isolation, growth, etc.

8. Review the 'Keep in Mind' section emphasizing important points. Encourage students to practice using Steps of Grief as a model for dealing with everyday stressors as well as catastrophic events.

B. 1. Distribute handouts and review as a class.

2. Review concepts as outlined in the PURPOSE and GENERAL COMMENTS.

3. Allow 10 minutes for students to complete.

4. Facilitate discussion and encourage students to:

    a) share as able, Steps of Grief in their personal lives not yet finished.

    b) share everyday life situations where knowing steps of grief might be beneficial.

    c) review importance of 'Keep in Mind' section as part of positive self-talk.

5. Process by asking students if this was helpful or healing and to explain.

6. Encourage students to practice using Steps of Grief as a model for dealing with everyday stressors as well as catastrophic events.

7. Possible follow-up activity: Instruct students to share concepts with loved ones and supports, recording feedback for subsequent class session.

Activity handout and facilitator's information originally submitted for Life Management Skills V by Marta Felber, M.Ed., West Fork, AR. Marta's M.Ed. is in Counseling. She used her experience from more than 30 years in helping professions, to heal herself after her husband's death. Felber lives in a Yankee Barn home on an Ozark mountaintop in Northwest Arkansas. She continues in her counseling role, with a focus on grief and loss and is the author of Grief Expressed: When a Mate Dies.

Adapted for SEALS III from LMS V by Elaine Hyla Slea, M.Ed., Euclid, OH,
adaptor of *SEALS+PLUS (Self-Esteem and Life Skills)* and *SEALS II.*

LAUGHING MATTERS

Constructing Your Humor Foundation

Identify three silly, awkward or embarrassing things you did or said during the past six months.	Who saw you do it?	How soon did the incident get shared and with whom?	Was there laughter at the time?	
1. At school	1.	1.	YES ☐ NO ☐	If **YES**, you can bet that's already one of your stories that will be revisited in years to come.
2. In public	2.	2.	YES ☐ NO ☐	If **NO**, you missed making that moment a laughing matter. Either look for the right moment for it to be recalled — this time with laughter — or be more alert next time you do something that should be shared with someone.
3. At home or while visiting others	3.	3.	YES ☐ NO ☐	

LAUGHING MATTERS

I. PURPOSE:

To instill an appreciation for humor as a coping mechanism.

To facilitate healing, communication, caring and creativity through storytelling.

II. GENERAL COMMENTS:

Humor is a sign of growth and confidence in an emerging adolescent. Girls will more often use verbal humor while boys are more likely to express humor in physical ways. As all children approach adolescence they are better able at expressing humor verbally and are better equipped to use humor as a coping mechanism. In doing so they are on their way toward handling the challenges and responsibilities of adolescence and adulthood.

Introducing playfulness and humor into a situation can relieve tension, ease sadness and build relationships. Revealing alternative ways of perceiving situations will enable one to revise problem-solving techniques. Humor helps to facilitate social relationships. It can also be a vehicle for dealing with painful situations.

How and when a person uses laughter says a lot about them. By briefly examining the healing benefits of humor, useful ways of dealing with the problems of everyday living may be discovered.

III. POSSIBLE ACTIVITIES:

A. 1. Introduce the topic and disclose one personal amusing story to the class.

2. Explain the purpose of session, distribute handouts and instruct students to complete.

3. Encourage sharing of at least one incident per student

4. Ask students "What is the value of story telling?" and "What is the value of laughing within a group, whether it is in class, at home, at work or at play?"

5. For a follow-up activity, ask students to bring to next session a photograph of themselves that evokes a humorous memory. Remind them to be prepared to tell the funny aspect of the story that was occurring when the photograph was taken.

B. 1. Discuss the difficulties, challenges and joys of being a member of this class.

2. Ask students to share one incident where they did something silly, awkward or embarrassing within the last six months, either at home, at school or in public, always being mindful of good taste and language.

3. Distribute handouts and complete as a class.

4. Suggest ways of increasing the possibility of building stories through laughter.

   a. Record silliness in photographs. Always have a camera loaded with film for a spontaneous moment, or for a reenactment of a laughable event.

   b. Transcend from tears (or humiliation) to laughter, ASAP! As soon as is conceivably possible, recall an uncomfortable event, bringing in observations of how funny it was (or must have seemed) to other than the person wishing/hoping no one had noticed.

   NOTE: This activity may sound very insensitive to those not well versed in the power of laughter. However, trust the experts on this one. As one becomes more adept at recognizing when and how to do this, students will spend much less time recovering from being 'emotionally shattered' and much more time recognizing that to err is human.

   c. Use props to prompt laughter. Suggest that at least once a year, no one leave the dinner table until the 'Table Game' has been completed. This game can involve props, i.e., wind-up toys, gag gifts, modeling clay that can, in some way, relate to some laughable family experience from the past year.

   d. Be alert to ways in which you can 'plant' chuckles into the lives of your loved ones. Notes in lunch boxes or left around the house, silly snacks that send double meanings, particularly tasteless table or room decorations, just to see if anyone would have 'the audacity' to comment (followed by you pretending to be serious, then laughing at the set up). Watch for funny little props as you travel and shop. Listen carefully to conversations so you can buy appropriate 'spin-off' gifts to be presented some day in the future.

   e. Plan a 'Game Night' inviting family and friends over for an evening of board games, fun and memory sharing and building. Search thrift stores or yard sales for copies of out of print board games or puzzles. Create funny certificates to be awarded as prizes. Lighten up and just have some fun!

5. Ask students to share suggestions of how to build stories through laughter.

6. Photocopy extra handouts and distribute to students, instructing them to complete it as a follow-up activity with their immediate family. Ask students to be prepared to discuss results and how this activity can be used to creating stronger family bonds.

Activity handout and facilitator's information originally submitted for Life Management Skills V by Shirley K. Trout, M.Ed., Waverly, NE. Shirley is Parent Education Director of the Nebraska Council to Prevent Alcohol and Drug Abuse and author of parenting books, including Light Dances: Illuminating Families with Laughter and Love.

Adapted for SEALS III from LMS V by Elaine Hyla Slea, M.Ed., Euclid, OH,
adaptor of *SEALS+PLUS (Self-Esteem and Life Skills)* and *SEALS II.*

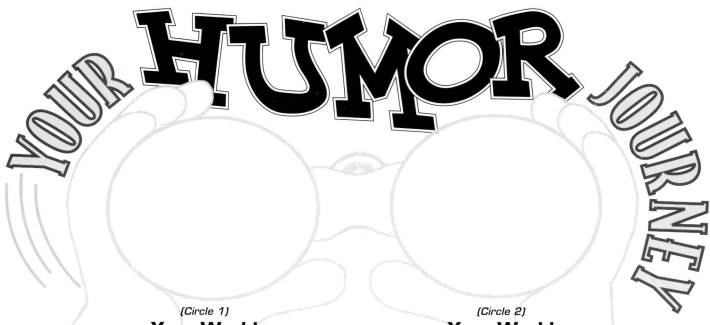

YOUR HUMOR JOURNEY

(Circle 1)
Your World
in the past week:
Draw a pie-shaped wedge (in Circle 1) that shows how much play, amusement or laughter you feel you have had in the past week.

(Circle 2)
Your World
as you would like it to be:
Draw a pie-shaped wedge (in Circle 2) that shows how much play, amusement or laughter you would like next week.

What are 3 things you do that allows you to smile, laugh and / or have fun?

0: ► *ex. Watch a favorite comedy show on TV*

00: ► *ex. Enjoying a pet*

1:

2:

3:

CREATIVE ACTION PLAN?
Of each of the 3 listed above, what will you do to ensure that these things happen?

0: ► *ex. I will videotape a show - or I will be sure to be home in time to watch reruns.*

00: ► *ex. I will find time to play with a pet and/or carry a picture of the pet.*

1: *I will*

2: *I will*

3: *I will*

Take the Humor Journey!
Shift your focus and move from Circle 1 to Circle 2.

I. PURPOSE:

To increase humor in one's daily life.

II. GENERAL COMMENTS:

Laughter, a natural part of elementary school, is often considered frivolous in secondary education situations as teachers focus on the 'serious' business of preparing students for the 'real' world. In fact, it has been found that humor is one of the best skills to have. Humor can relieve tension and pain. It can facilitate smooth flow of communication, breakdown attitudes and even draw students to learning.

Remind students to distinguish between laughter that hurts and laughter that heals. Jokes and teasing have tremendous power to injure others because they are based on ridicule. Humor that has a put-down quality, shows little or no compassion or empathy, and stems from ridicule, does not make us feel better about ourselves or others. A sense of humor that heals is warm, connected, broad and universal. It allows us to play with situations that are stressful instead of playing with others' pain to create laughter.

III. POSSIBLE ACTIVITIES:

A. 1. Before class, with the assistance of a biographical dictionary, make a list of famous persons who will most likely be known to the class. Print each name on a separate index card.

2. Demonstrate riddling technique by using the 'Famous Name' formula.
For example; Davy Crockett. Change the name slightly in order to create a (hopefully) humorous punch line for the riddle. Davy Crickett, Gravy Crockett, Davy Crew Cut, etc. Let your imagination run wild.

3. Think of a question that suggests the punchline. For example: What famous explorer chirped at night? What famous explorer makes turkey taste better?

4. Put the questions and the punchline together:
What famous explorer chirped at night?   Davy Crickett
What famous explorer makes turkey taste better?   Gravy Crockett

5. Using this example, ask the class to brainstorm other riddles and punch lines being mindful of good taste, appropriate language and political correctness.

6. Distribute the index cards. Instruct class to create a famous name riddle using the formula presented in class. Allow additional minutes for creativity.

7. Ask a few students to share their riddles and punchlines.

8. Discuss purpose of activity with class using information found in GENERAL COMMENTS as a guideline.

9. Distribute handouts and ask class to complete.

10. Share action plans as able, encouraging students' support, to increase humor in one's daily life and minimize those activities that do not enhance humor.

11. Process activity by asking remaining students who did not previously have the opportunity to do so to tell their famous names riddles.

12. As a follow-up activity, ask students to bring this activity home to share with family or friends. Share best riddles during next session to 'stump' the class.

B. 1. Ask each student to tell one recent 'funny' (joke, story, anecdote) they heard or experienced. Remind students to use good taste, appropriate language and to be aware of political correctness.

2. Distribute handouts and ask students to complete.

3. Ask students "Why is it important to include humor in each of your lives daily?"

4. Encourage the students to make a commitment to increase humor, laughter and play by asking them to take a 'humor oath'.

5. Ask class to raise their right hand, pat themselves on the head while they rub their tummies with their left hand. And finally, ask them to repeat after you:
"Starting right now, I will get more laughter and play in my life! So help me, _____."
(Fill in the name of a comedian to whom students can relate).

6. For further consideration, start a humor bulletin board to post cartoons, comics, jokes, etc., that tickle their funny bones.

7. Ask librarian/information specialist to assist students in obtaining copies of joke books, tongue twisters, riddles, joke web-sites, etc. Ask students to volunteer to read a humorous story, tell a joke, try a tongue twister, etc., to the rest of the class to set the pace along the "Humor Journey".

Activity handout and facilitator's information originally submitted for Life Management Skills V by Allen Klein, MA, CSP.
Allen is an award-winning professional speaker and best selling author of such books as
The Healing Power of Humor, Quotations to Cheer You Up and The Courage to Laugh. http://www.allenklein.com.

Adapted for SEALS III from LMS V by Elaine Hyla Slea, M.Ed., Euclid, OH,
adaptor of *SEALS+PLUS (Self-Esteem and Life Skills)* and *SEALS II.*

Getting a JOB?

WHAT DO THESE WORDS HAVE TO DO WITH GETTING A JOB?

Before we begin to seriously consider searching for that ideal position, we need to be aware of vocabulary frequently used in learning about jobs. Potential job applicants should understand the following terms:

career	application	short-range goal
job requirement	benefits	long-range goal
qualifications	salary range	minimum wage
apprentice	job security	professional
paraprofessional	GED	entry-level
technician	resume	interviewer
community college	union	applicant
retirement	employment office	disability

Look over the list.
How many terms do you know?

I. PURPOSE:

To identify words and terms used in conjunction with a job search.

II. GENERAL COMMENTS:

For a potential job applicant to be prepared, s/he needs to be familiar with a job-related vocabulary. Prospective employers, those who assist in job placement and other applicants will use this language. Knowing these basic terms will add a sense of confidence that is essential for success. Obtaining and maintaining a job is an important independent living skill.

III. POSSIBLE ACTIVITIES: This handout may be used in conjunction with the JOB READINESS section (S.E.A.L.S. II - pages 23-26). It may also be used in conjunction with APARTMENT HUNTING CROSSWORD PUZZLE (Supplemental page "A" - after page 80).

A. 1. Facilitate discussion on preparation for finding a job (e.g., understanding what kind of job we want, what our skills are, how to go about finding the jobs available).

   2. Encourage students to share their experiences about applying for, obtaining and maintaining a job.

   3. Distribute handouts. Define terms in language that all can understand. Bring classified ads, a resume, an application, class listings, or any example to demonstrate use/relevance of terms.

   4. Process by asking students to give examples (personal ones if possible) of each word (e.g., union — a union is a group of employees who join together to advocate for good working conditions and benefits. My father was a member of the teacher's union).

B. 1. Cut apart vocabulary cards; glue each on a 3" x 5" index card.

   2. Place cards face down on pile in center of table.

   3. Explain to students the value of knowing a job-related vocabulary.

   4. Instruct students, in turn, to choose top card, explain its meaning and give relevant implication.

   5. Continue until all 24 cards have been studied.

   6. Distribute handouts for further review.

   7. Ask each student to circle any words or terms that remain unclear. These can be discussed further at the next class.

   8. Process by asking each class member to use one previously unfamiliar term, correctly in a sentence.

Activity handout and facilitator's information originally submitted for Life Management Skills VI by Roberta Jean Ott, COTA, Allentown, PA. Roberta is a former elementary school teacher. She has worked at a state hospital for several years and is employed part-time at a local nursing home.

Adapted for SEALS III from LMS VI by Sandra Negley, MTRS, CTRS, Salt Lake City, UT, author of *Crossing the Bridge, A Journey in Self-Esteem, Relationships and Life Balance*.

H·O·U·S·I·N·G:
Exploring the Situation

I will be

living at _____

alone / with _____

Exploring the POSITIVES and NEGATIVES

Positive aspects	Negative aspects
1.	1.
2.	2.
3.	3.

Exploring INDEPENDENCE

Are you at a place in your life where you may be considering living in your own apartment? Before you jump into a situation you may not be ready for, evaluate your situation. Read the following questions to help you decide:

1. Do you have a prepared monthly budget? _____

2. Will your income be adequate for your rent, bills, and expenses? _____

3. Can you plan and cook your own meals? _____

4. Can you sort and do your own laundry? _____

5. Do you have any health problems that need to be attended to routinely? _____

6. Would you know how to handle an emergency should it arise? _____

Exploring SHARING

Roommates need to negotiate, compromise and even get along!
When sharing an apartment, it is wise to consider the following:

	You	Roommate
1. Whose name will be on the lease?		
2. Who will be responsible for paying the rent?		
3. Who will be responsible for paying utilities?		
4. Is smoking a problem?		
5. Who will pay for food?		
6. Who will shop for food?		
7. Who will do the cooking?		
8. Who will clean up?		
9. Who is responsible for laundry?		
10. Is listening to loud music a problem?		

I. PURPOSE:

To explore the 'pros' and 'cons' of independent living situations.

To increase awareness of independent living and of shared living responsibilities and considerations.

II. GENERAL COMMENTS:

Living independently is a giant step in developing one's autonomy. However, it is filled with many responsibilities. Taking a realistic look at different housing situations can assist those planning this transition. Emphasizing that no living situation is ideal; that all arrangements have pros and cons may allow some to feel more comfortable in their decision. The considerations of independent vs. shared living arrangements require time, honesty and support.

III. POSSIBLE ACTIVITIES: This handout may be used in conjunction with APARTMENT HUNTING CROSSWORD PUZZLE (Supplemental page "A" - after page 80).

A. 1. Explain to students that this session will allow an opportunity to explore and develop an awareness of independent living. This may avoid surprises, disappointments and perhaps even failures in future living choices.

2. Distribute handouts and pencils.

3. Facilitate discussion about independent living. Ask questions such as; "When would you like to move out on your own?", "Where would you like to live?". After discussion have students complete the top section of the handout.

4. Divide class into those who are expecting to live independently and those who are expecting to share living expenses with a roommate(s). Appoint one reader for each subgroup.

5. Allow each subgroup ten minutes as reader reviews questions aloud and encourages others to jot notes or place checks.

6. Reconvene and share thoughts and concerns.

7. Problem solve as a class specific issues - e.g., "If there is an emergency, who is the best person to contact? Do you have their phone number?"

8. Re-explore top section of 'pros' and 'cons'. Ask the class if they have discovered any additional 'pros' and/or 'cons'. Discuss and process.

B. 1. Discuss that transitions are oftentimes stressful. The decision of independent vs. shared living, the details/considerations of both, and the planning can be overwhelming.

2. Write 'pros' and 'cons' horizontally on flipchart. Write 'independent' and 'shared' vertically to form a comparison graph.

3. Ask class, "What are the 'pros' to independent living?" Write in responses. Then, ask students, "What are the 'cons' of independent living?" Write in responses. Continue process with the remaining two questions.

4. Distribute handouts and pencils.

5. Give students 15 minutes to complete bottom two sections of handouts, emphasizing honesty with oneself to get an accurate picture of concerns.

6. Review completed handouts.

7. Tally class for commonalties:
How many students are planning to live independently? What are their concerns?
How many students are planning to live in a shared environment? What are their concerns?

8. Assist students in effective problem solving. Bring resources that may be helpful to the students: phone numbers of local resources, blank daily schedules, bus schedules, etc. Direct role-plays for potentially difficult situations with roommates, parents, friends, etc.

9. Process by asking class members to complete top section and share.

Top third of activity handout and facilitator's information submitted by Marla Yoder-Tiedt, MSW, LISW and Sandi Miller, RRT, both employed at a psychiatric hospital in Columbus, OH, with 15 years and 22 years in the mental health field respectively. Middle and bottom third submitted by Joan Rascati, ADL's program manager, New Haven, CT. Joan has been employed at a mental health agency for 17 years and is involved in social, community and independent living skills programs.

Adapted for SEALS III from LMS VI by Sandra Negley, MTRS, CTRS, Salt Lake City, UT,
author of *Crossing the Bridge, A Journey in Self-Esteem, Relationships and Life Balance*.

MONEY $$$ MANAGEMENT SKILLS

Understanding how to manage money by balancing income and expenses is an important lifetime skill.

INCOME - the money we have coming in every month sets the stage for our budget. Although it can be difficult to spend within our means, managing money well is a major stress management technique!

◼ My current source(s) of income is: _____ .

◼ I receive $_____ per month.

◼ I have obtained a social security card: ☐ Yes ☐ No

◼ My social security number is: __ __ __ - __ __ - __ __ __ __ .

Check off one of the following:

◼ _____ I expect no major changes in my income in the next year.

◼ _____ I expect the following changes in my income in the next year:

_____

HOW CAN I SAVE $$$? – We all have expenses that take big bites out of our financial resources. Can we reduce these expenses, thereby using our money more wisely?

Under each expense below, list strategies that we could use to reduce these amounts.

1 CLOTHING:
    a. buy non-designer brands
    b. buy items 'on sale'
    c. _____
    d. _____

2 FOOD:
    a. pack a lunch
    b. limit trips to fast food
    c. _____
    d. _____

3 TRANSPORTATION:
    a. use bus ticket
    b. walk or bike
    c. _____
    d. _____

4 RECREATION:
    a. utilize free activities
    b. attend movie matinees
    c. _____
    d. _____

MONEY $$$ MANAGEMENT SKILLS

I. PURPOSE:

To introduce money management as a lifetime skill.

To identify one's income and ways one can save money.

II. GENERAL COMMENTS:

Managing money is a necessary life time skill. In order to manage money effectively one must gain knowledge and experience in balancing income and expenses. Talking about money (or the lack thereof) is difficult for many people, but it can be very worthwhile to openly and realistically discuss both income and expenses. Frustration, anxiety and/or stress often accompany money difficulties. It may be useful to examine one's income, analyze how one spends money and develop strategies for using financial resources more wisely.

III. POSSIBLE ACTIVITIES: This handout may be used in conjunction with MONEY MANAGEMENT section (SEALS+PLUS, pages 40-42), and LIFESKILL CIRCLE GAME (with $$$ Management Cards). It may also be used in conjunction with APARTMENT HUNTING CROSSWORD PUZZLE (Supplemental page "A" - after page 80).

A. 1. Ask class to brainstorm list of ways they spend money.

2. Facilitate discussion to share ways, in which expenses can, and have been, reduced, e.g.,
FOOD - Eating at home
CLOTHING - Swapping with a friend
TRANSPORTATION - Riding the bus
RECREATION - Going to free community concerts.

3. Distribute handouts and pencils. Review both sections aloud with the class explaining concept outlined in GENERAL COMMENTS above.

4. Give students ten minutes to complete both sections. Supply numbers and addresses of local Social Security offices if needed. Explain purpose of Social Security.

5. Share and compare ideas generated by items c. and d. in bottom section.

6. Process by asking students' input on how money and stress management are related.

B. 1. Introduce today's topic as 'Money Management'. Explain that it will be divided into two parts: income and expenses. Acknowledge that although looking at the truth may be difficult, it may also be stress reducing and strengthening in the long run.

2. Distribute handouts and pencils. Give students five minutes to complete the top section that focuses on income. Explain to students that it is important for all persons to have an accurate understanding of their finances so they can budget accordingly.

3. Supply needed information regarding Social Security office numbers and addresses, if needed.

4. Provide local telephone directories, newspapers, community recreation flyers, etc. Encourage participants to use these materials to find community resources that may help in reducing living expenses. Pose interesting questions to the group, such as:
"Which movie theater has the best bargains for matinees?"
"Which video store gives the best rates for movie rentals?"
"What store offers the best prices on today's styles?"
"Does the local bus authority have student discounts?"

5. Instruct students to complete bottom section of handout.

6. Review with the class that it is difficult to spend only what is within a budget, but the benefits may outweigh the stress, anxiety and frustration experienced and will allow savings for what is important.

7. Ask students to share one insight gained from this session.

Top half of activity handout and facilitator's information submitted by Marla Yoder-Tiedt, MSW, LISW and Sandi MIller, RRT, both employed at a psychiatric hospital in Columbus, OH, with 15 years and 22 years in the mental health field respectively.
Lower half of activity handout and facilitator's information submitted by Roberta Jean Ott, COTA/TASW of Allentown, PA, who has worked at a state hospital for several years and is employed part-time at a local nursing home.

Adapted for SEALS III from LMS VI by Sandra Negley, MTRS, CTRS, Salt Lake City, UT,
author of *Crossing the Bridge, A Journey in Self-Esteem, Relationships and Life Balance.*

BINGO CONNECTION

Circulate throughout the classroom and find people who match the descriptions in the boxes. Ask each one to write his/her name in the appropriate box. **A person is only allowed to sign one box on any sheet, even though they may meet requirements of another box.** Move on to find someone else. The person to get 5 in a row, horizontally, vertically, diagonally, or 4 corners, wins.

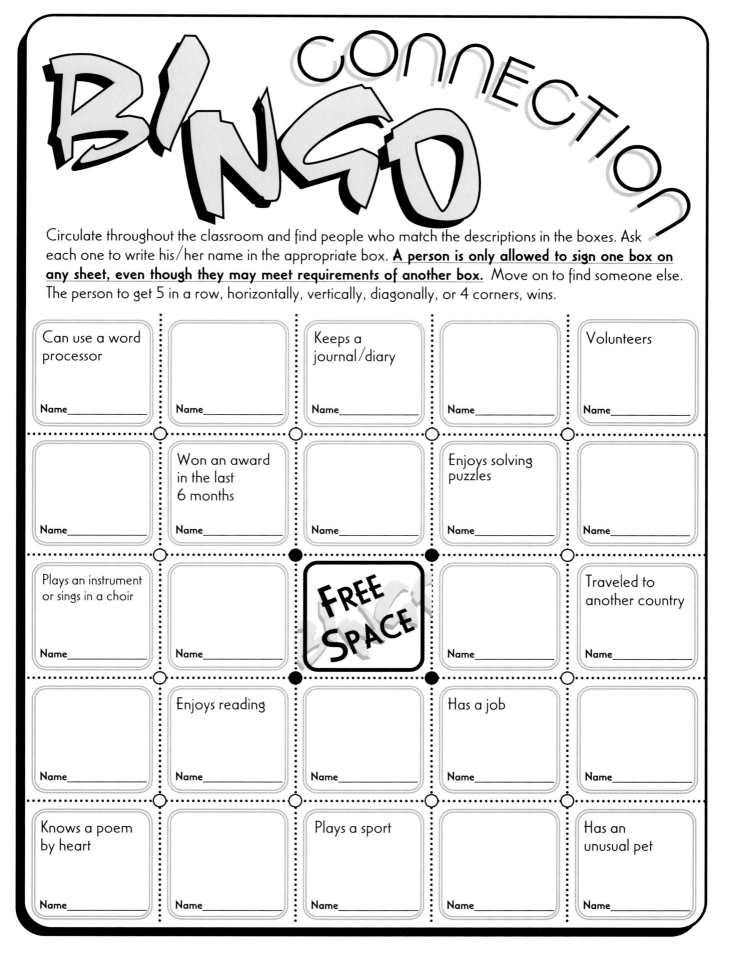

Can use a word processor Name_____	 Name_____	Keeps a journal/diary Name_____	 Name_____	Volunteers Name_____
  Name_____	Won an award in the last 6 months Name_____	 Name_____	Enjoys solving puzzles Name_____	 Name_____
Plays an instrument or sings in a choir Name_____	 Name_____	**FREE SPACE**	 Name_____	Traveled to another country Name_____
  Name_____	Enjoys reading Name_____	 Name_____	Has a job Name_____	 Name_____
Knows a poem by heart Name_____	 Name_____	Plays a sport Name_____	 Name_____	Has an unusual pet Name_____

I. PURPOSE:

To facilitate a non-threatening, comfortable learning atmosphere.

To promote social skill acquisition through group interactions.

To encourage group interactions.

II. GENERAL COMMENTS:

Most people recall games as part of the growing-up process. It is now recognized that games are not only for fun but can be used to prepare students for entry into the social system. Games, which also may be called structured exercises/activities/experiences within educational environments, can allow the participants to discover outcomes, rather than be told everything without trying it. The more comfortable participants feel with each other, the better the learning environment. The higher the comfort level, the more likely students are to participate in future activities and generate new ideas/awareness.

III. POSSIBLE ACTIVITIES:

A. 1. Photocopy handout along with SELF-ESTEEM ROAD TRIP (page 70). A different color paper for BINGO CONNECTION is recommended.

2. Distribute SELF-ESTEEM ROAD TRIP handouts. Instruct class to complete each section writing one positive accomplishment/goal about themselves in each of the four sections.

3. Distribute Bingo handouts. Instruct class to write one accomplishment/goal from SELF-ESTEEM ROAD TRIP in any blank square on the BINGO CONNECTION handout.

4. Instruct the class to switch BINGO CONNECTION handouts and repeat the process using a different accomplishment/goal.

5. Continue step 4 until all BINGO CONNECTION sheets are completed.

6. Instruct the class to take a BINGO CONNECTION sheet and 'circulate' throughout the classroom, finding students from the class who match the requirements of the boxes on the sheet. When they make a match, that person is to write his/her name in the appropriate box. A person is allowed to sign one box on any sheet even though he/she may meet the requirements of another box.

7. The first student to complete a line (horizontally, vertically, diagonally, or each of the four corners) wins.

8. Process by discussing previously unknown information about students in class, along with purpose of activity and its usefulness in personal goal setting.

B. 1. This handout can be used as an 'icebreaker' activity at the start of a new classroom environment/setting.

2. Before session, create a list of 12 new categories. These categories will be the criteria for completing BINGO CONNECTION handouts.

For example: Create a list of favorites, least favorites, most recent, or a mix of several different categories. If possible, tailor list to suit students' interests, hobbies, and activities, e.g.: favorite food, least favorite sports team, television program, favorite actor/actress, song, book, movie, least favorite school subject, dream car, most interesting teacher, season, time of the day, color, place to go shopping, music video, etc.

3. Distribute BINGO CONNECTION handouts.

4. Instruct students to write his/her answer to the first category from the new list in any square on the BINGO CONNECTION handout and pass the handout to another student.

5. Continue reading categories, writing answers and passing handouts until all of the handouts are completed.

6. Instruct the class to take a BINGO CONNECTION sheet and 'circulate' throughout the classroom, finding students from the class who match the requirements of the boxes on the sheet. When they make a match, that person is to write their name in the appropriate box. A person is allowed to sign one box on any sheet even though they meet the requirements of another box.

7. The first student to complete a line (horizontally, vertically, diagonally, or each of the four corners) wins.

8. Process by discussing previously unknown information about students in class, along with purpose of activity and its usefulness in personal goal setting.

Activity handout and facilitator's information created by Elaine Slea Hyla, M.Ed., Euclid, OH.
Elaine adapted SEALS+PLUS from Life Management Skills I and II, SEALS II from Life Management Skills III and IV and the portion of SEALS III originally from Life Management Skills V.

Communicating with "I" Statements

I feel . . .

The "I" statement is a way of communicating how another person's actions affect you without escalating conflict. Rather than making judgments about the other person, you are telling them how their actions affect how you feel and why. Then, you can tell them what you want or need to happen in the future, and, if necessary, what you will do in response. There are three, maybe four steps to the "I" Statement process:

> **STEP 1:** *"I feel . . ."*
> Make an honest statement about how you are feeling.
> > for example: *"I feel very frustrated right now . . . "*

> **STEP 2:** *"because . . ."*
> Tell the person what action or behavior of theirs has triggered your feelings.
> > for example: *"because you did not pick me up when you said you would and I ended up missing the movie."*

> **STEP 3:** *"I want or need . . ."*
> Tell the person specifically what you want or need from them now or in the future when similar situations arise.
> > for example: *"I need you to be on time from now on. If you have to change plans, I would like you to call me."*

> **STEP 4:** *"I will . . ."*
> This step is optional. Hopefully the other person will give you what you need after Step 3. However, if the problem continues, tell the other person what you are prepared to do in response. (But don't make threats you aren't going to follow through on.)
> > for example: *"If you're late without calling again, I will not go out with you anymore."*

NOW <u>YOU</u> TRY! Turn the following "You" statements into "I" statements using the four steps.

"You always make us get low grades on our projects. I do all the work and you never do your half. This time get your part done or else!"

I feel _____ because _____.

I want (or need) _____. (I will _____.)

"You are totally untrustworthy for telling my secret!"

I feel _____ because _____.

I want (or need) _____. (I will _____.)

"You're so loud all the time – why don't you just shut up!"

I feel _____ because _____.

I want (or need) _____. (I will _____.)

I. PURPOSE:

To increase interpersonal skills and assertiveness by communicating with 'I' statements.

II. GENERAL COMMENTS:

Irritation, frustration and anger can lead to a breakdown of communication. Oftentimes hurtful and blaming statements, name-calling, exaggerations and lengthy historical accounts are heard which can be damaging in any relationship. Using 'I' statements can be an effective assertive technique that can be helpful for many people.

III. POSSIBLE ACTIVITIES: This handout may be used in conjunction with AGGRESSIVE, ASSERTIVE, PASSIVE (page 7), PASSIVE, ASSERTIVE, AGGRESSIVE (page 8), SAYING "NO" (page 13 - all from SEALS+PLUS) and PASSIVE AGGRESSIVE (S.E.A.L.S. II - page 7).

A. 1. Distribute handouts and pencils.

2. Read handout aloud, explaining concepts as needed.

3. Divide class into pairs, allowing 10 minutes for pairs to complete bottom section.

4. Reconvene and share re-written 'I' statements, as a class/group.

5. Ask students to summarize possible benefits of this technique in personal, school and family relationships.

B. 1. Distribute one index card and pen per student.

2. Ask each student to write one 'You…' statement that they have heard recently, either in personal lives or on TV. Illustrate by listing the three examples on the bottom of the handout.

3. Collect cards.

4. Distribute handouts. Write the formula "I feel_____ because _____. I want (or need) _____. (I will _____".) on flip chart. Elicit list of consequences of 'You…' statements and benefits of using 'I' statements and write on another flipchart sheet.

5. Review top section together.

6. Allow 10 minutes for students to complete bottom section and share.

7. Place index cards in center of table. Ask each student to choose a card, one at a time and to change 'You' statements into 'I' statements with written formula.

8. Discuss the difference in how the 'I' and the 'You' statements feel to the listener, and how the listener is likely to respond as a result.

9. Process by asking students to summarize the new technique and the possible advantages.

10. Assign students to practice "I feel" statements and journalize until next class.

Activity handout and facilitator's information originally submitted for Life Management Skills VI by Kerry Moles, CSW, Bronx, NY. Kerry is a social worker and an Independent Consultant specializing in educating youth and youth workers on issues of domestic violence, sexual assault and independent living skills.

Adapted for SEALS III from LMS VI by Sandra Negley, MTRS, CTRS, Salt Lake City, UT, author of *Crossing the Bridge, A Journey in Self-Esteem, Relationships and Life Balance.*

COMMUNICATION

CONCEPTS WORD SEARCH

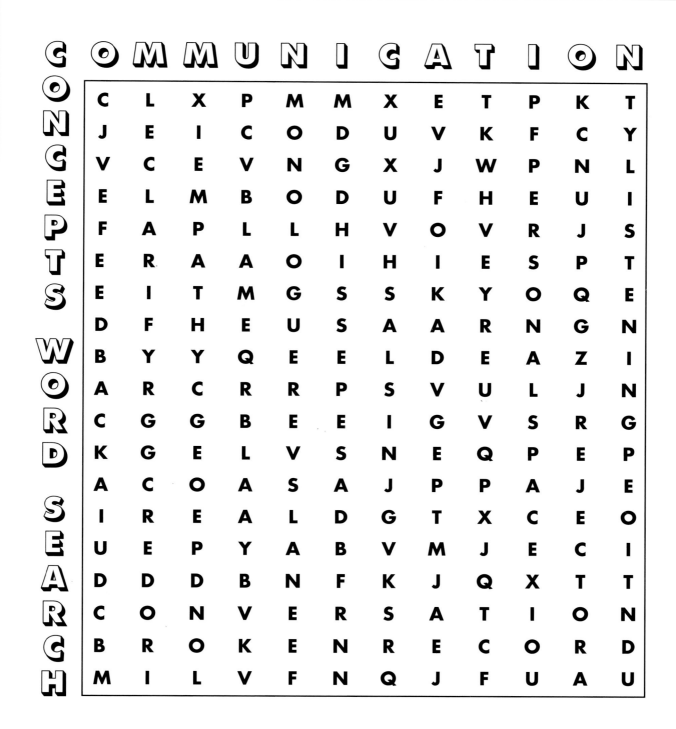

C	L	X	P	M	M	X	E	T	P	K	T
J	E	I	C	O	D	U	V	K	F	C	Y
V	C	E	V	N	G	X	J	W	P	N	L
E	L	M	B	O	D	U	F	H	E	U	L
F	A	P	L	L	H	V	O	V	R	J	I
E	R	A	A	O	I	H	I	E	S	P	S
T	I	T	M	G	S	S	K	Y	O	Q	T
D	F	H	E	U	S	A	A	R	N	G	E
B	Y	Y	Q	E	E	L	D	E	A	Z	N
A	R	C	R	R	P	S	V	U	L	J	I
C	G	G	B	E	E	I	G	V	S	R	N
K	G	E	L	V	S	N	E	Q	P	E	G
A	C	O	A	S	A	J	P	P	A	J	P
I	R	E	A	L	D	G	T	X	C	E	O
U	E	P	Y	A	B	V	M	J	E	C	I
D	D	D	B	N	F	K	J	Q	X	T	T
C	O	N	V	E	R	S	A	T	I	O	N
B	R	O	K	E	N	R	E	C	O	R	D
M	I	L	V	F	N	Q	J	F	U	A	U

AGGRESSIVE

BLAME

BODY LANGUAGE

BROKEN RECORD

CLARIFY

CONVERSATION

DIALOGUE

EAVESDROP

EMPATHY

FEEDBACK

ICEBREAKER

LISTENING

PASSIVE

PERSONAL SPACE

REJECTOR

ROLEPLAY

COMMUNICATION CONCEPTS WORD SEARCH

I. PURPOSE:

To improve interpersonal skills by increasing one's understanding of key communication-based terms.

II. GENERAL COMMENTS:

Effective communication skills and techniques are varied and numerous. The hidden terms in this word search are reflective of a variety of techniques and behavioral styles, both positive and negative.

III. POSSIBLE ACTIVITIES:

A. 1. Bring in supplies needed to create a peanut butter and jelly sandwich and a table covering for table or desk. Keep out of students' sight.

2. Distribute blank sheets of paper to class. Instruct the class to write the directions for making a peanut butter and jelly sandwich.

3. Collect instructions and retrieve sandwich supplies. Ask one student to read the instructions aloud as instructor attempts to make a peanut butter and jelly sandwich according to the students' instruction. NOTE: Interpret instructions literally, as if you have no experience making a sandwich. Follow students' directions exactly as written. Do not guess at or assume directions. Demonstration area might become a bit messy.

4. Present this activity to create a great deal of amusement and even perhaps frustration for your students.

5. Continue reading instructions and demonstrating sandwich-making skills.

6. Ask class to discuss objective of activity and its relevance to communication skills.

7. Distribute handouts.

8. Divide class into pairs, instructing pairs to find as many terms as time allows.

9. Tell students that terms are 'hidden' in horizontal, vertical and diagonal rows only. No terms have been inverted.

10. Reconvene and review results of word search with class.

11. Discuss definition and relevant meaning of each term identified. (For more difficult words, see GLOSSARY page C, in back of book.)

12. Process activity by reviewing benefits of being an effective communicator.

B. 1. Brainstorm on the board words associated with (or components of) effective and ineffective communication. This works particularly well when done as a review of previously taught concepts.

2. Distribute handouts, informing students that many of the terms hidden in the word search are similar (or the same) as those identified on the board.

3. Instruct students to independently complete word search noting that terms are 'hidden' in horizontal, vertical or diagonal rows. No terms have been inverted.

4. Review the location of the hidden words, discussing the meaning and application of each identified term. (For more difficult words, see GLOSSARY page C, in back of book.)

5. As a follow-up activity class can further explore the discussed terms in more detail, using examples from television, movies, novels, or comics to demonstrate.

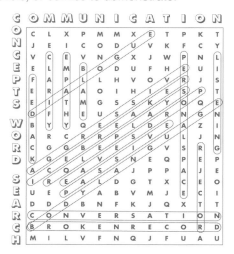

Activity handout and facilitator's information originally submitted for Life Management Skills V by Maggie Moriarty, M.S., COTA/L, Rocky Hill, CT. Maggie has been a practicing clinician in the behavioral health field over the past 22 years, creating and leading a variety of treatment groups. She is also an assistant professor of Occupational Therapy at a community college.

Adapted for SEALS III from LMS V by Elaine Hyla Slea, M.Ed., Euclid, OH, adaptor of *SEALS+PLUS (Self-Esteem and Life Skills)* and *SEALS II.*

Interacting & Coping with
DIFFICULT PEOPLE

There can be difficult people to deal with in our daily lives. It may be helpful to learn some new skills and coping strategies to deal more effectively with these difficult individuals.

It can be hard to deal with someone who is:

CRITICAL Abrasive Behavior out of proportion to problem Aggressive

Blaming Demanding Manipulative CONTROLLING

- **Can you think of someone in your life who has been especially difficult lately?**

Briefly describe a recent incident: _____

_____

- **What happens to me when I am around this person? How do I feel? How do I act?**

_____

- **What have I tried in the past to cope with this person?**

_____

Verbal	Non-Verbal	Did it work?
(For Example)		
▪ Blamed and yelled	▪ I sat, s/he stood	
▪ Gossiped	▪ Gave "dirty" looks	
_____	_____	Yes ☐ No ☐
_____	_____	Yes ☐ No ☐

POSSIBLE NEW COPING STRATEGIES

☐ Choose my battles
☐ Take care of myself
☐ Eliminate excuses
☐ Avoid "stirring" things up
☐ Avoid interrupting
☐ Be clear
☐ Avoid retaliating

☐ Practice assertiveness
☐ Detach with kindness
☐ Don't ignore behaviors
☐ Avoid grudges
☐ No put-downs
☐ See the other viewpoint

☐ Limit contact
☐ Accept reality
☐ Have patience
☐ Use body language
☐ No game playing
☐ Give the other person a "way out"

Many difficult people don't like who they are, won't face it, then judge and blame others for their problems. Nurturing your own positive self-image provides the tools to deal with difficult people in responsible ways.

Interacting & Coping with
DIFFICULT PEOPLE

I. PURPOSE:

To increase interpersonal skills by exploring ways to effectively cope with difficult people.
To review effective forms of verbal and non-verbal communication.

II. GENERAL COMMENTS:

Communication is a constantly evolving process of securing and delivering information, while building relationships. With difficult people, effective communication is especially challenging. Often times it is a struggle to deal with an individual whose nature is critical, controlling, manipulative, demanding or aggressive. It can be helpful to learn new skills, particularly assertiveness and self-care skills, to deal with these individuals more effectively.

III. POSSIBLE ACTIVITIES:

A. 1. Before session, obtain 10 paper cups (not Styrofoam), string and a wide rubber band. Tie six pieces of string 3 feet or longer to the rubber band, evenly spaced, making a 'starburst' pattern.

   2. Including yourself, select five student volunteers. Place paper cups upside down on a desk or table. Challenge group to use rubber band/string 'tool' to build a pyramid out of the paper cups.

   3. Students cannot use their hands to touch the cups. Instruct students to hold one end of each piece of string that is attached to the rubber band. The students are to then use this device to pick up the cups and place them on top of each other making a pyramid.

   4. Without informing the students, alter your participation in the activity to be as manipulating and controlling as possible for the students involved, demonstrating an interaction with a difficult person.

   5. Process introductory activity with a class discussion of feelings experienced while dealing with a difficult person.

   6. Distribute handouts.

   7. Continue discussion about what is challenging about dealing with 'difficult' people.

   8. Ask class to complete the question, "What happens to me...?" from the handout, either verbally or in writing. Include mention of stress or stress-related illness, if appropriate.

   9. Encourage discussion of different strategies students have tried in the past, to cope with difficult people.

   10. Focus on 'Possible New Coping Strategies' by explaining each strategy and how each can be put into practice. Demonstrate with appropriate examples from REAL LIFE SITUATIONS (end of book, page B, front and back), for role-play ideas, if desired.

   11. Process by asking each student to identify one benefit of learning to interact and cope with difficult people.

B. 1. Distribute handouts and pencils.

   2. Introduce topic and ask class to add verbal characteristics of difficult people to the ones listed on the handout (poor listener, judgmental, loud, tattler, crybaby, tantrums, etc.). Discuss non-verbal characteristics, (stands too close, stands over a seated person, pushes, points fingers, jabs finger, hand or fist into person, etc.)

   3. Instruct class to complete the question from the handout, "What happens to me..?" Refer to EMOTIONS© handout, (SEALS+PLUS page 24), or EMOTIONS© Poster.

   4. Invite class to share how they answered this question.

   5. Provide time to complete "What I have tried in the past....". Use the adage, "If you do what you've always done, you'll get what you've always got", to illustrate the need for developing new strategies.

   6. Ask for real situations with difficult people, being sensitive to confidentiality and privacy issues. Role play the situations (or simply discuss), incorporating ideas from the list of REAL LIFE SITUATIONS (end of book, page B, front and back), for ideas, if needed.

   7. Utilize the following handouts:

      SAYING "NO" (SEALS+PLUS - page 13)
      DEVELOPING BOUNDARIES (SEALS II - page 39)
      LIMITS (SEALS+PLUS - page 19)

Activity handout and facilitator's information originally submitted for Life Management Skills V by Nancy Day, O.T. Reg., Markham, Ontario, Canada. Nancy is an Occupational Therapist working in the mental health field, within the hospital sector. Her primary role as a group psychotherapist provides daily opportunity to design and facilitate group treatment. She believes it is a privilege to work in this capacity and witness the "magic" that occurs as individuals connect with one another and share in each other's growth.

Adapted for SEALS III from LMS V by Elaine Hyla Slea, M.Ed., Euclid, OH,
adaptor of *SEALS+PLUS (Self-Esteem and Life Skills)* and *SEALS II.*

Interview

with

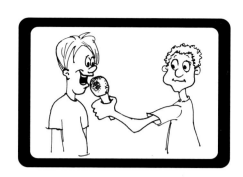

_____

Q. _____
_____ **?**

A. _____
_____ **.**

Q. _____
_____ **?**

A. _____
_____ **.**

Q. _____
_____ **?**

A. _____
_____ **.**

Q. _____
_____ **?**

A. _____
_____ **.**

Q. _____
_____ **?**

A. _____
_____ **.**

Q. _____
_____ **?**

A. _____
_____ **.**

Interview
with _____

I. PURPOSE:

To increase interpersonal skills between peers.

II. GENERAL COMMENTS:

Many people have difficulty interacting appropriately and comfortably with others. Social difficulties in conversations and meeting new people may be a contributor to social isolation. Extended social avoidance can contribute to problems later in life.

III. POSSIBLE ACTIVITIES: This handout may be used in conjunction with COMMUNICATIONS section (S.E.A.L.S. II - pages 3-8).

A. 1. Distribute a handout and pencil to each student. Explain that each letter 'Q' on the handout represents a question, and each letter 'A' represents an answer.

2. Instruct students to write down one question next to each 'Q'. Explain that questions should be....
   - specific enough to help a person get to know another person better (not yes/no questions)
   - generic, that everyone in the class could answer
   - comfortable to answer, not beyond reasonable social boundaries.

   Suggest topics if needed (current events, movies, weather, city born in, favorites, etc.).

3. Pair each student with another one with whom s/he is not acquainted or has little social interaction. Ask each student to write down his/her partner's answers next to each corresponding 'A'.

4. Instruct student to interview each other using the questions written on the handouts. Be sure that partners are ASKING each other the questions and not merely exchanging papers.

5. Process by asking thought-provoking questions, e.g.,

   How did you feel being the interviewer?
   How did you feel being the interviewee?
   What did you learn about your partner that you did not know before?
   Have you found that you share something in common with your partner?
   Are there more things you would like to learn about the person with whom you interviewed?
   Do you think you would be able to ask another person questions without having them written down beforehand?

B. 1. Explain to students that oftentimes it is difficult to get to know each other for a variety of reasons. Elicit insight from class members on this topic, e.g., Lack of trust? Little time? Paranoia? Don't know what to say? How to say it? Poor self-esteem?

2. Introduce today's activity as a safe place to get to know someone else. Distribute one handout and pencil for each participant.

3. Give students five minutes to brainstorm and write on the back of the handout ten questions that they might like to ask someone they don't know very well.

4. Instruct students to eliminate the four least favorable after considering the following questions....

   Could I ask this question to ANYONE in the group?
   Could this be thought of as offensive or invasive by ANYONE in this class?
   Will I get more of an answer than "yes/no" from my question?

5. Instruct students to write the six favorites in the "Q" lines on the front of the handout.

6. Ask students to pair up with someone that they are not well acquainted.

7. Give participants ten minutes to interview each other.

8. Reconvene and ask individuals to introduce his/her partner to the class with the most interesting question and/or answer.

9. Facilitate positive social interactions through sharing.

10. Ask entire class to vote on the most interesting or creative question/answer and give interviewee and interviewer token gift (perhaps that could be shared with the class, like package of small candies) as an award!

11. Process by asking class members for one insight into themselves from this experience, e.g., I do better one-to-one with people rather than in large groups. I enjoy talking about movies.

Activity handout and facilitator's information originally submitted for Life Management Skills VI by Elana S. Blachman, OTS, Woodmere, NY. Elana will be receiving her Master's degree in Occupational Therapy May 2000. Following the completion of her degree, she will be working for the Board of Education as a pediatric occupational therapist.

Adapted for SEALS III from LMS VI by Sandra Negley, MTRS, CTRS, Salt Lake City, UT, author of *Crossing the Bridge, A Journey in Self-Esteem, Relationships and Life Balance*.

defining LEISURE

Sometimes it is helpful to define, in your own words, concepts like leisure . . .

Finish one of the sentences . . .

1. I would define leisure

as _____

_____.

or

2. To me, leisure means

_____

_____.

Do you have leisure in your life?   Yes ☐   No ☐

Why is leisure important to you? _____

Can leisure be work (or vice versa)? _____

What happens when you do not incorporate leisure into your life? _____

_____

How can incorporating leisure into your life help you? _____

_____

I. PURPOSE:

To enhance one's understanding and develop personal definitions of leisure.

II. GENERAL COMMENTS:

Basic leisure exploration allows students to discuss their knowledge and values of leisure. It may also facilitate leisure awareness and an understanding of leisure in overall quality of life.

III. POSSIBLE ACTIVITIES: This handout may be used in conjunction with WHOLE YOU: BENEFITS OF LEISURE ACTIVITIES (SEALS III - page 38).

A. 1. Present the concept of leisure. Emphasize the importance of leisure, and the value and benefits of having a well-rounded life.

   2. Distribute handouts and pencils.

   3. Ask students to complete top section, choosing one of the two questions to answer.

   4. Discuss each student's response, listing them on a flipchart to be posted later.

   5. Divide class into pairs.

   6. Give pairs 4-5 minutes to interview each other and record partner's responses to the five questions in bottom section of handout.

   7. Reconvene and allow partners to introduce each other by sharing the most interesting response to one or two of the questions.

   8. Post flipchart as a physical reminder of leisure 'definitions'. Refer to chart in future classes addressing leisure.

B. 1. Explain to class that the concept of leisure may be difficult to grasp. Bring to class several possible basic 'definitions' of leisure written on index cards. For example: FREEDOM FROM RESPONSIBILITIES, GOING SNOWBOARDING, A "WANT TO" not a "HAVE TO", MY TIME, etc. Share definitions by asking students to read index cards to class.

   2. Distribute handouts and pencils.

   3. Give students 3-4 minutes to complete one of the two questions in the top section.

   4. Have students divide into trials and share responses.

   5. Emphasize that purposeful leisure is healthy and may assist in managing stress, provide exercise, decrease irritability, etc.

   6. Give students 5 minutes to complete the bottom section.

   7. Review the five questions in the bottom section, discussing the varied (and/or same) responses of class members.

   8. Discuss with students what each learned from class discussion and offer observations of possible student insights regarding their leisure awareness, interests or style.

Activity handout and facilitator's information originally submitted for Life Management Skills VI by Doris Lewis, CTRS, Lincoln, NE. Doris has clinical experience in physical rehabilitation, extended care, mental health and community sports programs. She has been in the therapeutic recreation field for 20 years.

Adapted for SEALS III from LMS VI by Sandra Negley, MTRS, CTRS, Salt Lake City, UT, author of *Crossing the Bridge, A Journey in Self-Esteem, Relationships and Life Balance.*

LOOKING AT YOUR LEISURE AND FREE TIME MAY BE REVEALING.

Answer these questions honestly:

1. How many times weekly (approximately) do you feel bored or express this to others?

   _____

2. How many hours of television do you usually watch daily?   (weekdays) _____ (weekends) _____

3. How many hours of video/computer games do you usually play? (weekdays) _____ (weekends) _____

4. How do you entertain yourself if the electricity goes off?

   _____

5. Check which of the following you might be likely to do if you spent time alone, without media entertainment:

   A. make a phone call _____   E. cook a special food _____

   B. write a letter _____   F. read _____

   C. make a card/gift _____   G. practice a skill _____

   D. enjoy a hobby _____   H. other _____

6. How do you feel when spending time alone?

   _____

7. Would you like to find new ideas for future activities?   Yes ☐   No ☐

   If yes, how could you do this? _____

8. What do you consider to be your talents and strengths?

   _____

9. What qualities in someone well-known do you admire?

   _____

10. Do you sometimes initiate plans for future activities with others?   Yes ☐   No ☐

    If yes, give a recent example: _____

Enjoying YOUR OWN Company...

I. PURPOSE:

To decrease reliance on media entertainment by exploring and developing the ability to enjoy one's own company.

II. GENERAL COMMENTS:

Media entertainment, namely television, computer and video games is how some define leisure. It is possible that television watching tends to promote the need for perpetual stimulation and entertainment. Other forms of media entertainment may replace avenues of personal development. In today's society, despite the advances and benefits of technology, have we become dependent on these forms of entertainment, that we can no longer enjoy our own company?

III. POSSIBLE ACTIVITIES:

A. 1. Discuss concept that leisure time and interests change throughout our lives. Pose the idea of reliance on media entertainment as potentially problematic.

2. Invite all students to name one current leisure activity that is neither related to television, computer or video game.

3. Distribute handouts with pencils.

4. Discuss results, tallying any interesting commonalties among the group, e.g., Does age make a difference? Does being involved in extra-curricular activities change responses? Boys-Girls?

5. Write on flipchart "Enjoying Your Own Company."
Brainstorm list of ideas the class has on what one could do if no media entertainment was available and they were all alone. Discuss how people entertained themselves in pre-television times?

6. Process insights gained from this activity.

B. 1. Discuss time management. Include the value of time for personal growth and development, healthy leisure, the benefits of a balanced schedule, etc. Present the notion that although media entertainment may be enjoyable, it may also be limiting. Ask for class input.

2. Distribute handouts and pencils.

3. Allow ten minutes for completion of handouts.

4. Discuss responses thoroughly.

5. Offer and support class with creative ideas to reduce media entertainment and to enjoy one's own company (5.h.): thinking quietly with a candle, exercising, playing an instrument, joining a youth group, playing game of solitaire, doing jigsaw puzzles, taking walk, etc.

6. Recognize people that participants admire. Ask class how these qualities are attained. Discuss relevance.

7. Process by asking class if any changes are needed in personal leisure time choices based on today's activity.

Activity handout and facilitator's information originally submitted for Life Management Skills VI by
Bettie E. Michelson, MS, Waukesha, WI. Bettie has developed creative educational units as a teacher
and materials for therapy and discussion groups as an occupational therapist working in mental health.
She is currently concentrating on writing.

Adapted for SEALS III from LMS VI by Sandra Negley, MTRS, CTRS, Salt Lake City, UT,
author of *Crossing the Bridge, A Journey in Self-Esteem, Relationships and Life Balance.*

MY LEISURE NEIGHBORHOOD

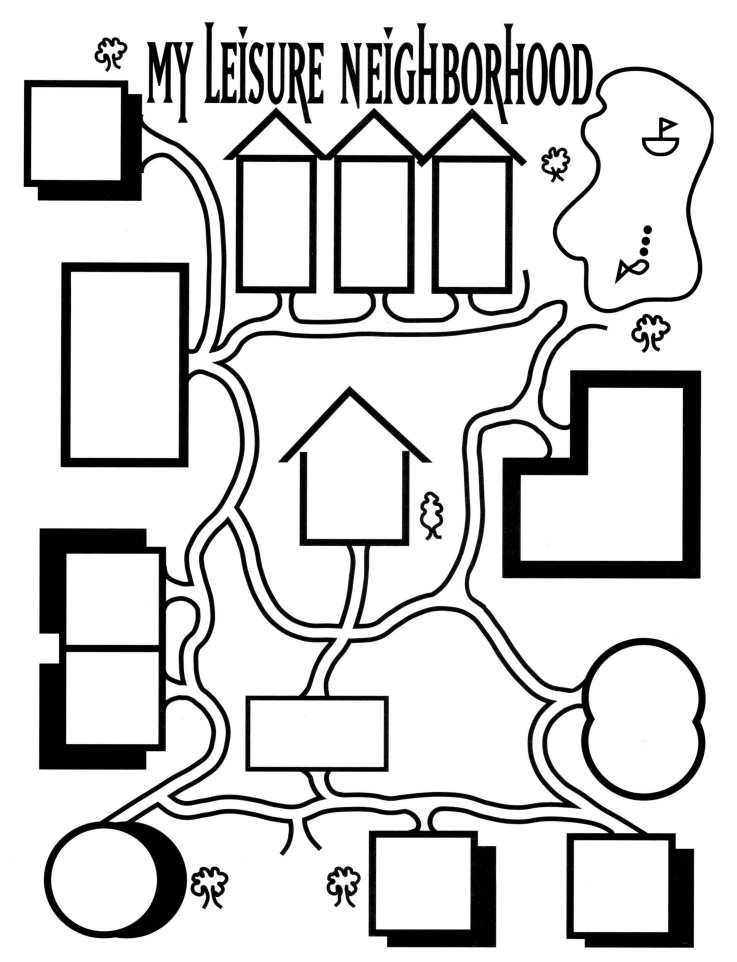

MY LEISURE NEIGHBORHOOD

I. PURPOSE:

To increase awareness of one's leisure participation patterns.

To explore changes one may make to increase leisure satisfaction.

II. GENERAL COMMENTS:

Adolescents are oftentimes challenged while attempting to fill their leisure time. In making public spaces open to all age groups, it is assumed that all teenagers will feel comfortable there. Young adults need places where they feel safe while allowing them a sense of ownership. For an adolescent, overly supervised fun can be no fun at all. To add to the matter, school boards, city councils and parents engage in ongoing debates about whose responsibility it is to provide quality leisure activities for young adults. Nonetheless, satisfying leisure activities can add to one's happiness and quality of life. Many adolescents may be unaware of leisure needs and patterns, as well as available resources. Investigating leisure options may lend itself to making positive changes. It is hoped that by making changes, adolescents can have a more varied and satisfying leisure life and will develop healthy life-long leisure values and skills.

III. POSSIBLE ACTIVITIES:

A. 1. Before session, collect a variety of local resources: telephone directories, newsletters, newspapers, magazines, entertainment guides, radio listings, associations or organizations, volunteer opportunities, museum, gallery or lecture schedules, concerts, etc. Include Internet sites that list community activities. In addition, provide one slip of paper for each student.

2. Discuss the meaning of a 'community leisure resource' (anywhere that people participate in leisure activities in the community). Present information from GENERAL COMMENTS above. Direct class to create a list of local community leisure resources, e.g., malls, friends' houses, parks, restaurants, gyms, museums, social clubs, etc.

3. Write list on board. Instruct class to classify resources according to the following leisure activity categories: Cultural, Outdoor, Relaxing, Social, Self-Discovery, Physical, Spectator, Adventure, Creative Expression, Educational, Solo, Escape, Self-Confidence, Volunteer, etc. Discuss the possible motivation for participation along with benefits of each identified category.

4. Distribute slips of paper. Poll students as to which activity category they would like to participate in by writing their names and activity category on the paper.

5. Collect written results of poll. Sort by matching responses. Divide class into groups based on this information. Distribute handouts along with a selection of community information to each group.

6. Instruct students to create a list of events, dates, locations, equipment needed, weather conditions and possible expenses on appropriate symbol on handout. For example: PHYSICAL LEISURE - water symbol ice skating or swimming, square: an athletic event, park symbol: hiking, house symbol: fitness video, etc. Encourage groups to locate opportunities available to them by searching listings of community resources if necessary. Encourage class to be creative yet practical. A request will be made to make a commitment to participate in one of the activities, either alone or with small group, before the next class session. Allow ample time for research.

7. Reconvene class and share results of research, instructing students to note on handouts any new leisure resource that might be of interest. Encourage feedback from class.

8. Process by affirming students' commitments to participate in community leisure activity selected. Instruct class to be prepared to participate in a discussion about completed leisure activity during next scheduled class session.

B. 1. List on board students' favorite leisure resources. Provide discussion based on   differences and similarities of leisure resources. Possible areas of discussion might include: changes in interests throughout school years, boys' selections vs. girls', motivations for participation, reasons for continued or renewed participation, etc.

2. Identify blocks and barriers to getting to each place, using information contained in GENERAL COMMENTS above for discussion guidelines. Ask class, "Are there other barriers involved in utilizing one's favorite community leisure resources?" Possible responses might include: money, family events, extra-curricular activities, part-time employment, limited transportation, no one to share activity or expenses, uncompleted assignments, thinking friends might not approve, etc. Instruct students to identify practical solutions for overcoming barriers.

3. Ask students to develop 5-10 categories of leisure activities. (Refer to A. 3. above for ideas)

4. Distribute handouts. As a class, identify and label each symbol according to categories of leisure activities provided by discussion above. This activity is two-part; the first is to develop a "Leisure Neighborhood Resource Map" listing as many related activities as possible represented by each symbol. For example, park symbol might include: golf, hiking, nature photography, in-line skating, biking, walking, running, swimming, kite or Frisbee flying, picnicking, etc. The second part is to outline as many benefits of the category or activity as possible.

5. Reconvene and share results.

6. Process by assisting students in forming goals related to how to make one's community leisure participation more satisfying.

Activity handout and facilitator's information originally submitted for Life Management Skills V by Martin B. Golub, CTRS, Rochester, NY. Marty enjoys Buffalo Bills football, the Chicago Cubs, all sports, crafts and hobbies. An avid bowler, Marty is involved in Rochester's G.R.E.A.T. Tournament each year. He hopes your Leisure Neighborhood is a happy one.

Adapted for SEALS III from LMS V by Elaine Hyla Slea, M.Ed., Euclid, OH,
adaptor of *SEALS+PLUS (Self-Esteem and Life Skills)* and *SEALS II.*

TEAM#
_____

WHEEL OF LEISURE

Brainstorm Ideas of Leisure Activities:

_____
_____
_____
_____
_____
_____
_____
_____
_____

Scoring:

Round 1
_____
_____
_____
_____
[_____]

Round 2
_____
_____
_____
_____
[_____]

Round 3
_____
_____
_____
_____
[_____]

Round 4
_____
_____
_____
_____
[_____]

TOTALS

Round 1
[_____]

Round 2
[_____]

Round 3
[_____]

Round 4
[_____]

GRAND TOTAL
[_____]

I. PURPOSE:

To increase awareness of leisure activities and their importance in contributing to the quality of life.
To assist students to discover new leisure activities and the diversity of participation options.
To encourage students to make leisure a priority in their lives.

II. GENERAL COMMENTS:

The benefits of leisure are endless. One expert reports that there are over 105 general and specific leisure benefits along with an array of associated benefits. It is during leisure time that many of life's most important decisions are made. It could be concluded that leisure provides more benefits to our total well-being than any other service or activity.

Futurists predict that by the first decade of the 21st century, leisure time will have increased accounting for more than 50% of lifetime activities. Therefore, leisure education, providing awareness opportunities for meaningful participation, will serve as a hedge against boredom brought on by too much free time. Leisure enhances health because it serves as a buffer to life's stressful events. It enables us to face negative events and still feel happy. Leisure activity has been related to depression: as leisure increases, depression decreases. It has been suggested that the relationship between leisure involvement and psychological well-being is reciprocal. While helping to boost morale, leisure contributes to the rebuilding of personal identities for those who experience traumatic or disabling events

III. POSSIBLE ACTIVITIES:

A. NOTE: Listing unusual, age-related, obsolete, seasonal, ethnic or geographically unique activities creates puzzles that are more difficult to solve, e.g., spelunking, Jai Alai, rappelling, kayaking, ice-sailing, snowboarding, curling, luge, lacrosse, etc.

  1. Open discussion about effects that stress can have on engagement of leisure activities. Discuss the importance of these activities in maintaining a healthy balanced lifestyle.
  2. Divide the class into pairs and number each team #1, #2, #3, and so forth.
  3. Distribute one handout to each pair.
  4. Explain to students that this game is based on the well-known TV game show, "Wheel of Fortune". If some individuals are unaware of this game, ask other students to explain.
  5. Give each pair 60 seconds to write as many interesting or unusual leisure activities as possible on the provided lines of the handout.
  6. Ask one member of team #1 to write on flip chart or board the same number of lines as are in the word or phrase. That is, if BINGO is selected, then five lines (_ _ _ _ _) would be written.
  7. Instruct a member from team #2 to roll one die. If they guess a letter in the puzzle correctly, they receive that number of points. (Note: if a person rolls a '1' then they are 'bankrupt' and lose all accumulated points.) If a letter is guessed correctly, give the team 10 seconds to solve the puzzle.
  8. Utilize the scoring section on the handout, each team keeping their own score. Facilitate healthy competition.
  9. Give team #3 a turn if team #2 does not guess correctly.
  10. Continue the game in this manner until the puzzle is solved. A new puzzle is now put on the board by team #2 and guessed by team #3. Play until all teams have had an opportunity to solve a puzzle and earn points.
  11. Process by asking students to identify the most unusual leisure activity that was heard during this session. Ask each to name one leisure activity that can be explored in the next week.

B. 1. Follow instructions as stated in A.1. to A.5. above, playing game as a variation of the TV game 'Password'. Team #1 selects a leisure activity from their list and verbally relates clues to team #2 consisting of two to three word terms associated with the activity. For example if leisure activity selected is Bingo, team #1 might say 'card', 'markers', 'four corners', 'free space', and so on. First clue is worth 10 points; second clue, 9 points, and so on until 10 clues have been given or the team guesses the activity-whichever occurs first. Team #3 is given a chance to guess if team #2 fails to correctly answer.
  2. Consider giving bonus points if a team can identify where that activity can take place within their community. For example, if the puzzle BINGO is solved, ask the team to name a bingo place in town.
  3. Award the winning team a token prize (e.g., homework pass, certificate of participation, etc.). Vote on a students' leisure activities that can be accomplished later in the week.
  4. Process activity by asking students, "Why is playing important?", "What is the value in leisure?" Encourage students to participate in at least one new leisure activity before next session, being prepared to share experience with class as able.

Activity originally submitted for Life Management Skills V by Barbara Lundberg, OTR/L, Sandra Netto, MSW, and Betty Welch, PhD, all employed at a Geropsychiatric Partial Hospitalization Program in Manchester, NH. Betty and Sandra specialize in geriatric mental health. Barbara has over 20 years experience in community mental health.

Adapted for SEALS III from LMS V by Elaine Hyla Slea, M.Ed., Euclid, OH, adaptor of *SEALS+PLUS (Self-Esteem and Life Skills)* and *SEALS II.*

THE WHOLE YOU

BENEFITS OF LEISURE ACTIVITIES

Many of us are unaware of the benefits of leisure especially while taking part in the activity. Listing the benefits will help you choose leisure activities that are satisfying and rewarding.

Write your leisure activities on the blanks provided below.

Then, analyze these leisure activities by placing a check in the appropriate response box.

LEISURE ACTIVITY I do . . .	1x year	1x month	1x week	1x day
▶ to relax is _____	☐	☐	☐	☐
▶ to socialize is _____	☐	☐	☐	☐
▶ for fitness is _____	☐	☐	☐	☐
▶ to be mentally stimulated is _____	☐	☐	☐	☐
▶ to compete is _____	☐	☐	☐	☐
▶ to be creative is _____	☐	☐	☐	☐
▶ to be alone is _____	☐	☐	☐	☐
▶ to learn something new is _____	☐	☐	☐	☐
▶ to help others is _____	☐	☐	☐	☐
▶ to help my spirit is _____	☐	☐	☐	☐
▶ as a spectator is _____	☐	☐	☐	☐
▶ for accomplishment is _____	☐	☐	☐	☐

BECOMING "THE WHOLE YOU" INVOLVES TAKING THE NEXT STEP. EXPAND YOUR LEISURE OUTLOOK!

MY LEISURE ACTIVITY ACTION PLAN:

I am interested in learning more about_____.

(list a new leisure activity)

I would invite_____ to join me on this date _____.

I. PURPOSE:

To identify leisure activities in which one participates.
To identify potential leisure activities for future participation.
To identify the benefits derived from engaging in leisure activities.

II. GENERAL COMMENTS:

Because the average adolescent spends from 6-7 hours in school daily, a large block of unstructured time remains. This time can provide a variety of opportunities for personal growth and development. Adolescence presents a vital opportunity for shaping enduring patterns of behavior that can set a young person on a healthy and successful course for life.

Some adolescents choose activities that increase confidence, teach teamwork, increase self-esteem, teach a sport or provide opportunities for spending time with friends. These activities have been shown to be linked to continued socialization, enhanced decision-making, improved problem solving and reduction in boredom. Some teens use leisure time to counterbalance challenges and pressures in their lives.

Many adolescents however, are reluctant to participate in activities that involve evaluation, criticism or judgment. They avoid activities that have the potential to create conflicts due to rules and structure, difficulty of quitting without guilt, or uncomfortable situations due to other participants.

By examining current available leisure opportunities, adolescents will be encouraged to develop lifelong positive attitudes and behavior changes towards leisure. Leisure education can make the connection between leisure satisfaction and life satisfaction.

III. POSSIBLE ACTIVITIES:

A. 1. Define the concept of 'a whole you.' Focus discussion towards impact of leisure activities upon a healthy lifestyle. Discuss benefits of leisure activities.
2. Select a time period during the school day where students have unstructured time for leisure activities, i.e., recess, lunch, study halls.
3. Distribute handouts. Encourage students to complete all, or most, of the 12 sentences using the context of being at school. Instruct students to list activities that they currently participate in to accomplish their leisure goals during unstructured times while at school. Possible responses might be: *"During lunchtime at school…A leisure activity I do to relax is reading. …A leisure activity I do to compete is softball."*
4. Allow 5-8 minutes for students to complete handouts.
5. Review responses, encouraging positive feedback from class. Instruct class to listen to classmates' responses, making additions to their own lists if necessary.
6. Instruct class to silently reread responses, placing a check in box that best describes student's current level of participation in activity.
7. Assist class in creating leisure activity action plans. Process activity by facilitating action plans. Encourage students to plan and organize leisure. Plan to implement students' action plans during next available unstructured time period.
8. Make extra copies of handout. Distribute to students providing encouragement to re-evaluate leisure activities focusing on personal time outside of school.
B. Before class session, use handout to create an overhead transparency.
1. Write 20-25 leisure activities on separate index cards and place face down in the middle of a desk or table.*
*Suggested activities might include: in-line skating, painting, shopping, board games, drawing, reading, doing crafts, photography, sports, exercise, volunteering, journalizing, composing e-mail, writing letters, gardening, clubs, scouting, dancing, listening to music, cooking, playing a musical instrument, talking on the phone, sewing, collecting, building models, martial arts, meditation, weight lifting or body training, massage, manicure, hair cut, dining out, swimming, learning new computer software, planning an event, fitness class or aerobics, performing community service, etc.
2. Using overhead projector, display handout.
3. Instruct each student one at a time, to choose a card and say aloud the leisure activity.
4. Direct each student to choose a sentence from overhead with which they could match the selected card and complete the phrase. For example, if the selected card lists READING, some participants might choose, 'An activity I do that HELPS ME SPIRITUALLY' while others might choose 'An activity I do TO BE ALONE.'
5. Distribute handouts.
6. Instruct class to complete handouts based on personal experiences. Share results, encouraging positive feedback from the class. Permit changes or additions to the lists as needed.
7. Discuss how the same leisure activities can meet different needs, depending on interests and leisure lifestyles.
8. Process and include goal setting, by using check boxes provided on front of handouts as guidelines.

Activity handout and facilitator's information originally submitted for Life Management Skills V by Doris Lewis, CTRS, Lincoln, NE. Doris has clinical experience in physical rehabilitation, extended care, mental health and community sports programs. She has been in the therapeutic recreation field for over 20 years.

Adapted for SEALS III from LMS V by Elaine Hyla Slea, M.Ed., Euclid, OH, adaptor of *SEALS+PLUS (Self-Esteem and Life Skills)* and *SEALS II*.

EATING
& your health

It may be time to examine your daily eating routines and consider making some changes in your eating behaviors. What affects your eating? ANSWER THE FOLLOWING QUESTIONS (check all that apply to you) and let's see what you can find out;

1. **What is your _body image_ and relationship to food? What do you see when you look in the mirror?**
a. _____ I am too fat/too thin.
b. _____ I'll never have the "perfect" enough body to fit in and be popular with the rest of my class.
c. _____ I feel guilty if I eat too much or if I binge on "forbidden" foods.
d. _____ My eating is out of control.
e. _____ I have used laxatives, water pills, tried bingeing or purging in order to lose or maintain my weight.

2. **Do you have any _emotional, medical or physical concerns_ that affect your eating? Do your _lifestyle choices_ affect your eating?**
a. _____ I prefer vegetarian or macro-biotic meals.
b. _____ I have to follow a special diet due to food allergies, asthma, diabetes, digestive or dental problems, weight, lactose intolerance, etc.
c. _____ A physical disability interferes with my ability to eat.
d. _____ I oftentimes use food to help me deal with stressful or painful situations.
e. _____ I need to learn more about counting calories, portion sizes or nutrition.
f. _____ Prescribed medications affect my eating.

3. **How do your _relationships_ affect your eating?**
a. _____ I feel lonely and don't like to eat by myself.
b. _____ While at home or school, conflicts frequently arise between myself and the person(s) with whom I usually eat my meals.
c. _____ I feel intimidated because someone comments about how I look.
_____ (for example, "You need to lose weight", "You're such a skinny runt.")
d. _____ I feel intimidated because someone comments about how I eat.
_____ (for example, "You eat too much", "You eat like a bird!")
e. _____ Most of my friends are obsessed with weight.
f. _____ My friends are my "eating buddies".

4. **How does your _financial situation_ affect your eating?**
a. _____ I have a part-time job which gives me some income.
b. _____ I spend money by eating out a lot, especially fast food.
c. _____ I have no outside sources of income other than an allowance.
d. _____ I have to ask my parents/guardians every time I need money.
e. _____ Oftentimes at home, food is just not available.

5. **How does your _daily schedule_ affect your eating?**
a. _____ I feel too stressed out after school or work to relax at a meal.
b. _____ I have so many obligations that I don't have time to sit down for a meal.
c. _____ I have to accommodate other people's schedules: babysitting, caring for siblings, staying late after school or work, clubs, activities, frequent phone calls during mealtimes, lessons, sports, friends, etc.
d. _____ I skip meals altogether or eat large meals late at night.
e. _____ I eat too fast.

Pick one of the problems with which you identify. _____

How much can you control this situation? _____

What changes could you make to improve your eating?

_____

When can you start this change? _____

I. PURPOSE:

To introduce the concept that one's nutrition and one's health status affect each other.

To generate suggestions for making changes in one's nutritional status.

II. GENERAL COMMENTS:

Habits allow people to simplify one's daily routine since the person does not have to expend thoughts or energy organizing and acting on conscious decisions. Often people who have physical, emotional, or mental health issues have developed habits, which adversely impact their general well-being. This may create a cycle in which the destructive habit further deteriorates the person's health, which encourages the use of habits in order to reduce fatigue. Developing new, more productive habits will require a challenge to the existing routine, exploration of alternative behaviors and practicing new routines.

This activity addresses the first two steps, reviewing eating habits in relation to one's health status and beginning to identify alternative behaviors.

III. POSSIBLE ACTIVITIES:

A. 1. Ask the class to discuss the following scenario: When a person grabs the hot handle of a pan what reaction is experienced by that person? Possible responses might be: pain, heat, burning, surprise, shock, concern for well-being, quick to let go, etc. What is the lesson learned by touching a hot handle? A possible response might be to avoid being burned in the future.

2. Ask the class why does a person never feel reluctant to letting go of a hot handle? How can this relate to the issue of habits? Why we are quick to let go of some negative habits while we are reluctant to let go of others? Relate discussion to activity topic of eating habits.

3. Distribute handouts.

4. Read handout aloud. Complete by instructing students to check statements that are appropriate and then add personal answers in blank lines.

5. Select a topic area from front of the handout for further discussion; body image, medical problems, relationships, financial situation or daily schedule.

6. Instruct class to analyze answers with respect to frequency of answers under a specific topic, or if any patterns emerge. Discuss each topic asking for personal comments, reflections or insights. Present definition of a habit as presented in GENERAL COMMENTS section and facilitate discussion of relationship of habits to introduction activity.

7. Instruct students to complete the bottom section and share responses as able.

8. Process by asking students to share insights gained from this activity.

9. Follow up by suggesting to students to set a goal for improved health and eating habits by journalizing.

B. 1. Lead discussion of information presented in PURPOSE and GENERAL COMMENTS SECTIONS ABOVE. Distribute handouts, and colored markers or highlighters.

2. Read handouts with students asking each to first check off areas they relate to, and then to highlight one issue for which s/he would like to receive suggestions for improvement. Allow students to verbally elaborate on their specific issue, if needed, for clarification.

3. Instruct each student to pass his/her handout to the left, writing a suggestion on the back of the page, and then, passing it to the next student on his/her left.

4. Continue in this manner until each student receives his/her own paper.

5. Ask each student to read his/her issue aloud, as well as the suggestions s/he received.

6. Discuss both the content of the suggestions and the process of asking and receiving help from others.

Activity handout and facilitator's information originally submitted for Life Management Skills V by K. Oscar Larson, OTR/L, MA, Alexandria, VA.
Oscar contributed to S.E.A.L.S. II and is a supportive colleague of Wellness Reproductions & Publishing, Inc.

Adapted for SEALS III from LMS V by Elaine Hyla Slea, M.Ed., Euclid, OH, adaptor of SEALS+PLUS (Self-Esteem and Life Skills) and SEALS II.

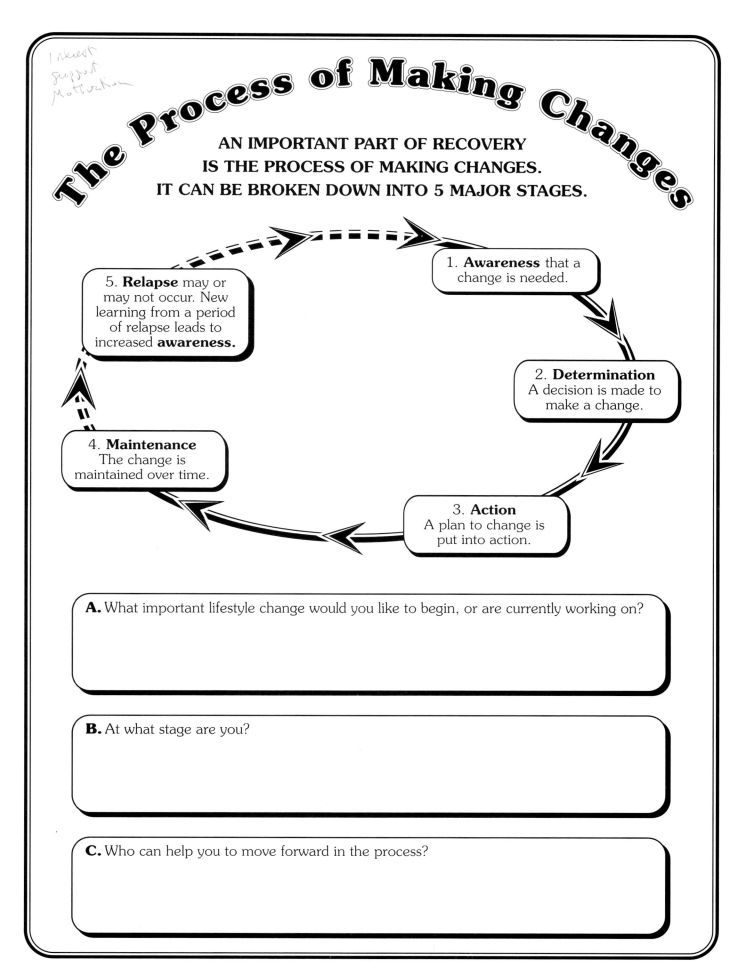

The Process of Making Changes

Interest
Support
Motivation

**AN IMPORTANT PART OF RECOVERY
IS THE PROCESS OF MAKING CHANGES.
IT CAN BE BROKEN DOWN INTO 5 MAJOR STAGES.**

1. **Awareness** that a change is needed.

2. **Determination** A decision is made to make a change.

3. **Action** A plan to change is put into action.

4. **Maintenance** The change is maintained over time.

5. **Relapse** may or may not occur. New learning from a period of relapse leads to increased **awareness.**

A. What important lifestyle change would you like to begin, or are currently working on?

B. At what stage are you?

C. Who can help you to move forward in the process?

The Process of Making Changes

I. PURPOSE:

To promote the concept that making change is a process.
To identify where one is in the process.

II. GENERAL COMMENTS:

Making change in our lives is an important part of moving towards a productive, responsible and healthy adulthood. It is an often difficult but a necessary part of growth. Individuals are often reluctant to change behaviors with which they have grown comfortable. Change involves establishing healthy relationships with others and ourselves along with healing and recovery. Adolescents often have difficulty with change due to perceived peer pressures and limited life experiences. There are a number of stages an individual undergoes as changes are made. Important learning about ourselves occurs at each stage, and all stages are valuable, as preparation for the next. A certain amount of back and forth movement between stages is a normal part of the process.

III. POSSIBLE ACTIVITIES: This handout may be used in conjunction with EATING & YOUR HEALTH (page 39).

A. 1. Using flipchart, board or overhead transparency, reproduce 'flowchart' (deleting text with correctional fluid or blank paper) from handout. Using flowchart, facilitate discussion of a skill students need to learn in stages, e.g., driving a car, studying a foreign language, learning a sport, studying a musical instrument, etc. Include discussion of desire, interest, support and motivation as important catalysts for change.

2. Relate discussion from activity A.1. to class topic by introducing concept of making changes in stages. Use information presented in GENERAL COMMENTS if needed.

3. Ask class to identify and share a change they would like to see occur in the community, country, or world. Use the flowchart (with text) from front of handout to demonstrate stages required to facilitate this change.

4. Distribute handouts.

5. Initiate a discussion review on the five major stages of making changes.

6. Ask students to complete the bottom section on a personal level and share responses.

7. Brainstorm the benefits of understanding this process. Review importance of changes occurring in stages as part of lifestyle or behavior changes.

B. 1. Distribute handouts.

2. Introduce the concept of making changes and review the 5 stages of change.

3. Ask students to complete the handout.

4. Divide class into pairs and ask each individual to interview the other regarding the three responses on the bottom of the handout. Request that students describe events, people, memories, etc. personally associated with each or any stage that 'triggered' change.

5. Reconvene and ask each individual to report on their partner's responses. For example, "Sarah is working on stress management. She became aware of this need for change after she contracted a stress-related illness. She is in the process stage of determination. She realizes that stress plays a large part in her health and energy levels. She is requesting that her friend and classmate, Anne, help her move forward as she is a good role model in this area and a reliable support for Sarah."

6. To process, ask students to share one thing they learned from this activity about the importance of making changes in a step-by-step process.

Activity handout and facilitator's information originally submitted for Life Management Skills V by Nancy Day, O.T. Reg., Markham, Ontario, Canada. Nancy is an Occupational Therapist working in the mental health field, within the hospital sector. Her primary role as a group psychotherapist provides daily opportunity to design and facilitate group treatment. She believes it is a privilege to work in this capacity and witness the 'magic' that occurs as individuals connect with one another and share in each other's growth.

Adapted for SEALS III from LMS V by Elaine Hyla Slea, M.Ed., Euclid, OH, adaptor of *SEALS+PLUS (Self-Esteem and Life Skills)* and *SEALS II.*

What do I Want To Change???

I want to:

○ Be able to say no

○ Stop a bad habit

○ Work part time

○ Stop negative thinking

○ Set a boundary

○ Be more organized in school

○ Learn more about the computer

○ Be on time

○ Learn to cook

○ Socialize with others

○ Develop a hobby

○ Ask for help when needed

○ _____

○ _____

○ Do volunteer work

○ End a destructive relationship

○ Like myself better

○ Attend religious/spiritually—enriching activity

○ Make new friends

○ Express my feelings

○ Stop overspending

○ Avoid yelling and screaming

○ Eat less junk food

○ Get fit

○ Handle anger better

○ Stop using obscene language

○ _____

Circle one item from the list above that stands out as being more important than the others.

The benefits for me in making this change are:

1. _____

2. _____

3. _____

What do I Want To Change???

I. PURPOSE:

To identify an area in which individuals want to make changes.

To consider potential benefits of making this change.

II. GENERAL COMMENTS:

Everyone at some time makes changes in their lives. In our lifetimes, change is inevitable and unavoidable in one form or another. Insight and personal growth are crucial in the process of changing. Many people struggle with change even after heartfelt commitment. Small steps towards change are just as beneficial as major ones. Change, especially for adolescents who are in the healing or recovery process, can be especially difficult. Slip-ups and relapses occur with higher frequency due to perceived and actual peer pressure. But slips and relapse can also have benefit. Experts claim that persons who slip or relapse have higher future success rates. However, coping strategies need to be in place before behavior can change. It is helpful to identify issues/conflicts/areas for change to ourselves as well as to others, asking for encouragement along the way. Awareness of the various benefits and 'steps' of making changes is important, as it increases motivation to persevere.

III. POSSIBLE ACTIVITIES:

A. 1. Use 'just do it-type' ads as a discussion prompt. Why does this advice really not work? If this advice is true and accurate then why do people often make the same New Year's resolutions? Ask class to discuss additional myths about change including: *"Change is easy"*, *"It just takes willpower"*, *"Some people can't change"*, *"Change means action"*, etc.

2. Distribute handouts.

3. Provide several minutes for students to complete the checklist instructing students to check off the 5 top things they want to change.

4. Divide into pairs and instruct each pair to share items checked off with reasons. Instruct pairs to determine if there are any common items between them.

5. Reconvene as a class and facilitate discussion on concepts of prioritizing, focusing on one issue at a time and the use of a step-by-step approach.

6. Instruct students to circle one priority item for change and share that with the class as able.

7. Ask students to determine benefits of making the change on the handout, either verbally or in writing.

B. 1. Before session print a list of student names in the class and cut into individual strips, placing strips in an envelope, box, or basket.

2. Instruct class to brainstorm a list of small changes that they have accomplished since the beginning of the term: Some examples might be; been on time to school everyday, kept locker organized, completed all assignments, volunteered, re-arranged personal space at home, passed state boards, standardized or proficiency tests, etc.

3. Use information contained in GENERAL COMMENTS for further class discussion.

4. Write the following sentence-starter on board, flip chart or overhead.
"A small change I've seen_____ make is _____."

5. Distribute strips, asking each student to share how they would complete the sentence-starter about that person whose name they have selected; For example: "A small change I've seen JOE make is that for the past two days he has been on time for class."

6. Elicit discussion about students' feelings on receiving this feedback.

7. Distribute handouts, and provide time for completion of entire page.

8. Invite students to share the item that was circled as a priority, as well as benefits of making this change.

Activity handout and facilitator's information originally submitted for Life Management Skills V by Nancy Day, O.T. Reg., Markham, Ontario, Canada. Nancy is an Occupational Therapist working in the mental health field, within the hospital sector. Her primary role as a group psychotherapist provides daily opportunity to design and facilitate group treatment. She believes it is a privilege to work in this capacity and witness the 'magic' that occurs as individuals connect with one another and share in each other's growth.

Adapted for SEALS III from LMS V by Elaine Hyla Slea, M.Ed., Euclid, OH,
adaptor of *SEALS+PLUS (Self-Esteem and Life Skills)* and *SEALS II.*

Highlight the Positive
ELIMINATE the Negative

Are you the type of person who sees:

the glass half full? ☐ ☐ or half empty?

it a little sunny outside? ☐ or a little gray outside?

life as challenges & Opportunities ☐ ☐ or life as a series of problems?

Let's ELIMINATE the Negative –

Are you the type of person who:

☐ asks family/friends to let you know when they see or hear you expressing negative language?

☐ says to yourself "Can I find a positive in this situation?" when you start to have negative thoughts about an upcoming situation or event?

☐ knows that the more we focus or talk about something, the more it happens in our life, both good and bad?

☐ is grateful for all the positives in your life?

There are many ways to learn to Highlight the Positive in our lives.

One way is to actively look at the good around us. Write a paragraph about a situation or event in your family, school, or community that you are happy about, satisfied with, admire, or find important.

I. PURPOSE:

To create a positive outlook by focusing on the positive and de-focusing on the negative.

II. GENERAL COMMENTS:

Developing a positive outlook may in fact be one of the most important life skills there is, because it enriches and strengthens all life roles. For some, this attitude comes fairly naturally; for others, an active process of re-thinking is ahead. These attitudes may be contagious, when we are around people who are positive, we often feel more positive and likewise the opposite is true.

III. POSSIBLE ACTIVITIES

A. 1. Distribute handouts. Instruct students to complete the top section. Explain that group members who checked off 2 or 3 on the left side, generally feel positive or optimistic. Conversely, explain that those who checked off 2 or more on the right side generally feel more negative or pessimistic.

2. List on the board in random order other words/phrases that further describe positive and negative people. For example, ***negative*** - brood, worry, little humor, poor self-confidence, nothing to look forward to, 'downers,' stomp out the spirit, frown often, unhealthy and ***positive*** - upbeat, look for challenges, high spirited, smile often, good self-confidence, faith in others, looks forward to future, pleasant to be around, healthy. Ask the students to identify what personality, positive or negative, those words describe. Ask students if they can identify some positive and negative people in their lives.

3. Read middle section aloud, as students check the boxes that identify them. Discuss how these choices affect relationships, risk taking, etc.

4. Instruct group members to complete the bottom section.

5. Allow students 10 minutes to share aloud their paragraphs.

6. Process by asking students to summarize this activity and insight gained.

B. 1. Distribute handouts. Instruct students to complete the top section. Explain that group members who checked off 2 or 3 on the left side, generally feel positive or optimistic. Conversely, explain that those who checked off 2 or more on the right side generally feel more negative or pessimistic.

2. Ask each student to identify positive and negative people in their lives. Ask them to describe what characteristics these people possess that led to the student identifying them as positive or negative.

3. Read middle section aloud as students check the boxes that identify them. Discuss how these choices affect relationships, risk taking, etc.

4. Ask each student to project themselves 10 years into the future (what will their age be, will they be married, what will be their occupation, etc.) and to describe how they would want a fellow co-worker or spouse to describe them. Discuss how they can foster those characteristics right now in their lives.

5. Instruct group members to complete the bottom section.

6. Allow students 10 minutes to share aloud their paragraphs.

7. Process by asking students to summarize this activity and insight gained.

**Adapted for SEALS III from LMS VI by Susan Miller, OTR/L, North Platte, NE
who works with adolescents in an outpatient partial hospitalization program.**

LOOK AROUND YOU...

**How you see the world when you look around you,
colors your attitude, thoughts and actions.**

So, look around you . . .
     and find 3 things that have blue in them. Go ahead and list them:

    1 _____

    2 _____

    3 _____

Did you notice that when you were looking for a certain color, it was easy to find, that the color jumped out at you? What happens when you *look around* and focus on things to smile about, the good in people, reasons to be positive?

      Now, look around . . . and find 3 things that make you feel:
positive / like smiling / warm inside / more alive or . . .! Go ahead and list them:

    1 _____

    2 _____

    3 _____

With a 'look-around-you mind-set', you'll find that things cause you to smile, jump out at you! In addition, when you smile, things and people seem to smile back! If you look-around-you for reasons to smile, you'll find them!

I. PURPOSE:

To develop a positive attitude by using a look-around-you-mind-set.

II. GENERAL COMMENTS:

Constantly focusing on the negative not only brings down the mood but also affects one's health. When one focuses on the negative, it causes one to be 'stressed-out'. Conversely, when one focuses on the positive, the results will be that of 'lifting-up'. Which each individual chooses is up to them.

III. POSSIBLE ACTIVITIES:

A. NOTE: This activity may take longer than one session. Plan accordingly.

1. Ask class to divide into triads. Distribute a piece of blank paper to each group. Instruct students to imagine that they are now the teachers. The curriculum states that the difference between a pessimist and an optimist must be taught. Instruct each triad to create an activity teaching this lesson: a game, a worksheet, a handout, a quiz, etc.

2. Allow sufficient time for students to create. Circulate among triads answering questions, defining terms, problem-solving, brainstorming, etc.

3. Reconvene and ask each triad to share results of activity.

4. Find common themes among their projects: For example: Did several triads create an activity that involved: use of colors, use of sayings, self-talk, vocabulary, was it a parody of a popular TV game show, etc. Did the triad members themselves discover an optimistic or pessimist in their triads. What is it like to work with them? What effect was felt by the rest of the triad?

5. Distribute handouts and instruct students to complete.

6. Share responses and discuss implications for viewing the world in a positive light.

B. 1. Distribute handouts and explain purpose.

2. Lead the class in completing the handout.

3. Ask the class to identify three stressors. List them on a blackboard or flipchart.

4. Pair the class into partners. Ask one of the partners to have a positive attitude, the other a negative attitude.

5. Have the pairs pick one of the stressors listed on the blackboard / flipchart. Instruct each pair to have a conversation with the 'positive partner' saying only positive things and the 'negative partner' saying only negative things about that stressor.

6. Stop the process after about a minute. Instruct groups to keep the same item but switch their attitude. The 'positive partner' now becomes negative and the 'negative partner' becomes positive. Continue the conversation for about a minute.

7. Reconvene and discuss the positive aspects the class found about each stressor.

8. Point out that every negative has a positive, and that it is up to each person to find it for themselves.

Activity handout and facilitator's information originally submitted for Life Management Skills V by Allen Klein, MA, CSP. Allen is an award-winning professional speaker and best selling author of such books as The Healing Power of Humor, Quotations to Cheer You Up and The Courage to Laugh. He can be reached at http://www.allenklein.com.

Adapted for SEALS III from LMS V by Elaine Hyla Slea, M.Ed., Euclid, OH,
adaptor of *SEALS+PLUS (Self-Esteem and Life Skills)* and *SEALS II.*

Things I am grateful for are:

_____

_____

_____

_____

_____

I am glad that I have a_____.

_____ is a blessing in my life.

Please continue to write your FEELINGS about things you are grateful for:

_____

_____

_____

_____

_____

_____

_____

_____

_____

_____

_____

_____

_____

_____

_____

_____

_____

GRATITUDE Journal

I. PURPOSE:

To increase one's positive outlook on life by realizing the reasons to be grateful.

II. GENERAL COMMENTS:

Our society, both old and new, says it is important for us to be thankful or have 'gratitude' for things we have or are given. We celebrate or 'give thanks' for all we have during our Thanksgiving holiday. Sometimes, especially when we are younger, we focus on all the things we <u>don't</u> have as opposed to all the things we <u>do</u> have. Sometimes it is helpful to review our lives and try to think in a more positive way about what we have.

III. POSSIBLE ACTIVITIES:

A. 1. Generate a discussion about the importance of considering the question: "What are we grateful for today?"

2. Explain to the group members that it is possible to be grateful for both small and large things and not only things we own but also family, friends, education, opportunities, etc.

3. Distribute handouts and allow students 5-10 minutes to complete the four questions.

4. Have each student share findings with the group. Encourage students to write other ideas from group members on the bottom portion, for them to write about later.

5. Ask students to complete the bottom of the page and journal how they feel about how grateful they are for things in their life, as homework. Propose thought provoking questions such as: "Are you happy about things you have? Are you angry that you don't get things you want? Are you sorry others don't have things you do? Are you jealous of things others have?"

6. Process by asking participants the possible results of doing this type of daily work on attitudes, life, conversations, health and relationships.

B. 1. Generate a discussion about the importance of considering the question: "What are we grateful for today?"

2. Distribute the handout and ask participants to complete the top four questions.

3. Write the words MATERIAL, HEALTH and RELATIONSHIPS on the board.

4. Ask participants to share items for each category from their papers.

5. Generate a discussion on which category we are most grateful for, is it material, health or relationships? Ask questions such as: Which category do they think their parents are most grateful? Their grandparents? Do they think as we get older we are grateful for different things?

6. Assign each member homework to complete bottom of handout by writing something new they are grateful for each day, for one week.

This handout was inspired by Loretta LaRoche, an international consultant for over 20 years in the field of stress management using humor. Loretta is the author of "Joy of Stress".

Adapted for SEALS III from LMS VI by Bonny Reed-Bell, OTR/L, Canton, OH who works in an inpatient adolescent psychiatric unit of a hospital.

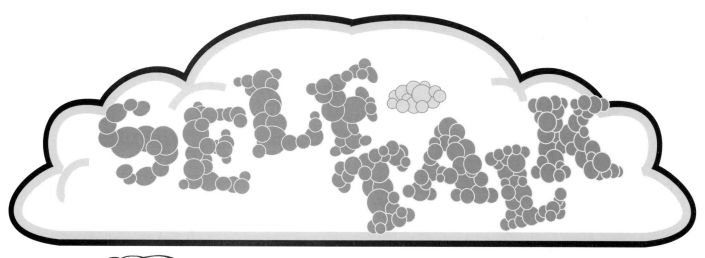

What is **self-talk**?

It is the SILENT conversation we have with ourselves in our heads all of the time.

Self-talk is SO powerful that we can talk ourselves into believing good things about ourselves (positive self-talk), or bad things about ourselves (negative self-talk). Negative self-talk can keep us from trying to reach our goals, positive self-talk can boost us into the sky!

With work, we may be able to change our negative thoughts into positive ones. Here are some examples:

DEFEATING PESSIMISTIC HURTFUL	NEGATIVE	POSITIVE	SUPPORTIVE UPLIFTING GOAL-DIRECTED
	"I really like to play basketball, but I know I'll never be good enough to get on the team."	"I really like to play basketball, and with some practice, I'll do well when I try out for the team."	
	"I am too tired to exercise."	"Exercising gives me energy and makes me feel good. I'll do it today!"	
	"I want my habits to be healthier, but it is hard to change the old ones. I don't know if I can do it."	"I can't change all my habits at once, but if I focus on making one change at a time, I know I'll be able to do it."	

NOW, it's your turn! What are some of the negative things that you tell yourself? How can these thoughts be changed to become POSITIVE, supportive, uplifting and goal directed?

Thoughts . . . | **can be changed to . . .**

I. PURPOSE:

To teach positive thinking, which students can use as a coping mechanism or a motivator.

II. GENERAL COMMENTS:

Learning to combat negative thinking requires awareness, effort and practice. Negative self-talk can be a life-long habit. Many young children hear negative messages about themselves and learn to use these messages in their self-talk. Negative self-talk is pessimistic, hurtful and defeating. We can learn to use positive self-talk instead. Positive self-talk is supportive, uplifting and can be used to help us achieve goals.

III. POSSIBLE ACTIVITIES:

A. 1. Survey several teachers or other school staff before meeting with your students to see if they have overheard positive or negative remarks lately. Write each remark on an index card.

2. Explain to your students the purpose and general comments as stated above.

3. Ask each student to select an index card and tell if the remark is positive or negative. Explain to your students that even though these were 'heard' comments and not 'self-talk,' these remarks give us an idea of the kinds of 'talk' that takes place in everyone's heads.

4. Distribute handouts and pencils. Review the handout and ask students to complete the bottom section. Assist them in changing negative thoughts into positive thoughts.

5. Discuss the consequences of negative self-talk and the value of positive self-talk.

6. Process by asking students to summarize what they learned in today's group. Ask them to practice their new skill by changing one thought per day for one week, and come to next week's group ready to discuss their experiences.

B. 1. Read the following to the students in your group: "Today's forecast is terrible! It is going to rain most of the day. You'll get all wet if you go out. Your shoes will get all wet, and then you'll have to dry them. Your umbrella is either lost or broken, so your hair will get all wet, too. Wherever you go, your dripping wet clothes will leave a puddle. You won't get anything done today, and you'll probably catch a cold from getting wet in all this rain! The sky will be full of gray clouds today, no sun at all. What a miserable day! It's best to go back to bed right now!"

2. Ask your students how they would feel and what they would do if they heard this forecast first thing in the morning. Help them understand how negative self-talk works by comparing our silent self-talk to this pessimistic weather forecast.

3. Distribute handouts and pencils.

4. Review the top section of the handout; give the students 15 minutes to complete the bottom section. Working in pairs may be helpful to your students.

5. Ask each student to share a negative thought and a new, positive thought.

6. Explain the assignment for your students' next group: For one week, keep a journal of negative thoughts. Practice turning these negative thoughts into positive thoughts and come to group ready to share some examples.

7. Process today's group by asking each student to imagine what their lives might be like if they could turn this new skill into a habit in the next 6 months. Encourage students to share their ideas with the group about how positive self-talk could change their lives.

Activity handout and facilitator's information originally submitted for Life Management Skills VI by Allison S. Unda, LMSW, Clemson, SC. Allison works as a maternal and child health social worker for a public health department.

Adapted for SEALS III from LMS VI by Sheila Freeman, MSW, CSW, who works with children in an outpatient mental health center.

My Relapse Prevention Plan

1 My diagnosis is:

_____

2 Three symptoms I experience with my illness are:

a. _____

b. _____

c. _____

3 Stressful events that endangered my health and put me in crisis:

_____

4 What can I do to avoid these types of stressful events in the future?

_____

5 Current stressors in my life today are:

_____

6 Three ways that I can reduce my stress are:

a. _____

b. _____

c. _____

7 Three of my positive qualities are:

a. _____

b. _____

c. _____

8 Supportive friends/family members that I call on a regular basis:

Name: _____ Phone number: _____

Name: _____ Phone number: _____

9 A daily community/leisure/healing activity I will engage in is:

_____

10 An activity I will definitely avoid is: _____

11 Three steps I will take to prevent relapse (when symptoms return or get worse) are:

a. _____

b. _____

c. _____

12 If I begin to relapse, I will: _____

My Relapse Prevention Plan

I. PURPOSE:

To empower all health consumers with a structured, tangible mechanism to maintain wellness and minimize the likelihood of relapse.

II. GENERAL COMMENTS:

Relapse prevention is oftentimes complicated, requiring knowledge, insight, support and determination. Many helpful ideas may be discussed with supportive peers and health professionals, but not organized into a unified, useable format.

III. POSSIBLE ACTIVITIES:

A. 1. Introduce the topic of relapse prevention.

   2. Distribute the handouts and pencils.

   3. Instruct the class to complete honestly and thoroughly.

   4. Review for accuracy, supporting group members for effort.

   5. Process ways of using the completed handout in the future. "Is it possible to place on refrigerator/visible place for a cue/reminder?" "Would it be helpful to share completed handout with a support/mental health professional?"

B. 1. Write the following on the board/flipchart:
     diagnosis
     symptoms
     stressors
     support
     healthy activities vs. unhealthy activities
     plan of action in case of relapse

   2. Discuss these relapse prevention concepts and explain as needed.

   3. Distribute handouts and pencils. Review each section offering observations and insights to assist class members in completing handouts thoroughly.

   4. Invite guest speaker(s) to address certain questions as needed (may be school counselor, representative from local health advocacy chapter, AA member if #10 is likely to elicit alcohol as a response, etc.).

   5. Introduce other issues that may be needed in a more personalized relapse prevention plan: e.g., MEDICATION(S) (name of medication, times to take, benefits/purposes, and side effects), PROFESSIONALS TO CONTACT (health professional, crisis hotline). These items may be addressed on the reverse side of handout.

   6. Facilitate discussion by asking students to discuss the benefits of developing relapse prevention plans.

Activity handout and facilitator's information submitted by Marla Yoder-Tiedt, MSW, LISW and Sandi MIller, RRT, both employed at a psychiatric hospital in Columbus, OH, with 15 years and 22 years in the mental health field respectively.

Adapted for SEALS III from LMS VI by Sandra Negley, MTRS, CTRS, Salt Lake City, UT, author of *Crossing the Bridge, A Journey in Self-Esteem, Relationships and Life Balance.*

Come to... RECOVERY ISLAND!

I. PURPOSE:

To increase awareness of one's personal recovery process.

To identify the obstacles to recovery and the tools necessary to enable one to reach 'recovery.'

II. GENERAL COMMENTS:

Reaching the "Island of Recovery" is the goal for people who are recovering from mental illness, physical illness and/or addictions. Yet, each person must reach the goal in his/her own way and in his/her own time. Visualizing how close or far one is from the goal, and reevaluating the tools needed to get there, may assist in the recovery process.

III. POSSIBLE ACTIVITIES:

A. 1. Distribute handouts and colored pencils.

2. Review the meaning of the island as the common goal of each individual, yet no two people will follow the exact same path or reach the island at exactly the same moment.

3. Ask class to draw themselves in the picture, as they are, with any tools or obstacles they are finding/using along the way. Offer minimal directions to stimulate imaginations. For further clarification, ask each student to pay attention to where they are in relation to the island. Are they in or out of the water? Are they swimming or traveling by some other mode? Is there anything in the water with them?

4. Ask students to volunteer in sharing and interpreting their pictures. Notice potential symbolism used by the originator (e.g., "What might the shark or boat represent on the path to recovery?")

5. Process the exercise by asking students what they learned. Encourage those who are closer to the island to help those who are feeling farther away.

B. 1. Open class discussion about recovery. Explain recovery can be from mental illness, physical illness and/or addictions. Ask the group, "What is required for one to be in recovery?"

2. Distribute handouts and colored pencils. Instruct students to not place names on handouts.

3. Ask students to draw themselves in the picture, as they are, with any tools or obstacles they are finding/using along the way. Offer minimal directions to stimulate imaginations. For further clarification, ask each person to pay attention to where they are in relation to the island. Are they in or out of the water? Are they swimming or traveling by some other mode? Is there anything in the water with them?

4. Encourage class members to draw pictures discreetly so others cannot see.

5. After drawings are complete, collect the pictures. Redistribute them so each student has someone else's picture. Encourage individuals to reflect on the pictures' meanings and then to guess the originator.

6. Allow for feedback and support. Discuss the best use of their 'Islands' - Therapeutic notebook? Bulletin board? Sharing with family or friends' meetings or visits?

Activity handout and facilitator's information submitted by Janell Horton, MSW, Long Beach, CA.
Ms. Horton is currently employed as a medical social worker specializing in oncology but has previously worked in psychiatric settings with the dually diagnosed population.

Adapted for SEALS III from LMS VI by Sandra Negley, MTRS, CTRS, Salt Lake City, UT,
author of *Crossing the Bridge, A Journey in Self-Esteem, Relationships and Life Balance.*

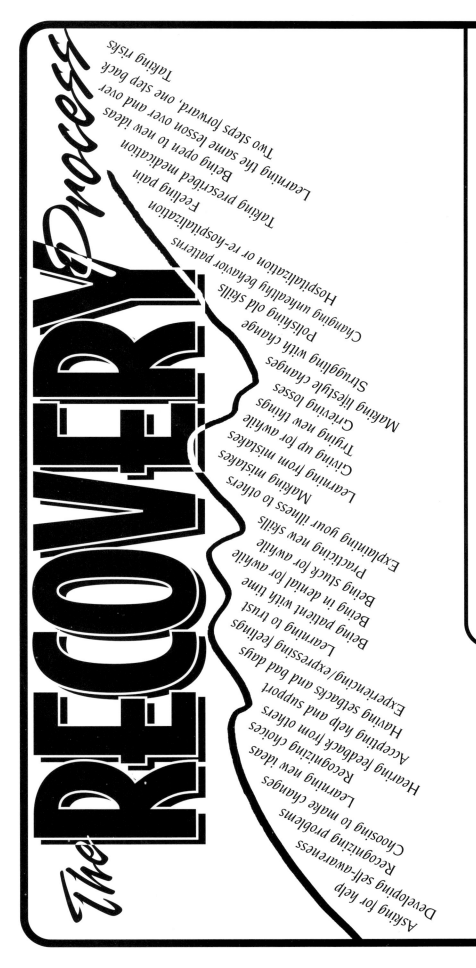

The RECOVERY Process

- Taking risks
- Two steps forward, one step back
- Learning the same lesson over and over
- Being open to new ideas
- Taking prescribed medication
- Feeling pain
- Hospitalization or re-hospitalization
- Changing unhealthy behavior patterns
- Polishing old skills
- Struggling with change
- Making lifestyle changes
- Grieving losses
- Trying new things
- Giving up for awhile
- Learning from mistakes
- Making mistakes
- Explaining your illness to others
- Practicing new skills
- Being stuck for awhile
- Being in denial for awhile
- Being patient with time
- Learning to trust
- Experiencing/expressing feelings
- Having setbacks and bad days
- Accepting help and support
- Hearing feedback from others
- Recognizing choices
- Learning new ideas
- Choosing to make changes
- Recognizing problems
- Developing self-awareness
- Asking for help

Recovery is a process full of steps, actions and changes as well as ups and downs. The recovery process is different for each person but often consists of many of the steps shown on the above graph.

Where are you in your recovery process? Circle the steps on the graph that apply to you . . . as many as you like.

Are there any other recovery steps you are currently working on, not shown here? What are they?

_____

_____

I. PURPOSE:

To increase understanding about the nature of the recovery/healing process.

To develop self-awareness about one's current 'place' in the process.

II. GENERAL COMMENTS:

Recovery can be a very challenging struggle for individuals with mental health, physical illness, and/or addiction issues. Many find it hard to see the bigger picture of changes, steps, stages, learning and movement in which they find themselves immersed and, at times, lost. Knowledge about what to expect in the recovery process can provide reassurance, self-awareness and increased motivation.

III. POSSIBLE ACTIVITIES:

A. 1. Provide blank paper and pens and ask participants to draw a 'line' (like a time line) to illustrate their recovery/healing over the past month. If necessary show an example on the flipchart, something like this:

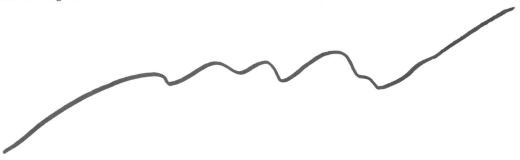

   2. Provide some time for sharing each student's 'recovery line.'

   3. Distribute handouts and instruct students to complete.

   4. Discuss students' observations, thoughts and reactions to this exercise.

   5. Encourage students to re-look at their 'recovery line' drawn at the beginning of class. Ask if anyone would draw his or her line differently now, with the knowledge gained from class.

B. 1. Write on flipchart a definition of process, e.g., "a set of actions or changes in a special order." Introduce the concept of process by using the flipchart, allowing time for exchanging ideas on the concept that recovery is a process.

   2. Brainstorm and list on flipchart what participants see as the steps/actions/changes/stages, etc., which occur in the process of recovery.

   3. Distribute handouts and pencils.

   4. Link the flip-charted ideas to the ideas on the handout.

   5. Provide time for participants to complete the handouts.

   6. Assign participants to subgroups and allow time for sharing.

   7. Reconvene and encourage discussion on any new learning gained from class.

   8. Pose question to students: "Is knowing there are stages, that consist of ups and downs to recovery, encouraging or discouraging?"

Activity handout and facilitator's information submitted by Nancy Day, O.T. Reg., Markham, Ontario, Canada. Nancy is an Occupational Therapist working in the mental health field, within the hospital sector. Her primary role as a group psychotherapist provides daily opportunity to design and facilitate group treatment. She believes it is a privilege to work in this capacity and witness the 'magic' that occurs as individuals connect with one another and share in each other's growth.

Adapted for SEALS III from LMS VI by Sandra Negley, MTRS, CTRS, Salt Lake City, UT,
author of *Crossing the Bridge, A Journey in Self-Esteem, Relationships and Life Balance.*

Creative Love, Creating Love

1. List the names of those closest to you. Briefly label their role in your life.

_____   _____

_____   _____

2. What qualities do you appreciate most in them?

_____   _____

_____   _____

3. What positive qualities do you bring to these relationships?

_____   _____

_____   _____

4. Can you usually express your feelings in an encouraging, non-threatening manner?

_____   _____

_____   _____

5. Can you think of ways in which these relationships could be improved?

_____   _____

_____   _____

6. Love for others may be expressed in many different ways. Match the name of the person(s) listed in #1 above, to one or more of the "creative love" expressions below. Write his/her name on the space(s) provided.

- scheduled (or unscheduled) quality time together _____
- a poem _____
- an art/craft project _____
- a special letter/card _____
- remembering favorites _____
- sincere compliments _____
- unexpected phone call or visit _____
- other _____

- completing an unassigned task or chore voluntarily _____
- hand-picked flowers _____
- original story _____
- framed photograph _____
- anything handmade _____
- listening _____
- a special food/meal _____
- other _____

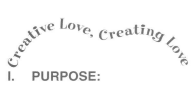

I. PURPOSE:

To provide a visual point of reference and expressive view of close relationships and to foster critical and creative ways of looking at them.

To experience the power of purposeful and meaningful gift giving.

II. GENERAL COMMENTS:

Supportive relationships help us live healthy, fulfilling and meaningful lives. Relationships can be assessed and improved through self-discovery and group input. Positive relationships require work. They don't just happen. Relationships that work are those in which people, who are attracted to each other, perceive the reasons for the attraction and then work steadily to keep those elements in the relationship. One element of a relationship involves purposeful gift giving. Gift giving is a fundamental form of human communication. They are tokens of status, respect and appreciation. Gifts create and cement alliances and partnerships. In close relationships, gifts are symbols of love; they signify what we think of, what we know of, how well we love and understand each other. Gifts are not always purchased in a store. Handmade items, as well as interests and a loving nurturing environment that help to positively influence a person's life, are the gifts of true significance.

III. POSSIBLE ACTIVITIES:

A. 1. Introduce topic of the vital importance of healthy relationships and gift giving, using the examples in O. Henry's (William Sidney Porter) short story "The Gift of the Magi."

2. Distribute handouts instructing students to complete. Explain as needed offering examples to illustrate, e.g., Section 6-remembering favorites: remembering a relative's holiday with a phone call, renting parent's favorite video and watching it together, making a cassette tape of best friend's favorites songs, etc.

3. Discuss the importance of honest, ongoing communication. Stress the basics, e.g., expressing one's own reaction to situations or behaviors is usually more effective than blaming others. Compile a list of words or phrases that tend to foster love and affection.

4. On reverse of handout, instruct students to set a goal of creating at least one personalized project for each person listed in #1.

5. Process by asking class what was learned by this experience.

6. Request that class complete creative expression of love, give them to significant other(s) and be ready to share the experience of purposeful gift giving during next scheduled session.

B. 1. Introduce the concept of close and healthy relationships.

2. Distribute handouts to students instructing them to complete. Explain as needed offering examples to illustrate, e.g., Section 6-remembering favorites: remembering a relative's holiday with a phone call, renting parent's favorite video and watching it together, making a cassette tape of best friend's favorites songs, etc.

3. Facilitate brief role-plays involving relevant issues for the class, encouraging creative responses. Try role-plays expressing feelings or ideas to improve relationships. Use REAL-LIFE SITUATIONS, (back of book, page B, front and back) for ideas.

4. Ask class to brainstorm ideas for additional creative love expressions that are low cost or no cost. Provide materials for creating love by creating expressions of love as class or individual projects.

5. Feedback may be encouraged after task completion.

6. Process by facilitating input on how to keep friends.

Activity handout and facilitator's information originally submitted for Life Management Skills V by Bettie E. Michelson, M.S. Bettie has developed creative educational units as a teacher and materials for therapy and discussion groups as an occupational therapist working in mental health. She is currently concentrating on writing.

Adapted for SEALS III from LMS V by Elaine Hyla Slea, M.Ed., Euclid, OH, adaptor of SEALS+PLUS (Self-Esteem and Life Skills) and SEALS II.

EVALUATE YOUR RELATIONSHIP

These questions are to help you think about what is important in your relationships with others. There are no right or wrong answers.

List four people in your life with whom you have important relationships.

1. _____ 2. _____ 3. _____ 4. _____

1. Name 3 things about him/her that you really like.

_____
_____
_____

Are there things about him/her you really dislike? _____
Does s/he encourage or discourage you to have other friends? _____
What activities do you enjoy participating in together? _____
Are there activities you participate in without this person? _____
Can you trust this person with personal information? _____
Do you think his/her relationship with family and other friends are healthy?
_____
Do you feel this relationship allows you to freely express your true self?
_____

2. Name 3 things about him/her that you really like.

_____
_____
_____

Are there things about him/her you really dislike? _____
Does s/he encourage or discourage you to have other friends? _____
What activities do you enjoy participating in together? _____
Are there activities you participate in without this person? _____
Can you trust this person with personal information? _____
Do you think his/her relationship with family and other friends are healthy?
_____
Do you feel this relationship allows you to freely express your true self?
_____

3. Name 3 things about him/her that you really like.

_____
_____
_____

Are there things about him/her you really dislike? _____
Does s/he encourage or discourage you to have other friends? _____
What activities do you enjoy participating in together? _____
Are there activities you participate in without this person? _____
Can you trust this person with personal information? _____
Do you think his/her relationship with family and other friends are healthy?
_____
Do you feel this relationship allows you to freely express your true self?
_____

4. Name 3 things about him/her that you really like.

_____
_____
_____

Are there things about him/her you really dislike? _____
Does s/he encourage or discourage you to have other friends? _____
What activities do you enjoy participating in together? _____
Are there activities you participate in without this person? _____
Can you trust this person with personal information? _____
Do you think his/her relationship with family and other friends are healthy?
_____
Do you feel this relationship allows you to freely express your true self?
_____

Evaluation Results: _____
_____
_____

I. PURPOSE:

To evaluate the positive and negative characteristics of relationships and identify principles of healthy relationships.

II. GENERAL COMMENTS:

People enter into and stay in relationships for a variety of reasons. It may be wise to take the time to reflect about the relationship to determine its overall health. This can serve as a good 'consciousness raising' activity for people who may be in unhealthy relationships or who limit the number of their relationships.

III. POSSIBLE ACTIVITIES: This handout may be used in conjunction with RELATIONSHIPS section (S.E.A.L.S. II - pages 35-43) and/or (Crossing the Bridge - pages 47-51).

A. 1. Introduce activity by telling students that it is important they make conscious decisions about what they want and what they do not want in a relationship.

2. Distribute handouts and pens.

3. Allow students ten to fifteen minutes to complete handout.

4. Promote honest sharing of responses in a supportive atmosphere. Provide input, as able, as to signs of a healthy relationship and signs of an unhealthy relationship.

5. Acknowledge the difficulties and obstacles when discussing potential changes in a relationship.

6. Ask students to identify any changes in their current relationships they would like to make. Brainstorm with class how they might implement important changes.

B. 1. On top left of flipchart write 'Healthy Relationships' and on top right, write 'Unhealthy Relationships'. Now brainstorm with class the elements of a healthy relationship and an unhealthy relationship.

2. Distribute handouts and pencils.

3. Allow students ten to fifteen minutes to complete.

4. Divide students into pairs.

5. Facilitate mutual sharing. It is not necessary to share the names of the persons listed on worksheet. Discuss the importance of actively listening during sharing of personal information.

6. Reconvene as a class. Write 'Evaluation Results' on flipchart. Explain to class that stopping to evaluate, to look at our insights, provides us with a knowing or realization about a situation, person, etc. Ask students to share their Evaluation Results from this activity. Role playing these changes is often helpful in processing with students.

7. It may be necessary to provide resources for anyone who is concerned about abusive relationships (hotlines, coalitions against domestic violence, rape centers, shelters, etc.). See HELP handout, (page 79).

8. Arrange, if desired, for local speakers to address relationship topics such as: teen support groups, domestic violence, healthy dating, date rape, etc.

Activity handout and facilitator's information submitted by Kerry Moles, CSW, Bronx, NY.
Kerry is a social worker and an Independent Consultant specializing in educating youth and youth workers on issues of domestic violence, sexual assault and independent living skills.

Adapted for SEALS III from LMS VI by Sandra Negley, MTRS, CTRS, Salt Lake City, UT,
author of *Crossing the Bridge, A Journey in Self-Esteem, Relationships and Life Balance.*

I. PURPOSE:

To identify positive/interesting characteristics/qualities of oneself and others.
To increase relationships by encouraging healthy friendships.

II. GENERAL COMMENTS:

One of the factors that can enhance or erode an adolescent's self-concept is the ability or inability to make and keep friendships. An analogy of an old fashioned community quilting bee can be made in respect to the need in today's society for quality friendships. It took many members of a community time and effort to make a quilt and it was an appreciated gift by the recipients. Likewise, developing friendships takes time and effort and a variety of people, and is a valuable gift. Healthy and dependable friends are those we can count on to 'warm' us like a quality quilt!

III. POSSIBLE ACTIVITIES:

A. 1. Introduce the concept of friendship. Generate a list of qualities that are important in a friendly relationship. Some students may protest that they have no friends. If this occurs, ask them to complete the activity by drawing pictures of friends that they would like to know and have.

2. Distribute handouts.

3. Instruct students to complete each corner by indicating their favorite color, hobby, food, and musical group or song. These four items can be creatively changed to meet the age and interest levels of the class. The four side panels should be designed to indicate the qualities that they find attractive in a friendship, e.g., interests, age, shared goals, sense of humor, spiritual beliefs, clubs, activities, sports, etc. Magazines can be used to cut out the representative items, or individuals can create drawings. The center of the square is left blank.

4. Give the class time to discuss their corners and side panels. Encourage and support aspects that are important in developing friendships.

5. If available, snap an instant picture of each student. This photograph is placed in the center of the 'quilted' square. If not, ask students to select a sign or symbol that best represents themselves or a quality that makes them attractive as a friend.

6. Mount all the completed squares on the wall to form a community quilt.

7. Process the activity by asking: "Was it difficult to complete your square?", "Was it hard to draw or find pictures to label the defined subjects or qualities?," "How do you feel about your finished square?," "How do you feel about letting others see it?," and/or "How do you feel about seeing other people's square?"

B. 1. Introduce the concept of friendship. Discuss qualities that are important in a friendly relationship.

2. Distribute handouts, photocopied on a variety of colored papers if possible, to promote individuality.

3. Assign each student an interview of a fellow classmate. Information on at least eight defined areas should be sought, e.g., favorite food, subject, teacher, sport, hobby, music, season, type of movie, greatest accomplishment, future plans, etc. These items will vary depending on the need and age of the class. Allow note-taking on the reverse side of the handout - not in the quilt squares!

4. Instruct each student to complete the corners and side panels of the quilt with information about the classmate just interviewed. Using any eight items of information just gathered, ask class to fill the four corners and four side panels of the quilt. Magazines can be used to cut out the representative items or individuals can create drawings. The center of the square is left blank.

5. If available, snap an instant picture of each student for the center or write student's name in the center, using decorative lettering or printing.

6. Create a 'QUILT OF FAME' by mounting all the squares on the wall to form a Friendship Quilt.

7. Process by asking each student to share the information in the square that was created. "Was it difficult to complete the assigned square?," "Was it hard to interview someone else?," "How was it to create something about/for someone else?," and/or "How do you feel about the finished quilt?"

Activity handout and facilitator's information originally submitted for Life Management Skills V by Lori Rosenberg, MS, CTRS, RTCR, University Heights, OH. Ms. Rosenberg has worked in a diverse set of health care and community settings where she has been responsible for developing a full complement of therapeutic recreation programs. She has written several articles and has spoken at both local and state Therapeutic and Activity Professionals' Conferences.

Adapted for SEALS III from LMS V by Elaine Hyla Slea, M.Ed., Euclid, OH, adaptor of *SEALS+PLUS (Self-Esteem and Life Skills)* and *SEALS II.*

Setting Boundaries

What IS A BOUNDARY?

A boundary is an invisible "barrier" between you and other people – limits beyond which you will not go and beyond which others are not welcome.

It is healthy to have a good sense of where your feelings and opinions start and stop, and where the other person's feelings and opinions start and stop.

It is especially important to know how to set boundaries with "difficult" people – particularly with those individuals who are critical, controlling, manipulative, demanding or aggressive.

How DO I COMMUNICATE MY BOUNDARIES TO OTHER PEOPLE?

Here are some words to use:

I HAVE A PROBLEM WITH THAT. _____

I DON'T WANT TO . . . _____

I'VE DECIDED NOT TO . . . _____

THIS IS WHAT I NEED. _____

THIS IS HARD FOR ME TO SAY . . . _____

I UNDERSTAND YOUR POINT OF VIEW BUT _____

I FEEL UNCOMFORTABLE ABOUT . . . _____

I'D RATHER NOT. _____

YES, I DO MIND _____

I'D PREFER NOT TO . . . _____

IT'S IMPORTANT TO ME. _____

I'LL THINK ABOUT IT. _____

THAT'S UNACCEPTABLE. _____

I GUESS WE SEE IT DIFFERENTLY. _____

Who DO I NEED TO BE ESTABLISHING CLEAR BOUNDARIES WITH?

_____

I. PURPOSE:

To increase awareness of what is meant by personal boundaries.
To improve language skills to communicate boundaries.

II. GENERAL COMMENTS:

Establishing and maintaining boundaries is an important assertive skill. Adolescents and young adults are often unaware of the need to have boundaries, and lack the necessary skills to set and maintain boundaries especially with peers and significant others. This skill is particularly useful when dealing with difficult situations or with difficult individuals.

III. POSSIBLE ACTIVITIES: This handout may be used in conjunction with INTERACTING AND COPING WITH DIFFICULT PEOPLE (page 32).

A. 1. Review 'What is a boundary?' using information contained in GENERAL COMMENTS as a guideline for discussion.

2. Give and ask for examples of boundaries, e.g.,
   "I don't permit others to use my e-mail account."
   "I don't loan my clothes."
   "I sleep late on weekends."
   "I never lend money."
   "I will not encourage or listen to gossip or spreading rumors."
   "I do not allow anyone to 'borrow' my homework."

3. Distribute handouts. Instruct students to complete above "starters", if able.

4. Share responses. Ask students to identify one personal boundary they need to establish immediately, and with whom (without naming names). For example: "a person who goes to this school", "a person who belongs to the same club that I do", "a person that I am related to", "a member of the faculty", etc.

5. Process by asking students to reverse the handouts and recall as much as possible from the front side, reinforcing points as they are mentioned.

6. Process by asking group members what might be a positive outcome of good manners.

B. 1. Ask the class to discuss the purpose of a fence. Ask why a homeowner would choose to build one around his/her property. Read Robert Frost's classic poem, "The Mending Wall," focusing on the meaning behind final line, "Good fences make good neighbors." This poem was written in 1914. Why is it still relevant today?

2. Distribute handouts. Review the 'What is a Boundary' section of the handout.

3. Divide class into sub-groups of 3 or 4 students each.

4. Ask sub-groups to brainstorm examples of personal boundaries they either presently have or want to have in their lives, in the classroom, other areas of school, home or at work. Instruct sub-groups to complete 'How do I Communicate My Boundaries' section using personal examples as a guide.

5. Give sub-groups five minutes to create one small role-play, which demonstrates how to communicate a boundary, utilizing some of the language from the list on the handout.

6. Reconvene as a class and encourage the sharing of role-plays with class.

7. Request that students identify with whom they need to be establishing clear boundaries, without naming specific individuals (see Activity A.4. above) and share as able by practicing the setting of boundaries through additional role-playing.

8. Process by identifying the benefits of setting boundaries.

Activity handout and facilitator's information originally submitted for Life Management Skills V by Nancy Day, O.T. Reg., Markham, Ontario, Canada. Nancy is an Occupational Therapist working in the mental health field, within the hospital sector. Her primary role as a group psychotherapist provides daily opportunity to design and facilitate group treatment. She believes it is a privilege to work in this capacity and witness the "magic" that occurs as individuals connect with one another and share in each other's growth.

Adapted for SEALS III from LMS V by Elaine Hyla Slea, M.Ed., Euclid, OH, adaptor of *SEALS+PLUS (Self-Esteem and Life Skills)* and *SEALS II.*

sticks and stones
may break my bones but words do hurt me!

Combating Emotional Abuse

Emotional abuse is an often overlooked form of abuse. Words CAN and DO hurt. An emotionally abusive person can be your boyfriend or girlfriend, coach, parent, instructor, friend, co-worker, etc. We must take steps to combat this form of abuse that leaves such everlasting internal scars.

What is emotional abuse?	Effects of emotional abuse
☹ Constant criticism, demands and rejections	☹ Low self-esteem: feeling inadequate, unworthy, devalued, unlovable
☹ Unreasonable jealously and jealous rage	☹ Hyperactive/disruptive behavior
☹ Deliberate flirting and unfaithfulness	☹ Anxiety
☹ Insults, rude nicknames	☹ Unrealistic fears
☹ Attacks on what a person is rather than what a person does	☹ Poor peer relationships
☹ Excessive or hurtful teasing	☹ Feeling responsible for the abuse
☹ Other _____	☹ Depressed, withdrawn, isolated

STOP PUTTING UP WITH PUT-DOWNS

YOU DON'T HAVE TO TOLERATE BEING:
☹ The object of cruel jokes
☹ Called names or nicknames
☹ Threatened
☹ Blamed
☹ Ordered around
_____

YOU DESERVE
☺ Understanding
☺ Respect
☺ Safety
☺ Security
☺ Strong positive relationships
_____

WAYS TO RESPOND
☺ "I" statements
☺ "I don't believe you"
☺ Talk to a counselor/friend
☺ Let the remark "bounce off of you"
☺ Don't match insult for insult
_____

MOST IMPORTANT!

Remind yourself:
You don't have to put up with emotional abuse!

STICKS AND STONES
COMBATING emotional abuse

I. PURPOSE:

To define signs and effects of emotional abuse.
To increase awareness of available strategies to combat emotional abuse.

II. GENERAL COMMENTS:

All forms of abuse are serious - no form should be dismissed. However, people repeatedly express that emotional abuse is the most difficult form of abuse to overcome and heal. Words can truly hurt. Relationships serve as mirrors of the inner self. We learn how valuable and worthy we are through interactions with others. This process is called self-building. Abuse occurs in a continuum that begins with hurting the feelings of loved ones and interferes with healthy self-building. Although some emotionally abusive people never physically abuse, physical abuse is always preceded by emotional abuse. Hurting never solves problems and only serves to create other problems such as continual resentment and hostility. Combating emotional abuse entails an awareness of the forms of emotional abuse, self-validation and strategies for healthy responses.

III. POSSIBLE ACTIVITIES: This handout may be used in conjunction with INTERACTING AND COPING WITH DIFFICULT PEOPLE (page 32) and HELP (page 79).

A. 1. Present a list of sayings to the class such as:
       "Children should be seen and not heard.", "Spare the rod and spoil the child."

2. Instruct the students to discuss the purpose of creating such sayings, the lessons/morals taught by each and the relevance of them.

3. On the board, write the topic sentence from the handout. Instruct the class to read what has been written and to discuss their personal observations/reactions.

4. Inform the class that today's topic is a serious one and introduce the topic of emotional abuse.

5. Distribute handouts.

6. Instruct class to read text in box. Instruct class to list reasons why emotional abuse is often overlooked.

7. Read and discuss 'What is Emotional Abuse' and 'Effects of Emotional Abuse.'

8. Allow students to share further examples, WITH AN AWARENESS OF ETHICAL AND/OR BOUNDARY ISSUES.

9. Instruct students that the bottom half of handout is designed to help them combat those 'sticks and stones' of emotional abuse.

10. Inform students that part of combating emotional abuse is focusing on the basics of what each individual deserves, e.g., understanding, respect, safety, security, strong positive relationships, etc.

11. Instruct class to silently complete section titled 'YOU DESERVE.' Ask for students to volunteer responses.

12. Discuss differences between *teasing, constructive criticism* and *emotional abuse*. Instruct students to list further examples by completing the middle section titled 'You Don't Have to Tolerate.'

13. Brainstorm with the class possible combating strategies by completing section titled 'Ways to Respond.'

14. Follow up by instructing the students to be aware of at least one instance of emotional abuse recognized from now until next session. Instruct students to select one strategy and put it into action. Ask the class to be prepared to discuss events and strategies during next session.

B. 1. Divide class into 5 sub-groups.

2. Distribute a sheet of blank paper to each group, instructing one student from each group to record group work.

3. Allowing ample time for completion, instruct one group to:
    a. write the lyrics to one popular song familiar to most members of the group.
    b. outline the plot of one television situation comedy familiar to most members of the group.
    c. outline the plot of a movie/video familiar to most members of the group.
    d. outline a music video familiar to most members of the group.
    e. list interactions with schoolmates (but not to identify specific names) that occurred from the beginning of the school day until the beginning of this session.

4. Instruct each group to share what they have written and to identify examples of emotional abuse in each. List examples on board.

5. Distribute handouts. Complete top half. Instruct class to list reasons why emotional abuse is often overlooked as related to introductory activity.

6. Review three parts of the combating strategy. Complete bottom half. Using list from board instruct students to supply healthy responses to the emotional abuses listed.

7. Set a class goal to actively practice combating emotional abuse in at least one area of their lives. Instruct class to be prepared to share success stories at next session.

Activity handout and facilitator's information originally submitted for Life Management Skills V
by Esterlee A. Molyneux, MS, SSW, of Logan, UT. Esterlee is a Program Coordinator at a Child Abuse Prevention Agency, teaching parenting and children's social skills classes as well as in-home parenting services.

Adapted for SEALS III from LMS V by Elaine Hyla Slea, M.Ed., Euclid, OH,
adaptor of *SEALS+PLUS (Self-Esteem and Life Skills)* and *SEALS II.*

TALKING about personal issues

Talking about your personal issues or concerns to friends, family, peers, teachers, or counselors can be challenging. Should you? Shouldn't you? How can you feel okay about discussing them? Or not discussing them? How much do you say? How about those awkward questions you sometimes get, when you're least expecting it? It's wise to give it some thought . . .

WHO·WHO·WHO·WHO·WHO·WHO·WHO·WHO·WHO·WHO·WHO

WITH whom are you comfortable being completely open and honest?

WITH whom or in what situations do you want to be more discreet, giving less information?

WITH whom do you want to completely keep your privacy?

Then, give yourself permission to respect these decisions.

WHAT TO SAY · WHAT TO SAY · WHAT TO SAY · WHAT TO SAY

☐ **THINK,** it may be helpful to think what to say before situations arise, so you're not caught off guard. Rehearse your response if you'd like. And remember . . . there's no right or wrong . . . find your own ways of talking about it.

☐ **SELECT** individuals who you feel you can trust with personl information, individuals who do not gossip or spread rumors about others.

☐ **DISCUSS** only the information you feel is important for the person to know. Telling the details or deep personal feelings might not be necessary.

☐ **AVOID** being negative, destructive, or blaming yourself or others when discussing personal concerns. It is important to stick to the facts and present the situation in an assertive manner.

☐ **EMPHASIZE** the positive aspects of what you are doing, e.g., "I am getting a lot of support." "The program I am in is teaching me a lot." "I have met with my teachers to improve my grades."

DO NOT WANT TO TALK ABOUT·DO NOT WANT TO TALK ABOUT

If you don't want to disclose anything, you have this right. Indicate the subject is off limits, in a pleasant but firm voice. Try something like, "I'm just not comfortable talking about it right now."

The term 'personal issues' covers a lot but without actually disclosing much, and avoids the problem of outright lying.

Acknowledge others' concern with "thanks for caring" or "I appreciate your concern." Practice quickly changing the subject, "How are you?", people might actually prefer talking about themselves anyway!

**TALK
ING
about
personal
issues**

I. PURPOSE:

To explore some of the 'how to' issues pertaining to self-disclosure.

To maintain and establish healthy and supportive relationships when talking about personal issues.

II. GENERAL COMMENTS:

Individuals with personal issues or concerns can be at a loss as to how to disclose information about their problems. It can be difficult for them to TALK about it and to NOT TALK about it with family, friends, teachers, counselors, peers and acquaintances. Maintaining and establishing healthy and supportive boundaries and relationships at this important time can be paramount in the healing process.

III. POSSIBLE ACTIVITIES:

A. 1. Ask students to complete the sentence starter (have it written ahead of time on flipchart): "One thing I have learned about having personal concerns is…."

2. Discuss with class why it can be difficult to talk about personal concerns to family, friends, teachers, peers or others. Write all responses on flipchart.

3. Distribute handouts and highlighters.

4. Review each section on handout and ask students for feedback on the ideas. Encourage students to add their own ideas on ways of disclosing to others.

5. Instruct students to review the handout one more time and to highlight the three most important items covered.

6. Facilitate role-plays using different approaches to discuss difficult subjects.

7. Ask each student to share aloud the one most helpful item covered in today's class.

B. 1. Ask students to share either a positive or negative experience when they disclosed personal information to someone.

2. Take one of the negative experiences and write on the board using no specific names. In B.4. below, the class will discuss how it might have been handled differently.

3. Distribute handouts. Review the points and facilitate discussion based on student's thoughts and ideas from the handout.

4. Develop list of likely questions/situations, with class input that may be posed to class members. E.g., The teacher said, "I was worried, your grades were slipping and you were missing so many classes….Are you okay?" Your friend says, "You haven't been like yourself lately, What's wrong?" Your father inquires, "You look so tired all of the time? Is something going on?" Use one on the flipchart and elicit others from the class.

5. Rehearse these aloud with class support. Integrate new phrases or concepts as outlined in the handout. Assure students that these are personal situations and need to be handled by each person individually.

6. Ask each student to identify a direction or goal each has, in respect to information discussed today.

Activity handout and facilitator's information submitted by Nancy Day, O.T. Reg., Markham, Ontario, Canada. Nancy is an Occupational Therapist working in the mental health field, within the hospital sector. Her primary role as a group psychotherapist provides daily opportunity to design and facilitate group treatment. She believes it is a privilege to work in this capacity and witness the 'magic' that occurs as individuals connect with one another and share in each other's growth.

**Adapted for SEALS III from LMS VI by Sandra Negley, MTRS, CTRS, Salt Lake City, UT,
author of *Crossing the Bridge, A Journey in Self-Esteem, Relationships and Life Balance.***

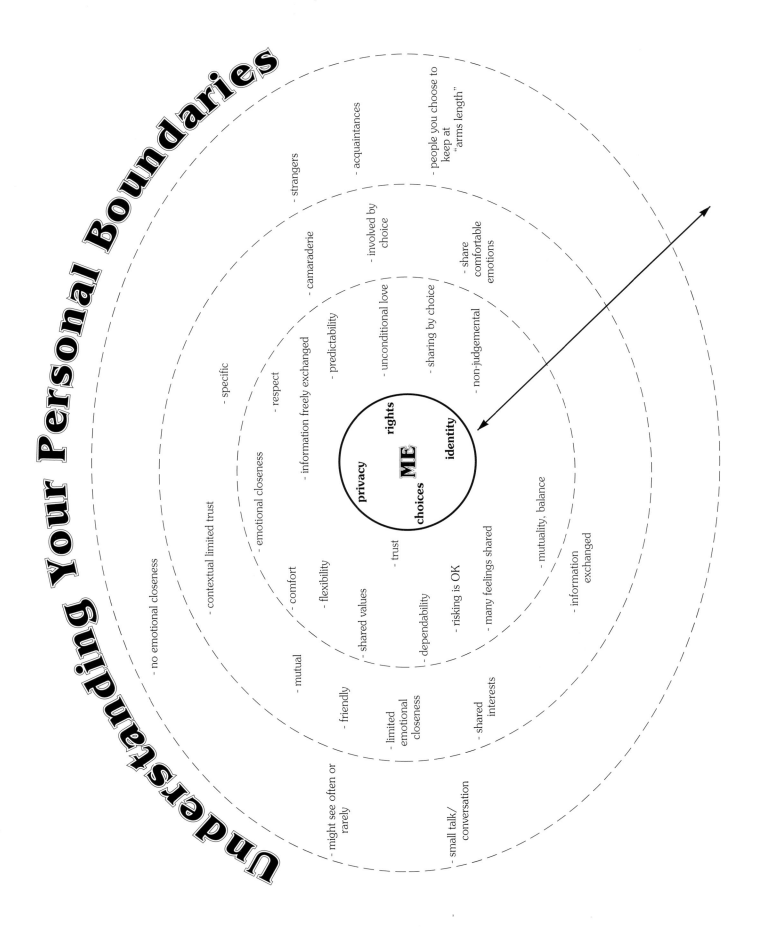

Understanding Your Personal Boundaries

ME
rights
privacy
choices
identity

- no emotional closeness
- contextual limited trust
- specific
- respect
- emotional closeness
- information freely exchanged
- predictability
- unconditional love
- sharing by choice
- non-judgemental
- involved by choice
- share comfortable emotions
- camaraderie
- strangers
- acquaintances
- people you choose to keep at "arms length"
- comfort
- flexibility
- shared values
- trust
- dependability
- risking is OK
- many feelings shared
- mutuality, balance
- information exchanged
- mutual
- friendly
- limited emotional closeness
- shared interests
- small talk/ conversation
- might see often or rarely

Understanding Your Personal Boundaries

I. PURPOSE:

To recognize appropriate personal boundaries in relationships.

II. GENERAL COMMENTS:

It is often times difficult to maintain healthy personal boundaries. Adolescents experiment with personal boundaries and those adolescents who have had poor role modeling of healthy relationships, may tend to find themselves perpetuating relationship struggles. They may open up to trust too quickly, get repeatedly hurt, or keep everyone at 'arms length' and unable to attain closeness.

III. POSSIBLE ACTIVITIES: May be used in conjunction with SETTING BOUNDARIES (page 52)

A. 1. Using large lettering, print each individual 'relationship characteristic' from front of handout on an index card and shuffle. Make a photocopy of handout. Using correctional fluid on all text except title and 'ME' in center of handout. Photocopy revised handout. Reproduce edited handout on board or flip chart. Bring a roll of tape to session.

 2. Distribute handouts. Explain the basic concepts of this model. Facilitate discussion about the appropriateness of always starting relationships in the outer ring and 'testing' the relationship for trust and respect by moving in, one 'ring' at a time. This way, even if trust is betrayed and comfortable feelings are shared, there is no major hurt. Distribute index cards to students. Ask students one at a time to read aloud information from index card and decide as a class where on model the behavior should be placed. Student then tapes index card on board or flip chart in appropriate position. Instruct the class to complete information on their handouts at the same time after verifying that placement is correct.

 3. Discuss different types of relationships, of friends, family, co-workers, etc., and assumptions about the 'rings' into which people should fit. Discuss the right to choose the distance that is set, regardless of expectation based on the nature of the relationship. Remind students that often individuals feel that certain family members or relatives should be in the closest 'ring', even if they are untrustworthy or disrespectful.

 4. Ask class to identify and write in the names of people in the appropriate 'ring'. Then, to rank their satisfaction in this relationship the way it is presently. (1=less satisfied, 5=most satisfied) in establishing personal boundaries. (example: Who to tell what to.)

 5. Assist students in appropriate and realistic goal setting for positive change.

 6. Process by asking students to share one goal with the class explaining the need for this change.

B. 1. Facilitate a discussion about relationships and personal boundaries. Ask students to define 'boundaries'.

 2. Distribute handouts.

 3. Discuss the reasons for a solid line around 'ME' and dotted lines around the others; my rights and choices are mine alone, and only I can choose what and when to share. If this line were dotted, we would not feel a sense of personal identity and would feel uncomfortably exposed to/controlled by person(s) around us. The dotted lines represent the ability to move people closer or further from us by our own choice; boundaries are not static.

 4. Discuss openly the characteristics of the different types of relationships. Encourage students to add other characteristics of each of the types of relationships.

 5. Process by asking students what was learned by this model of personal boundaries.

 6. Ask students to journalize using the following as a writing prompt: "Consider what personal changes you need to be making in order to develop or maintain healthy personal boundaries". Ask students to be prepared to discuss at a later session.

If appropriate, it may be helpful to talk about the fact that therapeutic counseling or other helping-professional relationships are different, in that there is often a need and assumption that communication must be honest and freely exchanged. There is not the same extent of mutuality and balance, and there is not always time for the slow development of trust. It may be helpful to draw a fourth ring (in a different color) just outside the 'closest' dotted ring to represent these types of relationships.

Activity handout and facilitator's information originally submitted for Life Management Skills V by Erika Pond Clements, B.Sc.O.T. (c). Erika is an Occupational Therapist and Program Manager in Toronto, Canada. She has worked in mental health and behavioral health settings for the past 10 years and has recently completed a diploma in Addiction Studies.

Adapted for SEALS III from LMS V by Elaine Hyla Slea, M.Ed., Euclid, OH, adaptor of *SEALS+PLUS (Self-Esteem and Life Skills)* and *SEALS II.*

eMOTIONS
Can Affect Your Eating

CIRCLE THE EMOTIONS THAT AFFECT YOUR EATING HABITS.

HAPPY	*PROUD*	*DISCOURAGED*	*LONELY*
NERVOUS	*STRESSED*	*DISAPPOINTED*	*EXCITED*
RELAXED	*SAD*	*ANGRY*	*ANXIOUS*
TIRED	*WORRIED*	*SELF-CRITICAL*	*SCARED*
BORED	*DEPRESSED*	*FRUSTRATED*	*CONTENTED*

Sometimes we may notice that we eat more or less when we feel a certain way. Sometimes we learn to eat due to an emotion. For example, parents may give a treat to their children when they are sad or hurt. Then, the child will learn to eat treats when he or she is sad or hurt. Over time, the result may be unhealthy eating and/or undesired weight loss or increase.

The next time a feeling 'makes' you want to reach for something to eat, or not eat, what can you do to help yourself?

☐ Talk about it.   ☐ Tell someone how you feel.   ☐ Take a walk.

☐ Ask for a hug.   ☐ Look at a favorite magazine.   ☐ Do some stretching.

☐ Create something.   ☐ Write in a journal.   ☐ Take deep breaths.

☐ _____   ☐ _____   ☐ _____

☐ _____   ☐ _____   ☐ _____

☐ _____   ☐ _____   ☐ _____

After considering the above options -

"The NEXT time I feel an emotion controlling my eating choices, I will

_____ *."*

I. PURPOSE:

To increase awareness of emotions that can contribute to unhealthy eating.

II. GENERAL COMMENTS:

Many people are not aware they eat or don't eat to feed emotions. The consequences are oftentimes unwanted: increase or decrease in weight, poorly controlled doctor recommended diets (low sugar, low salt, low fat, etc.), poor health choices and guilt feelings. Problem solving specific strategies may be empowering and helpful. Perhaps one may need further counseling on how to deal with these emotions in a positive manner.

III. POSSIBLE ACTIVITIES: This handout may be used in conjunction with EMOTIONS© (SEALS+PLUS - page 24).

A. 1. Introduce class to the topic of recognizing emotional reasons for eating.

2. Distribute handouts and pencils.

3. Instruct students to complete the handouts.

4. Discuss the different emotional reasons for eating that the students recorded on their handouts.

5. Discuss healthier alternatives when feeling a certain emotion.

6. Ask students to disclose personal plans for the next time participants have the urge to feed an emotion.

B. 1. Explain to the class that there are many things in our lives for which we have no control, e.g., the weather, who our parents are, the city we were born in, our first names, the neighborhood we grew up in, choices our children make, etc. Eating choices are within our control.

2. Introduce topic of emotions affecting eating choices. Ask students several questions to determine commonalties and differences within the class:
   "How many students overeat when upset, stressed?"
   "What do you tend to eat?"
   "How many students overeat at parties when feeling contented?"
   "How many students do not eat when feeling depressed?"
   "What foods are most appealing when you do eat?"
   Informally tally results.

3. Distribute handouts and pencils.

4. Give class ten minutes to complete.

5. Divide class into pairs.

6. Facilitate sharing of responses with partners.

7. Write on flipchart all possible strategies that students are considering.

8. Process by asking students to identify an interesting insight gained from this activity.

Activity handout and facilitator's information originally adapted from submission for Life Management Skills VI by Allison S. Unda, LMSW, Clemson, SC. Allison works as a maternal and child health social worker for a public health department.

Adapted for SEALS III from LMS VI by Sandra Negley, MTRS, CTRS, Salt Lake City, UT,
author of *Crossing the Bridge, A Journey in Self-Esteem, Relationships and Life Balance*.

EVERYTHING in moderation

Some people believe that anything is okay within limits.

Others believe that some things you can or can't do.

What's your opinion?

Is there a difference between using and abusing something?

Here is a list of people, things or activities that you might use or abuse.

Do you believe that some of these things can be used without creating problems in your life?

When do you cross over the line to begin to abuse it?

People, Things, Activities	Use	Abuse
FAMILY & FRIENDS		
ALCOHOL & DRUGS		
EXERCISE		
FOOD		
MEDICATIONS		
WORK		
SHOPPING		

EVERYTHING in moderation

I. PURPOSE

To develop awareness of controlled use versus abuse.

To facilitate healthy routines and health maintenance by discussion of…
- how one utilizes people, things or activities in a controlled manner, with constructive results
- how one abuses with destructive results, and
- how one may need to seek a different way to manage.

II. GENERAL COMMENTS:

Some people find that the commonly available approaches to problems (such as self-help books, support groups, talking to friends) present solutions that are too dogmatic, rigid or specific to relate to their situation. They may express annoyance as they experience giving up control, simplistic morality and / or one-size-fits-all advice. This activity is not intended to provide any specific answer by the end of the session, but aims at engaging in the process of reviewing behaviors and beliefs.

WARNING: This exercise can be quite confrontational and may not be appropriate for all group settings. Also, students who have connected with a specific group or coping procedure that provides guidance and structure may not benefit from this type of challenge.

III. POSSIBLE ACTIVITIES:

A. 1. Instruct the class, as a group, to provide definitions for the terms 'use' and 'abuse'.
2. Distribute handouts.
3. Instruct the students to look over the list of people, things and activities on the worksheet and to write down what they believe is the 'use' and 'abuse' of the subjects listed.
4. Organize students into small groups of 4-5 people.
5. Have each group select one individual to be a recorder and one to be a reporter.
6. Distribute one more copy of the handout.
7. Instruct students in their groups, to discuss each of the people, things and activities listed on the worksheet. Give the recorder the task of writing down what the students, as a group, determine to be the 'uses' and 'abuses' of the subjects. (Allow for discussion within the student groups as they attempt to define the 'uses' and 'abuses' of the subjects. They are going to discover that they may have different values and beliefs.)
8. Ask the reporters to share, with the class, their group's ideas of 'use' and 'abuse'.
9. Process with a reexamination of 'use' and 'abuse' and initiate discussion on how different value systems play a part in determining 'use' and 'abuse' in some subject areas, giving examples of cross-cultural beliefs that are in conflict with common practices where you live.

B. 1. Bring materials such as scissors, paper, poster board, markers, tape, etc. to class.
2. Instruct the class, as a group, to provide definitions for the terms 'use' and 'abuse'. Discuss how different belief and value systems may affect what is considered 'use' and 'abuse' in some subject areas.
3. Organize students into seven groups of two or more people.
4. Distribute handouts.
5. Assign each group one subject from the people, things and activities list on the worksheet. Consider having a drawing to determine what topic each group will have.
6. Instruct each group to devise creative ways to teach the rest of the class about their subject's uses and positive outcomes, as well as the 'abuses' and destructive results of the 'abuses'. (Suggest activities such as role-playing, poetry, writing a song, making a poster, etc.)
7. Give several minutes for each group to present their subject.
8. Allow for class discussion on each subject after each group presentation. Initiate discussion by asking for additional 'uses' and 'abuses' and consequences thereof. (Discuss topics not covered by any group.)
9. Process by inviting the students to think about the areas where they may be crossing over into the 'abuse' category. Encourage them to think about how they can prevent the abuse and the destructive results it may have on them now and in the future.

Activity handout and facilitator's information originally submitted for Life Management Skills VI by
K. Oscar Larson, OT, MA, Alexandria, VA. Oscar contributed to Life Management Skills IV and V and
is a supportive colleague of Wellness Reproductions & Publishing.

**Adapted for SEALS III from LMS VI by Lisa Kvas, Hibbing, MN,
an academic - career advisor in an Upward Bound program at a Community College.**

GROWING UP CAN BE A PUZZLE

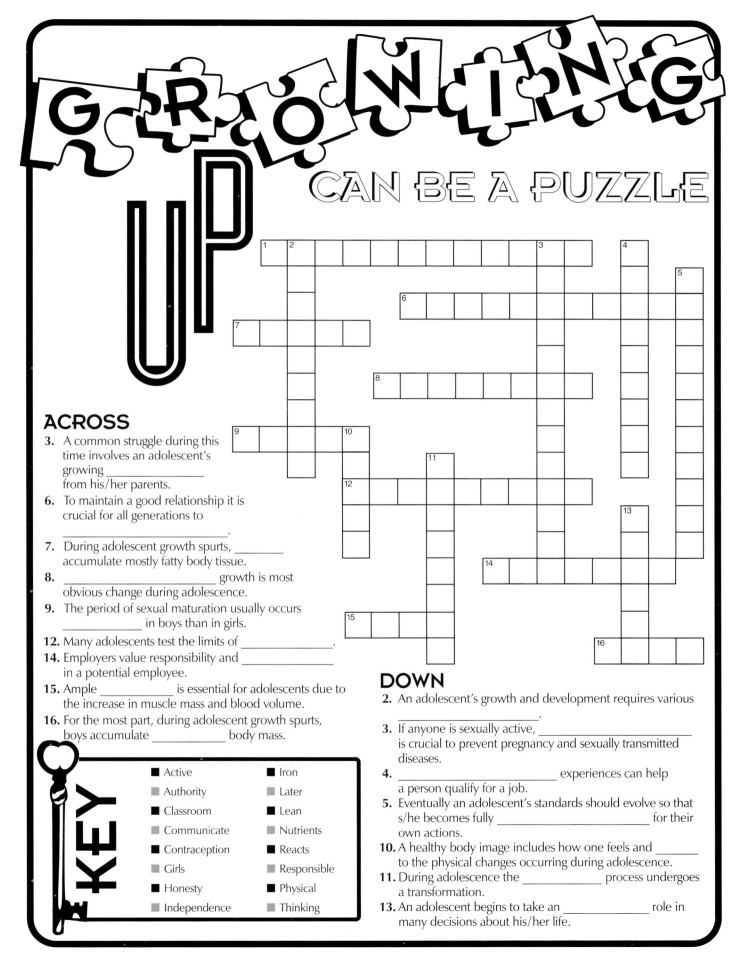

ACROSS

3. A common struggle during this time involves an adolescent's growing _____ from his/her parents.
6. To maintain a good relationship it is crucial for all generations to _____.
7. During adolescent growth spurts, _____ accumulate mostly fatty body tissue.
8. _____ growth is most obvious change during adolescence.
9. The period of sexual maturation usually occurs _____ in boys than in girls.
12. Many adolescents test the limits of _____.
14. Employers value responsibility and _____ in a potential employee.
15. Ample _____ is essential for adolescents due to the increase in muscle mass and blood volume.
16. For the most part, during adolescent growth spurts, boys accumulate _____ body mass.

DOWN

2. An adolescent's growth and development requires various _____.
3. If anyone is sexually active, _____ is crucial to prevent pregnancy and sexually transmitted diseases.
4. _____ experiences can help a person qualify for a job.
5. Eventually an adolescent's standards should evolve so that s/he becomes fully _____ for their own actions.
10. A healthy body image includes how one feels and _____ to the physical changes occurring during adolescence.
11. During adolescence the _____ process undergoes a transformation.
13. An adolescent begins to take an _____ role in many decisions about his/her life.

KEY

- ■ Active
- ▨ Authority
- ■ Classroom
- ▨ Communicate
- ■ Contraception
- ▨ Girls
- ■ Honesty
- ▨ Independence
- ■ Iron
- ▨ Later
- ■ Lean
- ▨ Nutrients
- ■ Reacts
- ▨ Responsible
- ■ Physical
- ▨ Thinking

Growing Up Can Be A Puzzle

I. PURPOSE:

To instill a realistic view of growing up and the special challenges and rewards that can accompany adolescent years.

To increase awareness of what teens face in terms of growth and development.

II. GENERAL COMMENTS:

A teenage boy or girl is not an overgrown child or an immature adult. The adolescent begins forging an identity that is separate from his/her parents. The teenage child continually strives to coordinate physical, intellectual and psychological growth and to develop a fully formed ego identity and sense of self. Adolescence is a time of conflicts, confusion, challenges and changes.

III. POSSIBLE ACTIVITIES:

A. 1. Instruct the class to share their perceptions about becoming an adolescent; specifically, fears, rumors, events that they are most looking forward to or least looking forward to. For example, if 9th grade is the first year in the senior high school, they might not be looking forward to attending a much larger school. On the other hand, they may be looking forward to the increased social opportunities.

2. Introduce activity as a way to help class dispel rumors, fears and preconceptions about adolescence and think more positively about the experience of growing up.

3. Before classroom session, first print each answer from the crossword on a 3" x 5" card. Then print each clue on a separate 3" x 5" card using a different color than the answer cards. Shuffle both sets of cards together.

4. Distribute all of the cards so that each student has one. If there is an odd number of students, include yourself in the activity.

5. Allow students a reasonable amount of class time to 'mingle', to locate the card that best completes the clue each student is holding.

6. After each student has located his/her partner, review each clue and answer, allowing time for questions and discussion.

7. Distribute handouts. Instruct students to complete puzzle in class as a pair.

8. Process by asking class to review clues and answers, identifying information that had provided new information or had dispelled fears about growing up.

B. 1. Distribute a blank sheet of paper to each member of the class.

2. List answers from puzzle on board or project list using overhead transparency.

3. Instruct students to silently read the list from the board, then group together the like or related terms (physical changes, intellectual, psychological, etc.), writing each group of related terms on the blank sheet of paper.

4. Review answers, allowing time for discussion and revision.

5. Based on opening activity, instruct the class to provide discussion topic.

6. Engage class in discussion of positive aspects of growing up.

7. Instruct class to write an original sentence about each aspect of growing up. Challenge the class to use as many words from each word group as possible in each sentence.

8. Ask for volunteers to read original sentences, allowing time for responses and discussion.

9. Distribute crosswords, complete as a class.

10. Process by asking the class if there were any surprise answers.

PUZZLE KEY:

ACROSS				DOWN			
1.	Independence	9.	Later	2.	Nutrients	5.	Responsible
6.	Communicate	12.	Authority	3.	Concentration	10.	Reacts
7.	Girls	14.	Honesty	4.	Classroom	11.	Thinking
8.	Physical	15.	Iron			13.	Active
		16.	Lean				

Activity handout and facilitator's information originally submitted for Life Management Skills V by Barbara Lundberg, OTR/L, Sandra Netto, MSW, and Betty Welch, PhD, all employed at a Geropsychiatric Partial Hospitalization Program in Manchester, NH. Betty and Sandra specialize in geriatric mental health. Barbara has over 20 years experience in community mental health.

Adapted for SEALS III from LMS V by Elaine Hyla Slea, M.Ed., Euclid, OH, adaptor of *SEALS+PLUS (Self-Esteem and Life Skills)* and *SEALS II.*

TAKE THIS QUIZ TO FIND OUT: How do you handle your ANGER?

This is a self-evaluation. Check the statements in all 4 columns that you would say are true about you, at least most of the time. Try to be as honest as you can!

COLUMN A

- [ ] I don't like to let others know my problems.
- [ ] Even when I'm upset, I usually portray myself in front of others as having it all together.
- [ ] If a family member or friend upsets me, I can let days pass without mentioning it.
- [ ] I tend to get depressed and moody.
- [ ] It is common for me to be resentful or bitter toward others, although many people would never suspect this.
- [ ] I frequently suffer from headaches or stomach aches.
- [ ] I often have trouble getting to sleep at night, or I wake up frequently in the night or early morning.
- [ ] There are times when I wonder if my opinions are really valid.
- [ ] Sometimes when I am confronted with an unwanted situation, I feel paralyzed.
- [ ] I usually won't initiate conversation about something that I know is a sensitive or troublesome issue.

COLUMN B

- [ ] I can be blunt and forceful when someone does something to upset me.
- [ ] When I talk about something I feel strongly about, my voice becomes increasingly louder.
- [ ] When someone confronts me with a problem they may be having with me, I am likely to react by criticizing them.
- [ ] No one has to guess my opinion; I am known for having strong viewpoints and letting everyone know what they are.
- [ ] When something goes wrong for me, I may focus so sharply on fixing the problem that I may overlook other people's feelings.
- [ ] I have a pattern of getting caught in arguing matches.
- [ ] I find it hard to keep my thoughts to myself when it's obvious that someone else is wrong.
- [ ] During verbal disagreements with someone, I tend to repeat myself a lot.
- [ ] I have a reputation for being strong-willed.
- [ ] I tend to give advice even when others have not asked for it.

COLUMN C

- [ ] When I am frustrated, I become silent, knowing it bothers others.
- [ ] I often sulk and pout.
- [ ] When I don't want to do something I will procrastinate. I can be lazy.
- [ ] When someone asks me if something's wrong, I will lie and say "no".
- [ ] There are times when I deliberately avoid someone's questions.
- [ ] I sometimes approach school or work projects half-heartedly.
- [ ] When an authority figure (teacher, parent or boss) talks to me about negative behavior, I stare straight at the floor and refuse to make eye contact.
- [ ] I complain about people behind their backs, but resist the opportunity to be open with them face-to-face.
- [ ] Sometimes I become involved in behind-the-scenes mischief or trouble making.
- [ ] I sometimes refuse to do something that has been asked of me knowing it will irritate the person asking me.

COLUMN D

- [ ] I am comfortable approaching my parent or a person in authority to ask questions, make requests and clarify expectations.
- [ ] When I get angry with a family member or friend, I address the issue without letting too much time pass or talking behind their backs. I discuss the reasons for my anger without escalating into yelling or personal put-downs.
- [ ] When confronting someone with a problem I have with them, I talk about how their actions affect me ("I get frustrated when you are late for appointments because it throws my schedule off"), rather than telling them what I think of them in a negative way ("You are so inconsiderate, you're always late for everything!")
- [ ] People around me usually know what to expect of me because I have clear limits and boundaries. They know I will not be "walked all over" but respond to reasonable requests.
- [ ] When I am having a conversation, I make eye contact most of the time and use body language that conveys confidence.
- [ ] I have a clear understanding of what my rights are in most situations, and when I feel my rights have been violated, I generally speak up about it.
- [ ] I don't usually hold grudges - when I have a problem with someone I try to work it out and then move on.
- [ ] When someone asks me to do something that I do not want to do, I feel comfortable saying "no".
- [ ] I am able to disagree with someone's point of view without putting him/her down. I can express my viewpoint and still respect their right to a different opinion. I don't feel the need to argue until I can prove I'm right.
- [ ] People usually feel comfortable talking to me about disagreements or problems they have with me – they know I will not "blow up" or attack them, and I never handle conflict with physical violence.

How do you handle your
ANGER?

I. PURPOSE:

To identify which anger management style one tends to use and to understand the consequences.

To recognize the different ways people manage anger.

II. GENERAL COMMENTS:

One might know that s/he doesn't handle anger as effectively as s/he might like, but be unsure how to respond differently. Anger issues are often scary, overwhelming and even intimidating to approach. A beginning place might be identifying the four different anger management 'styles' and looking at the consequences.

III. POSSIBLE ACTIVITIES: This handout may be used in conjunction with SEALS + PLUS, ANGER MANAGEMENT Module (pages 1-6) and S.E.A.L.S. II, PASSIVE-AGGRESSIVE (page 8, TRIGGERS (page 10).

A. 1. Distribute handouts asking students to complete or read out loud and explain concepts as necessary. Instruct them to complete handouts individually, checking the box for any statement that is true for them, at least most of the time.

   2. Ask students to count up the number of boxes checked in each column. If A's were mostly checked off, they probably handle anger in a passive style, mostly B's, aggressive, mostly C's, passive-aggressive and mostly D's would indicate an assertive style. There may be individuals who have an even amount of boxes checked off in two categories, which may display a combination of anger styles.

   3. Give students definitions and examples of each style and discuss whether they feel they tend to handle their anger in that way.

   4. Follow this activity with COMMUNICATING WITH 'I' STATEMENTS, (page 30).

   5. Allow each class member to choose one box checked off that is most troublesome to them, and to describe to the class what is especially bothersome about this. Ask students if it is problematic only to that class member or perhaps to others in the family, school, etc.?

   6. List on the board, with class input, the consequences of anger mismanaged.

   7. Briefly outline the assertive style and benefits.

   8. Process by asking students the best insight gained from this activity.

B. 1. Distribute handouts and pencils instructing students to complete.

   2. Ask students to count up the number of boxes checked in each column. If A's were mostly checked off, they probably handle anger in a passive style, mostly B's, aggressive, mostly C's, passive-aggressive and mostly D's would indicate an assertive style. There may be individuals who have an even amount of boxes checked off in 2 categories, which may display a combination of anger styles.

   3. Ask students if the style determined by this self-evaluation would be the same style that those closest to the individual would choose/guess for that individual. Ask student to openly discuss the consequences of this style on their personal lives.

   4. Discuss the four ways people react to anger: passive, aggressive, assertive and passive-aggressive. Utilize examples of the different styles using students real-life examples, movie clips, pre-designed scripts to be read aloud by students, etc. or other creative methods to illustrate/demonstrate the different styles.

   5. Process with students the value of this type of insight-oriented activity. Emphasize the value and benefits of the assertive style.

Activity handout and facilitator's information orginally submitted for Life Management Skills VI by
Kerry Moles, CSW, Bronx, NY. Kerry is a social worker and an Independent Consultant specializing in
educating youth and youth workers on issues of domestic violence, sexual assault and independent living skills.

Adapted for SEALS III from LMS VI by Sandra Negley, MTRS, CTRS, Salt Lake City, UT,
author of *Crossing the Bridge, A Journey in Self-Esteem, Relationships and Life Balance.*

Mindfulness INVENTORY

Mindfulness is a term that means to have an attitude of full awareness.

Adolescence is often a journey toward mindfulness. This path is not always easy nor is it a straight line. Ongoing attention and work along with self-monitoring and honesty is required. It often takes courage to stay on track. Go ahead . . . try it! Continue to move with and toward mindfulness. (Feel free to continue your responses on the back as necessary.)

1. What aspects of your life's journey right now excite you?
_____
_____

2. What benefits have you experienced since becoming an adolescent?
_____
_____

3. What drawbacks have you been able to identify and overcome since becoming an adolescent?
_____
_____

4. What/who helps you to stay on track?
_____
_____

5. How are you dealing with the changes in your life? How are other people (your parents/ guardians/grandparents) dealing with these changes?
_____
_____

6. How do you identify and manage your feelings (e.g., anger, boredom, excitement, frustration)?
_____
_____

7. How do you identify and manage stress? _____

8. What strategies help you to continue to develop and improve your . . .
a. physical health? _____
b. emotional health? _____
c. social skills? _____
d. spirit? _____

9. List at least 3 daily activities or routines that enhance your mindfulness lifestyle and describe how each is helpful to you.
_____
_____
_____

 *Mindfulness*
INVENTORY

I. PURPOSE:

To use journalizing as a method to explore experiences and solutions in the process of adolescent maturation.

To enhance students' feelings of competence by being mindful of successes and accomplishments.

II. GENERAL COMMENTS:

There are specific tasks of maturing that include identifying, experiencing and managing in new ways. In addition, there are coping strategies and routines that an individual might adopt and continue to use throughout one's lifetime. This inventory can be done at different times throughout the school term. It is important that an individual identifies and uses his or her own strengths, strategies and solutions.

III. POSSIBLE ACTIVITIES:

A. 1. Ask students to offer personal definitions of 'mindfulness'.

2. Distribute handouts.

3. Ask students to complete the handout as you read each numbered question.

4. Discuss whether task was difficult or easy and which questions were the most challenging.

5. Request that students share aloud the most helpful strategies.

6. Ask students to select three areas of their Mindfulness Inventory of which they are most proud or feel are most important and share with class as able.

7. Process benefits of this activity asking students if this would be helpful to do again and when. Supply the class with additional handouts for future use if needed.

B. 1. Initiate activity with a discussion of automobile maintenance: why it is necessary, when and who should perform it. Include a discussion of possible consequences for failure to maintain a regular schedule and the benefits of frequent safety checks. Relate opening discussion to the practice of journalizing and engaging in personal growth experiences.

2. Distribute handouts

3. Read top section aloud, elaborating on the concept, using information contained in GENERAL COMMENTS section, if necessary.

4. Discuss concept of balance between physical, emotional, social and spiritual coping strategies.

5. Give class 10-15 minutes to complete the handout.

6. Engage class in discussion of handout. Ask one student, "HOW DID YOU ANSWER…?" Explain to that student after their turn, that they may ask any classmate, "HOW DID YOU ANSWER…?" one question that is on the handout, i.e. Martha asks Jay, "HOW DID YOU ANSWER #7, How do you identify and manage stress?" Jay responds with his written answer for #7 on his handout. Jay, then, may ask another student "HOW DID YOU ANSWER…?"

7. Process by asking class to state one area of maturation that is going especially well right now and one area that needs improvement or support. Ask students to describe the ways in which the inventory contributes to a feeling of 'mindfulness'.

8. Ask students if there is a way to use this Mindfulness Inventory to create a daily/weekly plan. Offer additional handouts at students' request.

9. For additional assignment/extra credit, ask students to research origin and details of the 'mindfulness' concept.

Activity handout and facilitator's information originally submitted for Life Management Skills V by Erika Pond Clements, B.Sc.O.T. (c). Erika is an Occupational Therapist and Program Manager in Toronto, Canada. She has worked in mental health and behavioral health settings for the past 12 years and has recently completed a diploma in Addiction Studies.

Adapted for SEALS III from LMS V by Elaine Hyla Slea, M.Ed., Euclid, OH, adaptor of *SEALS+PLUS (Self-Esteem and Life Skills)* and *SEALS II.*

MY LIFE IS LIKE... MY LIFE IS LIKE... MY LIFE IS LIKE...

WHY USE SIMILES?

Similes enliven our lives through language. Similes can be more effective and rewarding than ordinary language. These thought-provoking comparisons create new meanings, allowing you to write about feelings, thoughts or experiences for which there are no easy words.

Certain issues, especially in regards to feelings can be so complex that you have no choice but to use similes.

PLACE a check mark (✓) in front of each simile that reflects an aspect of your life at the present time. Feel free to add additional similes on the spaces provided.

_____ A TREE	_____ A HOT BATH	_____ A FAMILY MEAL
_____ A LOAF OF BREAD	_____ A BASKET OF LAUNDRY	_____ A WALL
_____ A SUNRISE	_____ A BIRTH	_____ AN OASIS
_____ A MAZE	_____ A NUISANCE	_____ A SEARCH FOR MEANING
_____ A FUN HOUSE	_____ A BREAK	_____ A MUMMY
_____ AN ODYSSEY	_____ A HARD HAT	_____ A DESERT ISLAND
_____ A ROCK	_____ A DUMP TRUCK	_____ A BUTTERFLY
_____ A JOURNEY	_____ A HEADACHE	_____ A TORNADO
_____ A SUNSET	_____ A SPIRITUAL RETREAT	_____ A SUPPORT NET
_____ A FIRE	_____ A PIT	_____ A SAFETY-NET
_____ AN OCEAN	_____ A RACE	_____ A BLACK HOLE
_____ A PILE OF LUMBER	_____ A GAME OF CHESS	_____ A HIDE-AND-GO SEEK GAME
_____ A VOLCANO	_____ A MYSTERY BOOK	_____ THE LAYERS OF AN ONION
_____ A PUZZLE	_____ A BOXING MATCH	_____ A TRAP
_____ A GOOD NOVEL	_____ A TREADMILL	_____ _____
_____ A BAD DREAM	_____ A PANDORA'S BOX	_____ _____

I. PURPOSE:

To facilitate self-awareness and self-disclosure.

To identify areas for further exploration and assist in developing a protocol for continued personal growth.

II. GENERAL COMMENTS:

This informal tool is intended to facilitate purposeful self-awareness in a non-threatening environment. This exercise allows one to use similes to describe perceptions of the self. The types of similes may identify the attitude, degree of readiness, insight, level of motivation or resistance a student may be experiencing. For instance, someone who selects 'A TREE, A SUNRISE, A JOURNEY' may view this time in his/her life as a process of growth and exploration and therefore benefit from insight-oriented activities. One who selects 'A GAME OF CHESS, A MYSTERY BOOK' may view self-awareness activities as a learning experience and benefit from problem-solving oriented interventions.

III. POSSIBLE ACTIVITIES:

A. 1 Before session, cut blank sheets of paper into 2-inch wide strips. Cut enough to provide at least 12 strips for each student along with one blank sheet of lined paper for each student's completed activity.

2. Distribute the handouts. Ask the students to review the handouts and to honestly check off the similes, adding to the list as needed.

3. Present directions to the class for creating a "Found Poem." It is so called because the lines of the poem are found within another text (usually a piece of literature). In this context, however, students will be instructed to select the eight most powerful similes from their list that they checked and create an original poem about themselves using the similes selected. Limit poems to no more than 12 lines.

4. Distribute the cut strips of paper so that students can experiment with moving the order of the words, phrases or lines. This technique is often helpful as it frees the student to play with the words to convey meaning rather focus on style. The goal is to capture the essence of the student's feelings. Poems do not have to rhyme, phrases can be used in any order, phrases may be repeated for emphasis.

5. Instruct students to copy completed "Found Poem" on blank sheet of lined paper.

6. Ask for volunteers to share poetry as able.

7. Process activity by asking students to share benefits of similes as a self-awareness tool.

8. With permission, display students' poems as a follow-up activity.

B. 1 Distribute handouts to the class, giving students no more than 5 minutes to complete.

2. Place several magazines on a table in the center of the classroom to be used to make collages to describe feelings of "My Life is Like…"

3. Offer students a few minutes each to describe the similes they found or thought of while working on this project. Provide a supportive opportunity for students to discuss feelings, processing as able, e.g., linking together people who have similar feelings . . . do they have something in common?

4. Ask students to evaluate personal lists and recognize any patterns or themes in the items selected. Inquire what new insights the students have acquired through this activity about the direction their lives have taken.

5. Process activity by instructing the class to reflect on where they need to make changes from this point on.

6. Ask each person to date this work as it may be interesting to reflect back on these feelings in 1 month, 6 months, 1 year, 5 years, etc.

Activity handout and facilitator's information originally submitted for Life Management Skills V by K. Oscar Larson, OTR/L, MA, Alexandria, VA. Oscar contributed to S.E.A.L.S. II and is a supportive colleague of Wellness Reproductions & Publishing, Inc.

Adapted for SEALS III from LMS V by Elaine Hyla Slea, M.Ed., Euclid, OH, adaptor of *SEALS+PLUS (Self-Esteem and Life Skills)* and *SEALS II*.

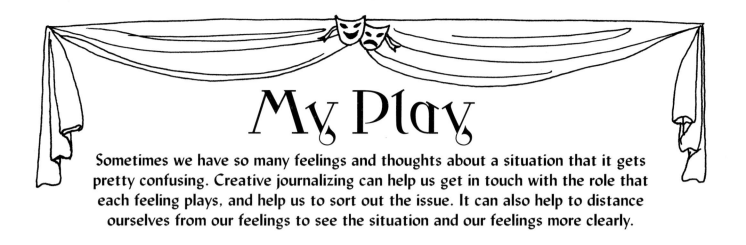

My Play

Sometimes we have so many feelings and thoughts about a situation that it gets pretty confusing. Creative journalizing can help us get in touch with the role that each feeling plays, and help us to sort out the issue. It can also help to distance ourselves from our feelings to see the situation and our feelings more clearly.

○ ○

Imagine that you are a playwright who is writing a scene in which a cast of characters is gathering together for a meeting. The characters are your different feelings, which all have some part in the play. Allow yourself to be as creative as you like in setting the scene. Describe each 'character' by how they might look, dress, etc. Then write lines for each, continuing your play onto the back of the sheet or onto additional paper until you come to an appropriate Finale to the scene.

● ● ● ● ● ● ●   **Cast of Characters:**   ● ● ● ● ● ● ●

Example: Anger, Reason, Fear, Patience . . .

_____

_____

Scene One:

Example:

Anger - a large man dressed in red, storms in and sits at the head of the table.

Reason - well groomed and dressed in a navy suit, calmly walks in, turns her cellular phone off, and smiles at the others.

_____

_____

Example:

Anger - (loudly with a sigh) Well, let's get started. Why is Patience always late? I don't have all day.

Reason - She sent word that she will be joining us a little late today, and that we should get started. Thank you for coming everyone, we're here to talk about . . .

_____

_____

_____

. . . continue with Scene Two, Scene Three and Finale . . .

My Play

I. PURPOSE:

To increase awareness of the usefulness of all feelings.

To introduce the process of sorting thoughts and feelings about a situation in a creative, fun and non-threatening way.

II. GENERAL COMMENTS:

Sometimes we lose sight of the fact that we are complex human beings with many layers of thoughts and feelings, especially when one or two feelings dominate a situation. When an individual loses sight of the other less dominant feelings, s/he may have trouble making rational decisions, or seeing him/her self as a well-balanced person, emotionally.

III. POSSIBLE ACTIVITIES: This handout may be used in conjunction with EMOTIONS© (SEALS+PLUS - page 24).

A. 1. Begin class by asking students if they ever get confused because they experience a number of feelings at once.

2. Discuss how they currently 'sort out' their feelings and are they able to keep their perspective in a given situation. How does this affect the decisions they make?

3. Introduce the topic of journalizing as one method to help in sorting feelings. Ask students if they've used journalizing in the past, what styles of journal writing are useful, and if they experience feelings of being 'stuck' when trying to write about their feelings.

4. Present this exercise as one possible journal writing style to use in situations where they are attempting to identify or 'sort out' feelings. Distribute pencils and handouts.

5. Give students twenty minutes to write their own 'play.' Make it clear that no one will have to share their 'play' with the class, unless they choose to do so.

6. Discuss what the experience was like, What was easy or difficult about it? Did they experience any surprises? What was helpful about using this style? What did they learn about themselves?

7. Allow those students who choose, to share their 'plays.'

B. 1. Begin class by asking students if they ever get confused because they experience a number of feelings at once.

2. Ask whether anyone has experience with drama. Discuss how it feels to play a part — does it allow any freedom not permitted in 'real' life? Do our lives actually unfold as a drama at times? For those without dramatic experience, discuss plays or movies in which characters play a one-dimensional role, e.g., the super hero, the klutz. Discuss how this creates comedy, sympathy, empathy and how the writer and director use this to make a statement about life.

3. Introduce this exercise as a way of identifying individual feelings and developing an understanding of the role of each feeling in making personal choices.

4. Distribute handouts and pencils. Allow twenty minutes for students to complete handouts and write own 'plays'. Instruct students that each will have an opportunity to direct their play by having class members act out the parts written. Allow ample time for acting of the plays.

5. Facilitate a discussion with class of what it was like to act someone else's feelings out for them, and what did they experience when seeing their own feelings acted out.

Activity handout and facilitator's information originally submitted for Life Management Skills VI by
Erika Pond Clements, O.T. Reg (Ont), Dip. Add. Erika is an Occupational Therapist in Toronto, Canada.
She has worked in mental health and behavioral health settings for the past 13 years.

**Adapted for SEALS III from LMS VI by Sandra Negley, MTRS, CTRS, Salt Lake City, UT,
author of *Crossing the Bridge, A Journey in Self-Esteem, Relationships and Life Balance.***

UNDERSTANDING THE RIPPLE EFFECT

Every action, behavior, decision that we make affects other areas of our lives. Identify one of your 'pebbles' and explore how it affects other areas of your life – 'THE RIPPLES'.

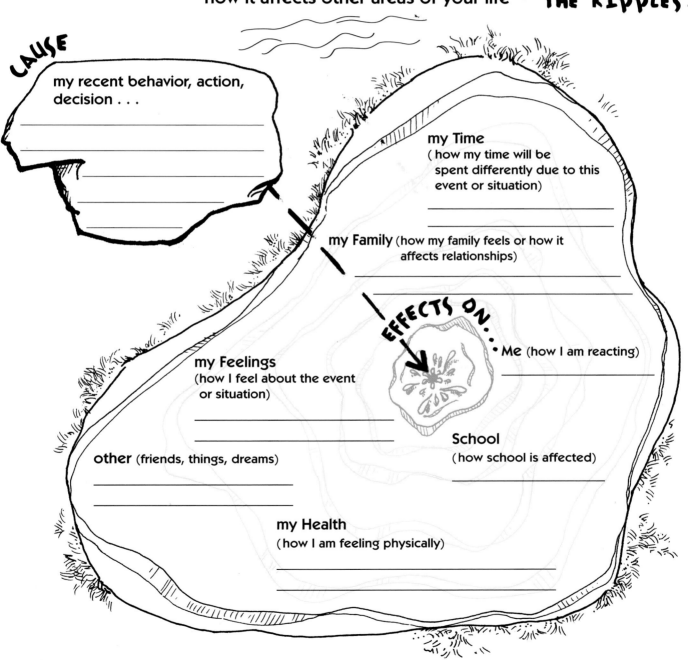

CAUSE

my recent behavior, action, decision . . .

_____
_____
_____

my Time
(how my time will be spent differently due to this event or situation)

_____
_____

my Family (how my family feels or how it affects relationships)

_____
_____

EFFECTS ON....

Me (how I am reacting)

_____

my Feelings
(how I feel about the event or situation)

_____
_____

School
(how school is affected)

other (friends, things, dreams)

_____
_____

my Health
(how I am feeling physically)

_____
_____

What did you learn from the event? _____

Would you do differently next time? _____

I. PURPOSE:

To increase personal responsibility by understanding how actions, behaviors and decisions affect other areas of our lives, directly or indirectly.

II. GENERAL COMMENTS:

Whenever one makes a decision regarding an action or behavior, other areas of life are affected. It is often easy to spot the action or behavior (the throwing of the stone), but sometimes one fails to recognize the impact this has on other areas of life (the ripples). By taking the time to consider the effects before the action or behavior takes place, one can accept personal responsibility and get a better handle on possible outcomes.

III. POSSIBLE ACTIVITIES:

A. 1. Introduce topic of the 'ripple effect' as cause and effect. Produce a simulated pond by taking a small round water container and tossing a pebble in it for all to observe.

2. Distribute handouts and pencils.

3. Instruct group members to complete handouts and review.

4. Process by discussing how the 'ripple effect' is both positive and negative, offering examples from the group or hypothetical ones. (For instance: Fighting in school affects relationship with family and friends and how? It affects school how? etc.)

B. 1. Introduce topic of the "ripple effect". Produce a simulated pond by taking a small round water container and tossing a pebble in it for all to observe.

2. Present topics that may be appropriate to this specific group ranging in intensity to...
   • smiling at new people on the unit
   • offering assistance/volunteering
   • taking better care of my body today
   • cursing in front of others
   • abusing alcohol/drugs
   • being involved in an abusive relationship

   Instruct group members to complete handouts without their names.

3. Collect handouts and then redistribute randomly.

4. Ask group members to take turns reading handouts aloud, giving feedback and guessing original writer. Allow for feedback/support from the rest of the group.

5. Process with the group possible benefits of this type of image work and thinking.

Activity handout and facilitator's information originally submitted for Life Management Skills VI by Rick Germann, MA, LPC, Park Ridge, IL. Rick is a coordinator of Psychosocial Rehabilitation and also teaches undergraduate education and graduate counseling courses in a University.

Adapted for SEALS III from LMS VI by Jennifer Campo, COTA, Bridgewater, NJ.
Jennifer works as a behavioral specialist in child/adolescent psych.

An Affirmation is a GIFT to myself

Do negative thoughts and messages produce negative results and behaviors?

Negative thoughts

and messages we often tell ourselves are . . .

- "I am not worth it."
- "I am not lovable."
- "It's too late."
- "I'd be better off dead."
- "I just can't."
- "I'm too fat."
- "I will never amount to anything."
- "I'm too tall."
- "I'm too short."
- "I'm too skinny."
- "I never do anything right."
- "I am so stupid."
- _____
- _____

What is the result of these negative thoughts and messages?

_____
_____
_____

Do positive thoughts and messages produce positive results and behaviors?

AFFIRMATIONS

are statements about a desired outcome as if it is already coming into reality.

They are positive statements about who we _really_ are. When we begin to recognize the negative messages we tell ourselves, we can then start to re-program them into positive messages by using positive affirmations like:

- + "I am lovable."
- + "I can do anything I set my mind to."
- + "I am smart."
- + "I am strong enough to be who I am."

- + "I will."
- + "I matter."
- + "I am big as I have to be."
- + "My life is important."
- + "I am creative."
- + "I do exist."

Here are a few hints to making affirmations work:

1. Keep them short and simple. **2.** Choose only positive words.
3. Make sure the affirmation fits <u>you</u> and expresses <u>your</u> desires.

Now, it's **your turn to write your own affirmations:** _____

_____
_____
_____

Try positive affirmations . . . they help boost self-esteem • help diminish fears and self-doubts • improve self-confidence • help you see the _real_ you!

An Affirmation is a GIFT to myself

I. PURPOSE:

To increase awareness of how using affirmations regularly can positively influence the way people think and feel about themselves.

To provide practice in using affirmations to counteract negative thoughts, beliefs and behaviors.

II. GENERAL COMMENTS:

It has long been recognized that everyone (and especially adolescents) can one day feel as if they are on top and the next day hit rock bottom. All of us know how easy it is to get stuck or lost in a stream of negative thoughts. What we may not be aware of, is that often these thoughts might have been 'taught' to us from the messages received at an earlier age. A systematic use of affirmations can 'reprogram' self-esteem to a new life affirming way of thought and action. As a teaching tool, affirmations promote 'readiness'. Students are made ready to: give effort, believe that they can achieve, fit in, belong and learn. The need to give and receive affirmations is constant throughout one's lifetime. Hints for teachers who are helping students to create positive affirmations are: Affirmations must be believable. Students especially need affirmations while experiencing change. The need for affirmation never diminishes. Affirmations should have 'no strings attached.'

III. POSSIBLE ACTIVITIES:

A. NOTE: Students are most likely to express negative self-talk during test taking. This activity needs to be scheduled immediately following a test or examination.
   1. Record students' reactions to test taking as you distribute test papers. Also note student responses as you return the graded tests.
   2. Using humor, improvise a brief skit or monologue using only the responses recorded above. Allow students to see the negative messages and the consequences.
   3. Distribute handouts. Review concepts and complete as a class.
   4. Assist class in developing personalized affirmations that meet the interests and vocabulary levels of the students. Instruct class to use blank side of handout to create a positive affirmation using their name, initials or school's monogram to complete one (or all) of the following prompts, e.g.,

   Cathy **L**ynn **A**dams. I am **C**apable, **L**oving and **A**ssertive.

   A dictionary and/or a thesaurus will be helpful for students with challenging initials. If too difficult, that person could use school initials, e.g.,

   East **M**iddle **S**chool - I am **E**nergetic, **M**agnificent and **S**trong.

I am ____, ____ and ____.	I look ____, ____ and ____.
In all situations, I am ____, ____ and ____.	My life is ____, ____ and ____.
I express my feelings with ____, ____ and ____.	I look for ____, ____ and ____ in others.
I have ____, ____ and ____.	I love ____, ____ and ____ about myself.

   Adapt this activity for students with 2 or 4 initials.
   5. Ask class to process activity by explaining basic concepts. Discuss their importance after sharing personalized affirmation with class.
   6. If available, an additional activity might be to purchase iron-on transfer paper for ink jet printers. Using a pre-packaged graphics program, allow students to create and print (in reverse) personalized affirmations. Artwork can then be transferred to students' T-shirts by using a hot iron or laminating press with caution and adult supervision. Schedule a day when students can wear T-shirts to reinforce positive self-talk and affirmations.

B. 1. Bring a glass of water to session. Ask the class, "What is most likely to occur, if you tell yourself repeatedly that you are going to spill the glass of water?" Predicted response will be that you will most likely spill the glass of water. Discuss the outcome if the self-talk is positive. Predicted response might be that the water would not be spilled. Relate demonstration to handout topic.
   2. Divide class into pairs.
   3. Read the statement from the front of the handout defining 'affirmations'.
   4. Distribute and review handouts.
   5. Instruct each pair of students to take 5-10 minutes to ask the other to identify one or two negative messages that they tell themselves or have been told.
   6. After identifying one or two negative messages, ask each pair to take another 5-10 minutes to then identify one or two affirmations
   7. Reconvene and ask students to share the negative message(s) and affirmation(s).
   8. Explain that affirmations can be stated daily (or several times daily) to oneself to become integrated. Problem solve ways of further integrating these positive messages (e.g., written affirmations on index cards, on locker door, making audiotapes to listen to, etc.)
   9. Process the benefit of sharing as validation and the importance that positive affirmation can have in our lives.

Activity handout and facilitator's information originally submitted for Life Management Skills V by Nan Muder, COTA/L, Tallahassee, FL. Nan has worked in acute care mental health and substance abuse. She enjoys occupational therapy in the mental health arena as it provides the framework to address clients' needs in practical and holistic ways.

**Adapted for SEALS III from LMS V by Elaine Hyla Slea, M.Ed., Euclid, OH,
adaptor of *SEALS+PLUS (Self-Esteem and Life Skills)* and *SEALS II*.**

FLY AWAY AND LET GO...

 The nickname or name I was/am called that I hate(d) is . . .

_____

 The part of my body I hate the most is . . .

_____

 My teacher(s) always complain(ed) about my . . .

_____

 A mistake I made that still really bothers me is . . .

_____

 The negative thing I say to myself *most* often is . . .

_____

 The thing that bothers me the most about other people is when they . . .

_____

 The one characteristic I have that I always kick myself for is . . .

_____

I. PURPOSE:

To increase self-esteem by identifying negative aspects of self, as seen by self or others, and 'letting go' of them.

II. GENERAL COMMENTS:

People often carry excess 'baggage' which becomes a heavy burden and can damage one's self-esteem or self-concept. Oftentimes this excess baggage comes from comments others have made about us, particularly in early childhood. Sometimes, this 'excess baggage' is reflected in the things we say about others.

III. POSSIBLE ACTIVITIES: This handout may be used in conjunction with SELF-ESTEEM handout (SEALS+PLUS - page 55.)

A. 1. Discuss the concept of 'excess baggage' and its potential negative affect on personal well-being.

2. Distribute handouts and pens.

3. Instruct group members to answer each of the lead-in questions, after thinking about their current and past experiences.

4. Allow 15-20 minutes for completion.

5. Ask if any group members would like to share their responses and discuss how they impact their self-esteem.

6. Discuss what it means to 'let go' of the 'excess baggage.' Instruct group members to fold the handout into a paper airplane, using the fold lines **✱**, and 'fly' the excess baggage into a garbage can placed in the center of the room.

7. Discuss what symbolism means and process by asking group members how it feels to have symbolically let go of negative aspects of self. Ask group members to consider that maybe, by letting go of the negative aspects, room was made for more positive aspects to be noticed, developed and nurtured.

B. 1. Prepare for group by cutting each question into a strip of paper adding other appropriate questions if desired to have enough questions for each group member. Place in a basket in the center of the table.

2. Discuss the basic premise of the activity.

3. Instruct each group member to take a slip of paper from the basket and respond. Encourage sharing and support for peers.

4. Make a list with the group of possible negative impact of holding on to 'excess baggage,' For example, How does holding on to 'excess baggage' affect relationships? Health? Sleep? Trust? Forgiveness in others?

5. Distribute handouts and pens, instructing group members to answer each of the lead-in questions, after thinking about their current and past experiences.

6. Discuss what it means to 'let go' of the 'excess baggage'. Show the group members how to fold the handout into a paper airplane, using the fold lines **✱**, and 'fly' the 'excess baggage' into a garbage can placed in the center of the room.

7. Ask each group member to explain, in one word, how each feels right now.

✱INSTRUCTIONS TO FOLDING PAPER AIRPLANE:
Fold in half, lengthwise ①
Fold corners down ② to folded end;
Bring newly created corner to folded edge ③
Same corner, fold up to slanted edge ④

Activity handout and facilitator's information originally submitted for Life Management Skills VI by Barbara Lundberg, OTR/L, Sandra Netto, MSW, and Betty Welch, Ph.D., all employed at a Geropsychiatric Partial Hospitalization program in Manchester, NH. Betty and Sandra specialize in geriatric mental health.
Barbara has over 20 years experience in community mental health.

Adapted for SEALS III by Julie Stoelzel, MSW, LICSW, School Social Worker, Revere, MA.

GAINS GRAPH

Putting your accomplishments on paper can help you discover the real you. ALL gains, no matter how small ARE IMPORTANT. Consider the areas below, or feel free to create your own. List them in the column on the left. Write today's date in the space labeled #1. Then graph your gains. Continue to graph on a regular basis. Can you see any patterns or progress?

↺ a goal accomplishment
↺ a positive thought you've had
↺ an improvement in your mood

↺ a new skill practiced
↺ a personal strength discovered or rediscovered

↺ a new friend made
↺ a compliment you received
↺ a small step taken

↺ a treat you gave yourself or gave someone else
↺ a task completed

Areas for Consideration

| #1 Date___ | #2 Date___ | #3 Date___ | #4 Date___ | #5 Date___ | #6 Date___ | #7 Date___ |

GAINS GRAPH

I. PURPOSE:

To increase self-concept and sense of accomplishment by bringing attention to gains made during a short time period.

To recognize the importance of being aware of positive gains.

II. GENERAL COMMENTS:

Gains graphing is the simple act of recording what is happening in one's life. The results of this may be making the hidden meaning of life or behaviors more visible. Being able to monitor one's development may enhance goal seeking, reveal values or beliefs, produce motivation, and create memories for future reflection. There may be patterns worth recognizing in a gains graph. Focusing on the positive gains one experiences may be a vital coping skill for enduring life's tasks in the future!

III. POSSIBLE ACTIVITIES:

A. NOTE: This activity can be especially effective at the close of the school day or the end of a class period.

1. Reproduce overhead on flipchart, board or overhead transparency. Activity will be implemented as two-part process: class and individual gains graphing.

2. Explain activity as described in PURPOSE and GENERAL COMMENTS.

3. Using overhead, flipchart or board, discuss areas of consideration for gains graph. Allow class to decide areas, which, as a class, they will select for graphing and fill in bar graph for that day's gains.

4. Distribute handouts. Instruct class to complete the procedure this time listing personal areas of consideration on the gains graph. Allow a few minutes for completing the bar graph for today.

5. Discuss feelings, difficulties, or any insights gained from working on handout.

6. Schedule a portion of classtime during subsequent class sessions to complete class and individual gains graphs.

7. Process activity after seven sessions by encouraging students to discuss class gains and to share individual progress with insights.

8. Provide additional handouts, if requested, and encourage students to continue gains graphing.

B. 1. Ask each student to share an accomplishment experienced this week. Facilitate feedback if students are unable to note personal progress.

2. Discuss the benefits of identifying and sharing an accomplishment.

3. Ask for reasons why it might have been difficult for some students to share an accomplishment (e.g., not being able to think of one, too embarrassed to mention it, minimizing any actual progress.) List on board, flipchart or overhead transparency.

4. Distribute handouts and provide time for students to complete the block for today only.

5. Divide class into pairs. Encourage partners to share responses.

6. Reconvene and discuss feelings about activity.

7. Ask for possible ideas on how to use the handout for the six remaining sections to be graphed. Consider the support that partners may be able to give during the subsequent sessions. Allow class to decide on a course of action for the handout.

Original handout and facilitator's information submitted for Life Management Skills V by Nancy Day, O.T. Reg., Markham, Ontario, Canada. Nancy is an Occupational Therapist working in the mental health field, within the hospital sector. Her primary goal as a group psychotherapist provides daily opportunity to design and facilitate group treatment. She believes it is a privilege to work in this capacity and witness the 'magic' that occurs as individuals connect with one another and share in each other's growth.

Adapted for SEALS III from LMS V by Elaine Hyla Slea, M.Ed., Euclid, OH,
adaptor of *SEALS+PLUS (Self-Esteem and Life Skills)* and *SEALS II.*

I'm Ready for the World with...

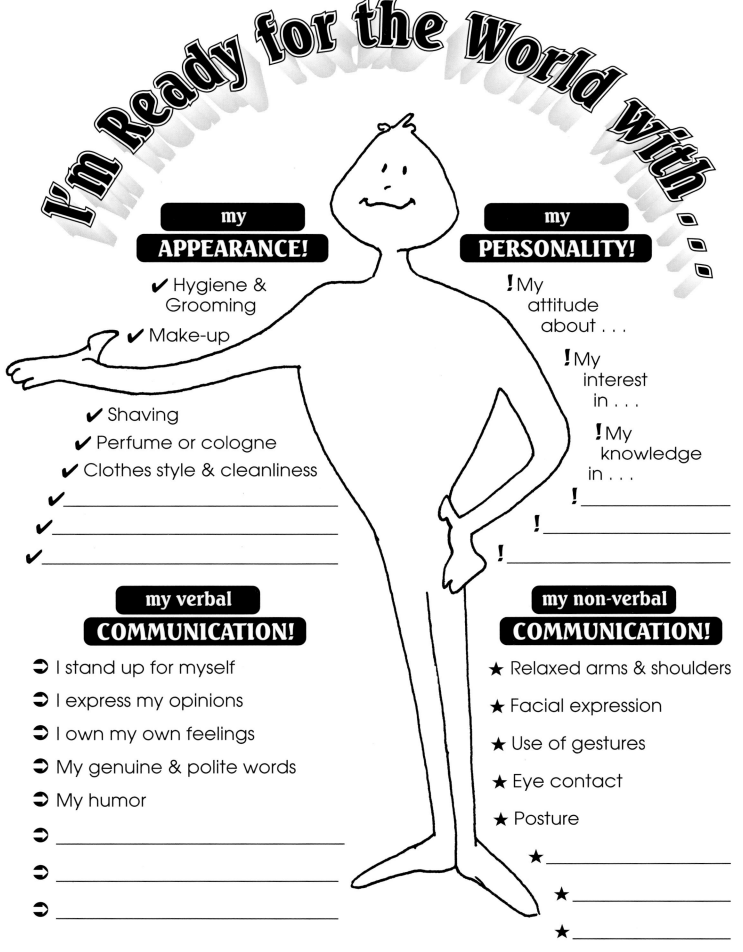

my APPEARANCE!

✔ Hygiene & Grooming

✔ Make-up

✔ Shaving

✔ Perfume or cologne

✔ Clothes style & cleanliness

✔ _____

✔ _____

✔ _____

my PERSONALITY!

! My attitude about . . .

! My interest in . . .

! My knowledge in . . .

! _____

! _____

! _____

my verbal COMMUNICATION!

➲ I stand up for myself

➲ I express my opinions

➲ I own my own feelings

➲ My genuine & polite words

➲ My humor

➲ _____

➲ _____

➲ _____

my non-verbal COMMUNICATION!

★ Relaxed arms & shoulders

★ Facial expression

★ Use of gestures

★ Eye contact

★ Posture

★ _____

★ _____

★ _____

I'm Ready for the World with . . .

I. PURPOSE:

To increase one's awareness of the importance of social presentation.

To increase one's feelings of self-esteem through successful social presentation.

II. GENERAL COMMENTS:

Being aware of one's social behaviors is a vital component for social acceptance. Humans are social creatures who rely on social interactions (relationships) in order to enhance the quality of their lives. However, during the latency and adolescent years many individuals struggle to understand acceptable social behavior.

III. POSSIBLE ACTIVITIES:

A. 1. Distribute handouts and pens.

2. Request that each student review and fill in areas for 'attitudes,' 'interests' and 'knowledge.'

3. Ask the class which of the four topics they would like to address first:

My Appearance

My Personality

My Non-Verbal Communication

My Verbal Communication.

4. Encourage the students to give specific examples of the behaviors discussed. To enhance discussion, use movie clips as examples of inappropriate social behavior or to observe others' reactions to behaviors.

5. Ask each student to identify one behavior that s/he can practice this day.

B. 1. Distribute handouts and pencils. Briefly review aloud with class.

2. Ask students to look at each other and to think about their interactions during or before class.

3. Proceed around the room asking students to take notice of some aspect of another student's appearance, communication or personality that they admire.

4. Have each student describe what s/he likes about that other class member by phrasing it in a compliment, e.g., "Joe, I like how you styled your hair", "Amanda, I like how you help new people around here feel comfortable." If class grasps the concept of the exercise, ask each student to write another compliment on a piece of paper without identifying the other person's name. Read each comment and ask the class to try to identify who the compliment is about and who wrote it.

5. Ask students to review handout independently by next class and to complete all blank sections.

Activity handout and facilitator's information submitted by K. Oscar Larson, OT, MA, Alexandria, VA.
Oscar contributed to SEALS II and is a supportive colleague of Wellness Reproductions & Publishing.

**Adapted for SEALS III from LMS VI by Sandra Negley, MTRS, CTRS, Salt Lake City, UT,
author of *Crossing the Bridge, A Journey in Self-Esteem, Relationships and Life Balance*.**

Time to do an about-face . . .

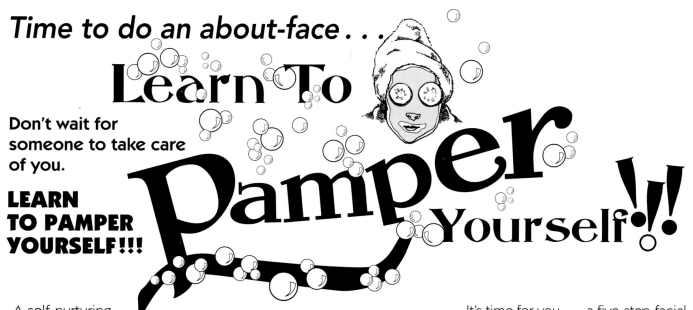

Learn To Pamper Yourself!!!

Don't wait for someone to take care of you.

LEARN TO PAMPER YOURSELF!!!

A self-nurturing activity can really lift your spirits, and it doesn't require a lot of money. You can bring the spa into your own personal space.

It's time for you . . . a five-step facial – like having a spa at home! There are many masks on the market targeted to different skin types, or you can mix your own with some basic kitchen ingredients.

Identify your skin type and treat yourself to the personal facial that works best for you.

○ **DEHYDRATED SKIN:** Mix together: Juice from half a cucumber
2 teaspoons cornstarch
1 teaspoon olive oil

○ **DRY SKIN:** Mix together: 2 teaspoons cornstarch
1 teaspoon honey
A few drops of strong chamomile tea (cooled)

○ **NORMAL TO DRY SKIN: COMBINATION**
Mix together: 2 to 3 teaspoons bran
1 teaspoon olive oil
1 egg yolk

○ **OILY SKIN:** Mix together: 1 egg yolk
A few drops of lemon juice

To bring the spa into your home, wash your hands and follow the steps listed below:

1. Clean your face with a gel or milky cleanser.
2. Remove impurities from your face by steaming the skin for 5 to 7 minutes. Position your face above a bowl filled with steaming hot water. Add to the water a few drops of chamomile oil (soothes) or lavender (acts as a mild antiseptic).
3. After steaming, gently exfoliate your skin: make a homemade scrub of 2 Tablespoons of oatmeal blended with 3 Tablespoons of hot water to make a paste. Let paste cool. Apply using a circular motion. Rinse with lukewarm water.
4. Apply the mask appropriate for your skin type (listed above). Leave on for 15 minutes.
5. Rinse with cool water and apply moisturizer.

TAKE TIME FOR YOU!!! YOU ARE WORTH IT!!!
Manage your stress by taking the time and energy to take care of yourself.
DO AN ABOUT FACE!!!

I. PURPOSE:

To introduce the value and importance of self-nurturing (taking the time to be good to oneself.)

II. GENERAL COMMENTS:

All too often people spend so much time taking care of others that they neglect themselves and/or wait for someone else to do something for them in return. It is critical that individuals learn to initiate self-nurturing activities as part of a process of learning to value themselves. (This is an effective and enjoyable activity for girls, especially those in which self-esteem, stress management and getting in touch with one's spirit are central.)

III. POSSIBLE ACTIVITIES: This handout may be used in conjunction with TREAT YOURSELF (S.E.A.L.S. II - page 30).

A. 1. Distribute one handout, to students, stapled on top of 3 blank sheets of paper.
   2. Discuss concepts of self-nurturing, and barriers that students have to taking time for oneself, etc.
   3. Discuss the need for self-care and how it affects self-esteem.
   4. Write on the board: "How I can bring a spa into my home?" On the board, brainstorm list of possible ways to make this a reality within the students' budget/capabilities. Encourage students to list these on remaining sheets in packet. Include activities such as bubble bath, doing nails, shaving legs, using a hair conditioner, lighting a candle, aroma-therapy, having friend give back rub/massage, etc. If appropriate for class, facilitate mutual 5-minute back rubs with students standing in circle so that all participants get a massage.
   5. Review handouts and assign class 'homework' of giving self a facial by next class time. As part of the assignment, ask students to journalize on one of the sheets, "How I felt before facial," "How I felt after facial."
   6. To end class ask students what s/he learned from this activity. Remind class that they each have the power to treat themselves with the same kindness and caring that they bestow on others.
   7. Review packets next week for journal entries and discuss at-home facials.
B. 1. Prepare for class by bringing or having participants supply the following:
   - ribbons to tie back hair
   - juice from one cucumber
   - bran
   - lemon juice
   - facial cleanser (gel or milky)
   - cornstarch
   - eggs
   - water
   - uncooked oatmeal
   - olive oil
   - honey
   - bowl of water for each participant

   Have access to a sink and a source to heat water (range, microwave, coffee maker).
   2. Introduce topic by briefly discussing the importance of 'being good to yourself.' Distribute handouts and review.
   3. Facilitate the class in the following steps maintaining a fun, casual atmosphere fostering socialization and laughter.
   - Ask students to tie back hair (if necessary).
   - Have students cleanse their faces.
   - Have students steam their faces by positioning themselves over a bowl of steaming water. (This step can be eliminated if no heat source is available for water.)
   - Exfoliate skin with oatmeal paste (see handout).
   - Have each student make own facial mask per instructions on handout.
   - Have students apply mask and leave on face for 15 minutes.
   - During this step, (for 15 minutes) ask students "When was the last time you did something nice for yourself?" and "What stops you from doing pampering things for yourself?"
   - Have students rinse faces.
   - Have students apply moisturizer.
   4. Elicit feedback from the class and generate discussion by asking each student what they learned from this activity.

Activity handout and facilitator's information originally submitted for Life Management Skills VI by Deena Baenen, COTA/L, LSW, North Royalton, OH and Joanne Garofalo, COTA/L, Willowick, OH. Deena teaches occupational therapy assisting and is a field work coordinator at a local college and was a recipient of the Recognition of Achievement Award in Fieldwork Education from AOTA in 1998. Joanne is a school-based occupational therapy assistant working within a private practice.

Adapted for SEALS III from LMS VI by Sandra Negley, MTRS, CTRS, Salt Lake City, UT, author of *Crossing the Bridge, A Journey in Self-Esteem, Relationships and Life Balance.*

A Letter to Myself

Dear_____,

I am a _____ and _____ person.

I am especially good at _____.

If I had to choose two words to describe me, they would be _____

and _____. Other people have told me that I am good at

_____. One thing I would like to do better is

_____, and I know I can accomplish this because

I have the qualities to do so.

Sincerely,

_____

A Letter to Myself

I. PURPOSE:

To increase self-esteem by recognizing positive attributes.

II. GENERAL COMMENTS:

Positive self-esteem is vital in overcoming adversity, may it be a small disappointment, a major setback, or a serious condition or illness.

III. POSSIBLE ACTIVITIES: This handout may be used in conjunction with POSITIVE AFFIRMATIONS (S.E.A.L.S. II - page 59), JOURNAL KEEPING (S.E.A.L.S. II - page 16, GAINING INSIGHT INTO SELF-TALK (Crossing the Bridge - page 20), and BRIDGE OF SELF-CONFIDENCE GAME.

A. 1. Introduce the topic of self-esteem.

   2. Discuss the concept of positive self-talk and negative self-talk.

   3. On the left side of flipchart or white board draw a "+" (positive) symbol and on the right side make a "–" (negative) symbol.

   4. As a class, brainstorm "+" qualities we admire in others or self and "–" qualities we see in self or others.

   5. Give each student a blank piece of paper and instruct them to write a goal (something they hope to accomplish) on the top of the blank piece of paper.

   6. Instruct students to write under the word 'GOAL' personal positive qualities/traits that will help student accomplish this goal.

   7. Ask class members to share their goals and attributes.

   8. Give each student a blank handout as a homework assignment; instruct them to bring to next session.

B. 1. Lead a brainstorming session by asking students to name someone they admire, (family members, popular celebrity, artist, and political figure.)

   2. Discuss the positive qualities/traits this person possesses.

   3. Divide class into pairs

   4. Distribute handouts and pencils.

   5. Instruct students to write a letter to their partner.

   6. Ask each student to read letter aloud to class.

   7. Facilitate group applause at the end of each reading.

   9. Discuss how it is often easier to see and share positive qualities about other people. However, seeing positive qualities in one's self is also important.

  10. Give each student a new blank letter and ask him or her to now write a letter to themselves.

  11. Ask students to volunteer to share their letters with the class.

  12. Invite students to hang letters somewhere they can read daily.

     Additional Suggestion: Make posters of famous men and women. Show posters (like flash cards) to class and discuss positive qualities/traits they admire in these individuals.

Activity handout and facilitator's information submitted by Marla Yoder-Tiedt, MSW, LISW and Sandi Miller, RRT, both employed at a psychiatric hospital in Columbus, OH, with 15 years and 22 years in the mental health field respectively.

Adapted for SEALS III from LMS VI by Sandra Negley, MTRS, CTRS, Salt Lake City, UT, author of *Crossing the Bridge, A Journey in Self-Esteem, Relationships and Life Balance.*

Self-Esteem Road Trip

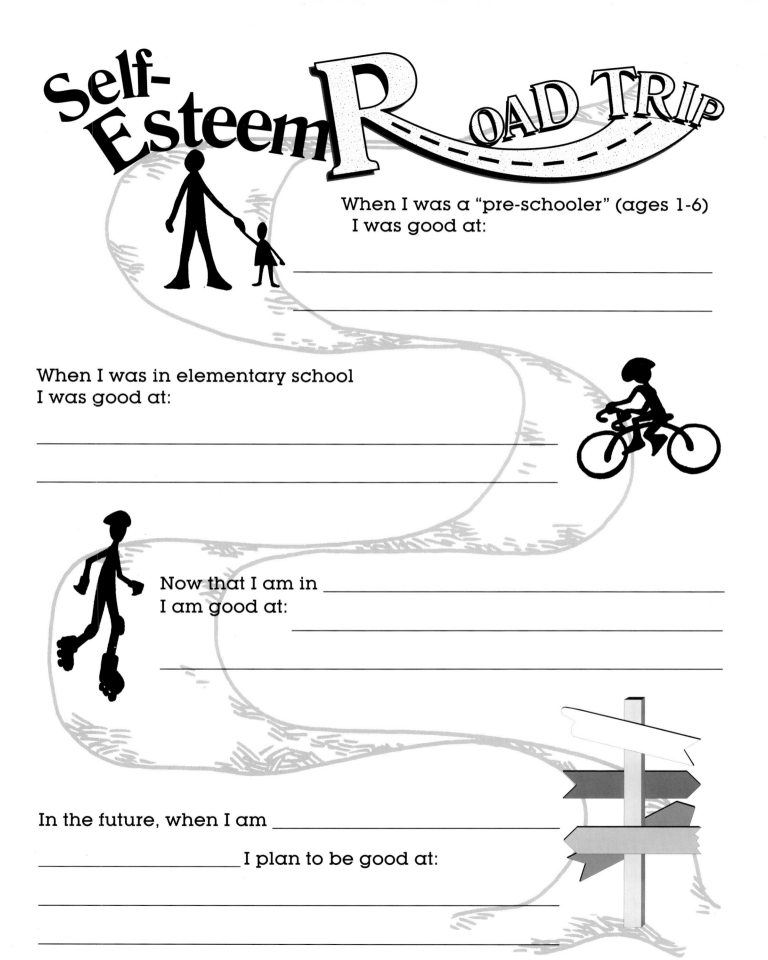

When I was a "pre-schooler" (ages 1-6)
I was good at:

_____

_____

When I was in elementary school
I was good at:

_____

_____

Now that I am in _____
I am good at:

_____

_____

In the future, when I am _____

_____ I plan to be good at:

_____

_____

I. PURPOSE:

To increase healthy self-esteem and self-efficacy.

To practice realistic goal setting based on an inventory of prior strengths and interests.

II. GENERAL COMMENTS:

Self-efficacy is the confidence in our ability to learn, understand and accomplish tasks that are needed to achieve goals that we have set. It also gives us the confidence to deal and cope with life's problems. It is helpful to reinforce self-esteem and self-efficacy by reviewing past accomplishments as well as current strengths and abilities. Comparing and contrasting these accomplishments over the student's school experience can aid in career goal setting.

III. POSSIBLE ACTIVITIES:

A. 1. Before session, bring scissors or papercutter and a timer to class.

2. Instruct the class to share who among the class is excited about growing up and beginning high school and why.

3. Discuss the important decisions that they will need to prepare to make about themselves and their futures before they graduate. Possible answers might include,

   College - *which major, which college, how much will it cost, who will pay?*
   Work - *what kind of job, additional training needed, can I support myself?*
   Family - *do I want to get married and when, how many children, if any?*

4. Ask the class to discuss how they will go about making these decisions.

5. Distribute handouts and discuss purpose as listed above.

6. Instruct class to complete each section and to also write his/her name by each section.

7. Collect handouts and cut each sheet into 4 individual sections and place in a box or envelope.

8. Divide the class into two teams. Introduce them to the game "Pictionary."

9. One person from each team will select one slip of paper and must communicate by drawing the listed accomplishment/goal within a 2-minute time limit.

10. Each team earns 1 point for guessing the accomplishment/goal.

11. Each side takes a turn, giving each student an opportunity to draw. Optional activity: ask writer to volunteer to identify him/herself.

12. After everyone has taken a turn within the class time period, the team with the most points wins.

13. Process activity by reviewing new facts learned about classmates and shared accomplishments/goals. Follow-up with discussion of why process of taking inventory of past successes can aid in goal setting.

B. 1. Photocopy 2 sets of handouts. Use a different color for second set if desired.

2. Distribute first set to class. Discuss activity using information contained in GENERAL COMMENTS section as guideline. Instruct students to complete handouts as able.

3. Distribute second set of handouts. Instruct students to ask parents /guardians to complete second handout using recalled information about the student as able. Instruct students to then compare and contrast their own handouts with those of parents/guardians.

4. Request that students be prepared to discuss activity during subsequent session, paying particular attention to new information learned, differences and similarities of answers between parents/guardians.

5. Lead discussion using probing questions: *How did your parents/guardians respond to this activity? Were your parents/guardians proud/indifferent/excited/ annoyed to share their memories with you? Did you find it easy/difficult to complete this activity with your parents/guardians? How was it for you to hear all 'good stuff' about yourself?*

6. Process activity asking students how this activity can be an aid in career goal-setting.

7. ADDITIONAL SUGGESTED ACTIVITY: This handout can also be used as an 'icebreaker' for any new classroom setting in conjunction with BINGO CONNECTION (page 29).

Activity handout and facilitator's information originally submitted for Life Management Skills V by Barbara Lundberg, OTR/L, Sandra Netto, MSW, and Betty Welch, PhD, all employed at a Geropsychiatric Partial Hospitalization Program in Manchester, NH. Betty and Sandra specialize in geriatric mental health. Barbara has over 20 years experience in community mental health.

**Adapted for SEALS III from LMS V by Elaine Hyla Slea, M.Ed., Euclid, OH,
adaptor of *SEALS+PLUS (Self-Esteem and Life Skills)* and *SEALS II.***

SPEAKING POSITIVELY about others!

I. PURPOSE:

To strengthen the power of self-acceptance.

To facilitate the ability to express positive feelings towards another person.

II. GENERAL COMMENTS:

People who have high self-esteem not only talk and think positively about themselves, but also about others. It is oftentimes easier to find positives in others, before they become apparent in ourselves. The lifelong task of developing and maintaining a positive self-image is essential. A positive self-image strengthens the power of self-empowerment and self-acceptance.

III. POSSIBLE ACTIVITIES:

A. NOTE: Materials needed for activity will include strips of paper, 3" x 14", colored markers, and tape or a stapler.

1. Explain PURPOSE and GENERAL COMMENTS.

2. Arrange chairs in a semi-circle. Place the teacher's chair facing the semi-circle (the teacher participates in the exercise).

3. Distribute a strip of paper and marker to each student. Instruct each student to turn to his/her left and think of one positive statement about the person s/he is facing. Examples are: "Sarah is always ready to listen," and "Mark is wearing a cool outfit." For participants who are well acquainted with each other, ask that a statement describing the person's personality, achievements, or a virtue admired about the person be stated. Examples include, "David plays the guitar like a professional", "Linda is always kind to everyone she meets", "Rob is friendly to everyone." For those students less well-acquainted, more superficial statements will take place.

4. Instruct students to write his/her positive statement on the slip of paper. Allowing a few minutes for completion, ask students to read each affirmation one at a time. Comment on each positive statement and emphasize that people with high self-esteem are people who see the good in others and verbalize this often. After each student reads, the ends of the paper strip are stapled together forming a 'link'. The student who has just read passes the link to the person on his/her left. That person follows the same procedure as described above, stapling his/her 'link' through the previous link forming a 'friendship chain'. Continue until entire class has read his/her affirmation and the 'friendship chain' is completed. Display the chain in a place where all students and visitors to the classroom will be able to see it.

5. Distribute handouts and read aloud. Instruct students to complete the two blank bubbles at the bottom of the handout by the next session and return the handout. The bubbles can be filled with positive statements overheard by others or statements that the students themselves made.

6. Process the activity by reflecting on certain statements (made in this session about others) that included key virtues such as respect, dignity, kindness, sensitivity, etc., reminding students that these are all characteristics of people with high self-esteem.

B. 1. Arrange chairs in a full circle. The teacher stands outside the circle and does not participate.

2. Instruct each student to stand up and make a positive statement about the student sitting to the left and right of him/her. See examples in A.3. above. Write the following three topics on the dry/erase board: VIRTUES, POSITIVE ADJECTIVES and ACHIEVEMENT.

3. List the responses under each of the three topics, e.g., write 'honor roll' under ACHIEVEMENT. Review all three columns and emphasize that people with high self-esteem speak positively about themselves and others, focusing in on the stated virtues, achievements and positive adjectives. Reflect on the POWER of positive speaking!

4. Distribute handouts, complete and process.

Activity handout and facilitator's information originally submitted for Life Management V by Michele Vitelli, Skippack, PA. Michele is a teacher of self-esteem workshops for youth aged 7 to 18. Most of her students are youth-at-risk; however, she has addressed adult audiences on how to instill self-esteem into their children. Helping our future adults feel good about themselves and have pride for who they are, is the core of their self-esteem and the entire basis for her workshop. Currently, she is a graduate student of Education.

Adapted for SEALS III from LMS V by Elaine Hyla Slea, M.Ed., Euclid, OH,
adaptor of *SEALS+PLUS (Self-Esteem and Life Skills)* and *SEALS II.*

Taking care of self is #1

"I realize that to take care of my responsibilities, I must see to it that I take care of myself."

By signing this, I acknowledge the above to be a true statement and will make a commitment to take care of myself.

_____ signature

It is OK to take care of myself by . . .

1. ....
2. ....
3. ....
4. ....
5. ....
6. ....

So I can better take care of my

RESPONSIBILITIES ...

Taking care of self is #1

I. PURPOSE:

To increase awareness of the importance of taking care of oneself.

II. GENERAL COMMENTS:

It is easy to become overwhelmed with everyday responsibilities and lose sight of the importance of keeping oneself emotionally and physically well.

III. POSSIBLE ACTIVITIES:

A. 1. Ask class to define 'responsibility'. Write 'response-ability' on the board. Explain that it is important to have the 'ability to respond' to difficult situations and challenges.

2. Develop a list of varied responsibilities that this specific class might have, e.g., clubs, babysitting, volunteering, homework, church, tutoring, athletics, class or school leadership, scouting, exercise, therapy, family obligations, part-time jobs, etc. Next, list barriers to responsibility such as: feelings of depression, feelings of being overwhelmed, feeling stressed out, acknowledging students' feelings.

3. Facilitate brief discussion of the importance of taking care of oneself.

4. Distribute handouts, instructing students to complete.

5. Discuss responses and process.

B. 1. Prior to the class, develop a small deck of cards entitled "Taking Care of MYSELF". See IT'S YOUR CHOICE (page 5) for additional ideas. Include realistic ways that this specific class is capable of taking care of themselves, considering: cognitive abilities, financial status, community supports, environmental constraints, etc. Examples may include: speak up for self, exercise, sleep eight hours each night, play cards, manicure nails, talk to a friend/support, say "no", allow others to take responsibility for selves, don't focus on the past, journalize, maintain a positive attitude, read, ask for help, be punctual, smile, network, avoid worry, etc. Prepare 2-3 cards per student.

2. Divide class into two teams. Instruct one student at a time from each team to select one card from the deck. Using board or flipchart, encourage students to play the game "Pictionary" to convey the card to his/her team. Students must convey information from card by drawing pictures about the card. Words, letters or numbers may not be used. Give one point to the team if they correctly guess the card in less than two minutes. Give the other team a chance to guess if the first team fails to correctly identify the card. Alternate teams and student 'artists'. Award a meaningful token gift to the winning team.

3. Distribute the handout, instructing students to complete.

4. Discuss the importance of taking care of oneself in order to take care of other responsibilities, as well as setting realistic goals in this effort, beginning today.

Activity handout and facilitator's information originally submitted for Life Management Skills V by Glenda Pritchett, Ed.S., LPC. She is director of an inpatient psych program in Louisiana, maintains a private practice and is a Marriage and Family Therapist-Clinical member. Glenda offers her more than twenty years experience via her daily radio show, The Next Step, and as a regular contributor to SHOWCASE Magazine's Health Column.

Adapted for SEALS III from LMS V by Elaine Hyla Slea, M.Ed., Euclid, OH, adaptor of *SEALS+PLUS (Self-Esteem and Life Skills)* and *SEALS II.*

expressing our spiritual self through Nature

The expressing of ourselves as spiritual beings incorporates **ALL** of our senses.
Think of . . .

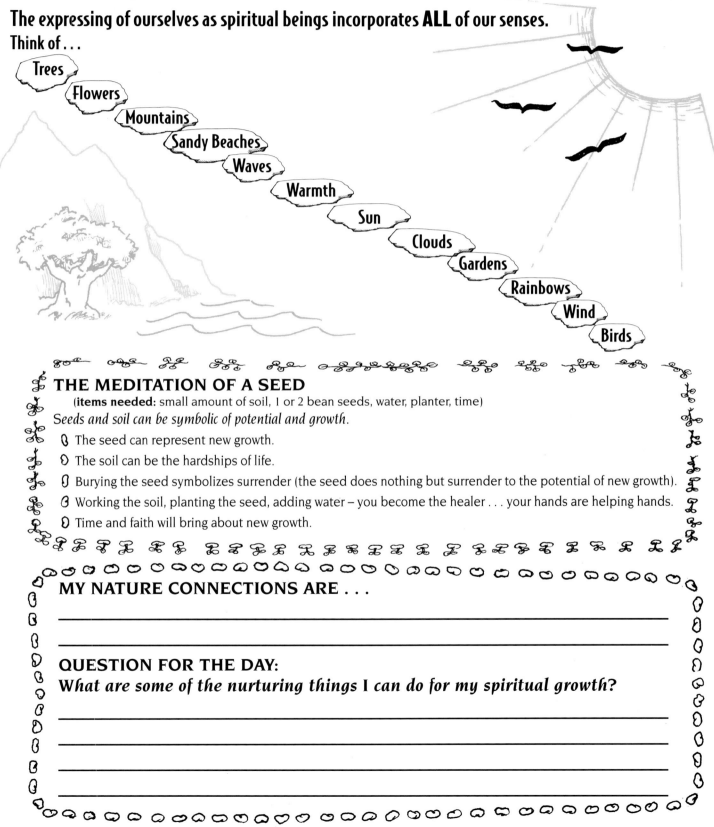

Trees
Flowers
Mountains
Sandy Beaches
Waves
Warmth
Sun
Clouds
Gardens
Rainbows
Wind
Birds

THE MEDITATION OF A SEED

(items needed: small amount of soil, 1 or 2 bean seeds, water, planter, time)

Seeds and soil can be symbolic of potential and growth.

- The seed can represent new growth.
- The soil can be the hardships of life.
- Burying the seed symbolizes surrender (the seed does nothing but surrender to the potential of new growth).
- Working the soil, planting the seed, adding water – you become the healer . . . your hands are helping hands.
- Time and faith will bring about new growth.

MY NATURE CONNECTIONS ARE . . .

_____

_____

QUESTION FOR THE DAY:
What are some of the nurturing things I can do for my spiritual growth?

_____

_____

_____

_____

expressing our
spiritual self through Nature

I. PURPOSE:

To introduce how spiritual symbolism, solace and healing can be found in Nature.

To connect healthy spirituality with the variety of expressions of Nature.

II. GENERAL COMMENTS:

Often students view standard symbols of spirituality and religious objects with suspect and fear, attaching negative experiences or ideas to them. Nature is universal and can be used to redefine and expand spiritual symbols or touch-points as part of the journey of personal growth.

III. POSSIBLE ACTIVITIES:

A. 1. Describe a peaceful place in Nature, e.g., a garden, wooded area, beach, seashore, grassy field, or mountain scene.

2. Explain the concept of Nature as a way/place to feel connected spiritually and to heal.

3. Distribute handouts along with soil, bean seeds and planters. Provide water and instruct group members to plant bean seeds and to water.

4. Review the top two sections of the handout and plant seeds.

5. Assign the bottom section for homework.

6. Process by asking group members to briefly describe the most spiritual place in Nature each has experienced.

B. 1. Take the group outside to a tranquil place or gardened spot for today's session.

2. Distribute handouts along with soil, bean seeds and planters. Read handout aloud. Provide water and instruct group members to plant bean seeds and to water.

3. Provide participants with Native American prayers/poems or those from another culture that describe a connection between our environment and ourselves. (Examples are "The River and the Clouds", by Thich Nhat Hanh and "A Prayer for the Redwoods". These and others can be found on the Internet and/or public library.)

4. Review handouts focussing on bottom section. Discuss 'What are Nature connections' and "What are nurturing things one can provide for spiritual growth?".

5. Divide group into pairs, assigning each pair to discuss one of the two ideas.

6. Ask each person to share one new insight about Nature, spirituality and/or healing.

For one follow-up activity, ask group members to describe a peaceful place you remember; i.e., cottage, garden, wooded area, beach, seashore, grassy fields, hills, mountains. Instruct them to design a place where each felt spiritually uplifted. What would it look like? Where would it be? Examples are:

- a large house with a soaking tub facing a picturesque window
- a bench placed in the middle of a garden
- a small house-of-worship with just one seat

Suggest that group members use paint, markers or a magazine collage to portray their image.

For another follow-up activity, go on a short walk and search for natural objects that are personally symbolic. For example, a smooth stone or pebble, a wildflower, driftwood, seashells, twigs and leaves. Incorporate the objects into a group collage of nature or create individual shadows boxes. Then share about the experience and one thing each learned from the exercise.

Activity handout and facilitator's information originally submitted for Life Management Skills VI by Rev. Donald Shields, BRE., MTS, Markham, Ontario, Canada. Rev. Shields is a graduate of Tyndale College and Seminary in Toronto. After receiving formal SPE training, Donald has worked as Chaplain in Long Term Care and Acute Care settings. He is presently employed as coordinator of spiritual and religious care at a Hospital in Markham, Ontario, Canada. He is married with two teenaged girls.

**Adapted for SEALS III from LMS VI by Robin Teoli, PhD, Martins Ferry, OH,
a marriage and family therapist specializing in children and adult counseling.**

Our Spiritual SELF
...a Sensory Expression

The expressing and healing of our selves as spiritual beings is a sensory experience.

Pictures

COLORS

Shades

Sculpture

Beauty

Music

Touch

BRIGHTNESS

Shadows

Symbols of faith and spirituality can draw us close or push us away. Write or draw in the two boxes below, pictures, objects or symbols that affect you positively or negatively.

POSITIVE - comforting

NEGATIVE - distressing

I. PURPOSE:

To introduce how spiritual symbolism can be found in Arts and Fine Arts.

II. GENERAL COMMENTS:

Often students view standard symbols of spirituality and religious objects with suspect and fear, attaching negative experiences or ideas to them. This exercise can be used to redefine and expand spiritual symbols or touch-points as part of the journey of personal growth.

III. POSSIBLE ACTIVITIES:

A. 1. Describe how spirituality has used art as an expression using examples such as the cross, stained glass, church bells, Star of David or the Yin-Yang circle..

2. Bring in some religious icons and symbols and redefine them as expressions of spirituality rather than symbols of oppression and control. A few examples may include:
   • The Chalice is a symbol of inclusion inviting participants to share equally.
   • The Menorah represents Jewish identity and history.
   • The Buddha represents collective wisdom and thought.
   Elicit other examples, including ALL group members.

3. Distribute handouts and drawing materials, instructing group members to complete bottom section after reading top section together.

4. Encourage an atmosphere of support and acceptance as students share personal drawings.

5. Process by asking group members how to use the insights gained from this activity into their personal lives.

B. 1. Discuss the concept that our spiritual selves can be expressed and healed in many ways; through the gift of sight, hearing, touching, etc.

2. Provide participants with a variety of pictures or slides and have the group describe how each interprets these pictures/slides. Provide for a wide variety using shade, light, facial expressions, colors and animate and inanimate objects.

3. Distribute handouts and drawing materials instructing group members to complete bottom section after reading top section together. Play music that the group might consider relaxing/spiritual, if group desires.

4. Share personal drawings offering opportunity for those that wish to interpret their work for the group to do so.

5. Provide several colorful readings or poems that incorporate vivid symbolism emphasizing the value of bringing forth the visual aspects of spirituality to promote healing, e.g., Maya Angelou.

Activity handout and facilitator's information originally submitted for Life Management Skills VI by Rev. Donald Shields, BRE., MTS, Markham, Ontario, Canada. Rev. Shields is a graduate of Tyndale College and Seminary in Toronto. After receiving formal SPE training, Donald has worked as Chaplain in Long Term Care and Acute Care settings. He is presently employed as coordinator of spiritual and religious care at a Hospital in Markham, Ontario, Canada. He is married with two teenaged girls.

**Adapted for SEALS III from LMS VI by Robin Teoli, PhD. Martins Ferry, OH,
a marriage and family therapist specializing in children and adolescent counseling.**

Writing Our Own Prayer

What I'd like to say to a Power greater than myself.

To assist you in completing this personal project, here are 4 prompts:

To: (can be left blank or even have our own name)

_____

Content: (what's on my mind, what am I concerned about – use an image, impression, picture and/or words, emotions, persons, actions, etc.)

_____
_____
_____
_____
_____

I am concerned because: (how if affects me) _____

_____
_____
_____
_____
_____
_____

From:_____

Mode of Prayer: (silent, poetic, musical, loud, soft, telling the facts, asking for help, sharing, apologizing, grateful, etc.)

_____
_____
_____

Writing Our Own Prayer

I. PURPOSE:

Sometimes we don't pray in traditional ways. But we all can express our feelings, needs and desires in creative ways to find a sense of spiritual serenity.

To connect healthy spirituality with a variety of expressions of prayer-song, drama, poetry, dance, prose, dialogue, silent, loud, angry, joyous and sad.

II. GENERAL COMMENTS:

Often students view traditional prayers or symbols of spirituality with suspect, fear or disappointment, perhaps attaching negative experiences or ideas to them. Redefining and expanding prayer may be inclusive, empowering and spiritually healing as part of the journey of personal growth.

III. POSSIBLE ACTIVITIES:

A. 1. Provide participants with a wide variety of different prayers from various faiths and spiritual traditions. Ask participants to volunteer to read, or read around a circle with permission given for those who wish to pass.

2. Discuss types of feelings — sad, happy, angry, fearful — and how prayers can help us to verbalize how we feel.

3. Distribute handouts and pens, giving group ten minutes to complete.

4. Allow group five to ten minutes to share in pairs or triads.

5. Process group by asking group members to share what was learned in this activity.

B. 1. Read aloud colorful readings or poems that are prayer-like in quality. Provide readings for all group members to read aloud if s/he chooses.

2. Distribute handouts, explaining concept that writing a prayer might be one way to reach a new spiritual level. Allow ten minutes for group members to write prayers.

3. Ask group members to share prayers aloud if comfortable.

4. Discuss the following questions:

   • What sorts of things can we say in prayers and when do we find ourselves needing to pray?

   • What could make us feel uncomfortable about praying?

5. Collect all prayers and compile (if group is comfortable) and prepare a notebook for others (family members, friends, and staff) to read.

Activity handout and facilitator's information originally submitted for Life Management Skills VI by Rev. Donald Shields, BRE., MTS, Markham, Ontario, Canada.Rev. Shields is a graduate of Tyndale College and Seminary in Toronto. After receiving formal SPE training, Donald has worked as Chaplain in Long Term Care and Acute Care settings. He is presently employed as coordinator of spiritual and religious care at a Hospital in Markham, Ontario, Canada. He is married with two teenaged girls.

Adapted for SEALS III from LMS VI by Robin Teoli, PhD. Martins Ferry, OH,
a marriage and family therapist specializing in children and adolescent counseling.

figure it out!

Sometimes, it's hard to know when we are on the path to wellness . . . what is actually helping? Does a certain activity really work? How much? Should I continue using it . . . or should I stop?

One way to monitor possible progress is to keep a record before and after each activity.

Generally it is recommended to try all symptom management techniques for 3 - 4 weeks.

Record your "BEFORE" and "AFTER" responses below.

0-10 scale: 0 = lousy ➜ **10 = great!**

Date __/__/__ Before I _____ , I feel _____. After, I felt _____ .

Date __/__/__ Before I _____ , I feel _____. After, I felt _____ .

Date __/__/__ Before I _____ , I feel _____. After, I felt _____ .

Date __/__/__ Before I _____ , I feel _____. After, I felt _____ .

Date __/__/__ Before I _____ , I feel _____. After, I felt _____ .

Date __/__/__ Before I _____ , I feel _____. After, I felt _____ .

Date __/__/__ Before I _____ , I feel _____. After, I felt _____ .

Date __/__/__ Before I _____ , I feel _____. After, I felt _____ .

Date __/__/__ Before I _____ , I feel _____. After, I felt _____ .

Date __/__/__ Before I _____ , I feel _____. After, I felt _____ .

I. PURPOSE:

To assist in developing an awareness of successful relapse prevention strategies.

II. GENERAL COMMENTS:

Different relapse prevention tools work for different people. It is oftentimes difficult when trying one or more techniques, methods or tools, to determine how beneficial a specific activity is or is not. At times, nothing feels like it is working, but in more careful analysis, small increments of improvement may be happening. Or perhaps it's time to try something new and avoid possible frustration for all involved!

III. POSSIBLE ACTIVITIES:

A. 1. Develop list of possible relapse prevention strategies with class. These may include...

- relaxation/guided imagery
- music
- hobbies
- art
- taking medications
- exercise
- spending time outdoors
- leisure/recreation
- meditation/prayer

- crafts
- dancing
- going to counseling
* assertiveness
- journalizing
- setting goals
- time alone
- eating right/sleeping well
- etc.

2. Explain to class that all strategies may be beneficial to certain people, but most likely, not all will be successful for everyone. A good way to determine effectiveness is trial periods of 3-4 weeks. This is a general rule and needs to be adapted for certain individuals. Obviously, if someone has an uncomfortable reaction in a guided imagery exercise, s/he does not need to try it daily for 3 weeks! An alternate activity may be explored.

3. Distribute handouts and explain concepts offering examples of how to complete. Use the following example or one of your own: Let's say I try exercise, walking 1 mile per day. Before the 1-mile walk, I feel like a '4' out of '10' (1-lousy, 10-great). I'm feeling lethargic, focusing on little things that bother/hurt me. After the 1-mile walk, I feel like a '6', slightly more energetic and less irritated. I record similar results 3 times/week for 3 weeks, and I see that the rating consistently went up 2 to 3 points. I figure I'll keep walking 3 times per week (maybe even more). Ask the group to develop a hypothetical scenario when a strategy was not as favorable.

4. Utilize the handout by doing a 20-minute relapse prevention tool that may be helpful for this particular class. Ask each student to complete the first two sections in the box: "Date and Before...". Encourage students to consider "I feel" in all realms - emotionally, physically, spiritually, etc.

5. After the activity, instruct students to complete the last section, "After..." and discuss.

6. Discuss the benefits of carefully analyzing which relapse prevention tools work and which ones do not.

B. 1. Distribute handouts, explain concepts and offer real or hypothetical examples to illustrate.

2. Allow each student to choose an activity that could reasonably be done in class, that each feels may be helpful in, managing their symptoms, etc. Each class member can be doing a completely different activity. Before beginning activities, instruct students to complete the first two sections of the handout, "Date and Before...".

3. Give each group member 20 minutes to complete the activity.

4. Reconvene after the 20 minutes, and complete the "After..." section of the handout.

5. Develop relapse prevention plans with each individual of 2-3 tools/activities that s/he is committed to trying for 3-4 weeks and record those on handout.

6. Meet one time/week for 3-4 months, calling this group "Figure-it-out." Monitor students' progress and discuss updates.

7. Make changes to plans according to findings, encouraging students to be persistent, even vigilant in determining which relapse prevention tools work and which do not.

Adapted for SEALS III from LMS VI by Sandra Negley, MTRS, CTRS, Salt Lake City, UT, author of *Crossing the Bridge, A Journey in Self-Esteem, Relationships and Life Balance.*

Silly Stress Strategies

Match the 15 "Silly Match-Ups" on the left with the
well-known "Stress Strategies" on the right. Draw a line to connect the correct strategies.

I
SILLY MATCH-UPS

1. Happy Birthday to me

2. Enroll in Turtle Academy

3. Proclaim Yourself a Hero

4. Retire from the Supreme Court

5. Shoot for the Stars

6. Don't Take the Hinges off to Walk through the Door

7. Avoid Leaping Contests with Leap Frogs

8. Go to a Cave, or Lock Yourself in the Bathroom

9. Don't Take Candies from Babies

10. Make Lemonade

11. Plan for Rain on a Picnic

12. Call out Sherlock Holmes

13. Use the Gas in the Tank

14. When Lost in the Dark, Continue to Look for a Flashlight

15. Take a Vacation from your Island

II
STRESS STRATEGIES

A. Give and Take

B. Humans are Social Creatures and need each other.

C. Make the Best of it

D. Plan for what Might Happen

E. Take a Time Out

F. Under Pressure . . . Act don't React

G. Treat Myself Special

H. Use What you Have

I. Get to the Bottom of Things

J. Slow Down

K. Don't Judge

L. Be Proud – Don't Wait for Others to Reward You

M. Compare Myself to Who?

N. Reach Beyond – Have Dreams & Goals

O. Simplify!!

Silly Stress Strategies

I. PURPOSE:

To increase knowledge and awareness of simple stress strategies.

II. GENERAL COMMENTS:

Stress management often sounds like a mysterious and difficult skill to master. However, many stress management strategies are common sense and can be broken down into teachable units. Humor, also used in this exercise, goes hand-in-hand with stress management.

III. POSSIBLE ACTIVITIES:

A. 1. Facilitate discussion with the class around the concept of 'stress' and the importance of managing one's stress.

2. Introduce the stress management skills on the handout as 'silly stress strategies' that are really practical well-known ways of taking care of one's self. Remind the class of the role and importance of humor in managing stress.

3. Divide the class into pairs or triads.

4. Distribute one handout to each sub-group. Explain that the handout has 15 stress management strategies expressed in humorous terms. The 15 'Silly Stress Strategies' are to be matched to their practical stress strategy partner.

5. Give the sub-groups 15 minutes to match the strategies.

6. Reconvene as a class and review each 'Silly Stress Strategy' and the answers selected. Encourage discussion about each strategy.

7. Process benefits of remembering these strategies and re-emphasize the use of humor.

B. 1. Introduce the stress management skills on handout as 'Silly Stress Strategies', practical well-known ways of taking care of one's self. Remind students of the role and importance of humor in managing stress.

2. On a flipchart or white board write all of the 'Stress Strategies' (column II) listed on the handout.

3. Take the 15 'Silly Match-ups' (from column I) and make them into 15, 3" X 5" cards. Write one per card.

4. Place cards in a stack in the center of table, face down.

5. Divide class into two teams, depending on size of class. More teams may be necessary.

6. Play game as follows:

a. Team one draws a 'Silly Match-Up' card. They have one minute as a team to match it with a 'Stress Strategy' listed on the board. If they are unable to match strategies correctly Team 2 gets an opportunity to correctly match strategies. Each correct answer receives one point. Play the game using the idea of a familiar TV game show.

b. Continue sequence until each of the 15 strategies has been played. The winning team could receive some token prize to be shared with all participants.

7. Distribute handouts and pencils reviewing and matching strategies. Discuss which strategies students feel require additional work or implementation in own lives. Elicit specific examples if possible.

8. Process by asking questions:"What role does humor have in stress management?" "Why is it important to know and understand stress management tools?", "How can you use, or remind yourself, about these strategies?"

Matching Answers:

I	II
1	G
2	J
3	L
4	K
5	N
6	O
7	M
8	E
9	A
10	C
11	D
12	I
13	H
14	F
15	B

Activity handout and facilitator's information submitted by Robin Wildbur, OTR, Royal Oak, MI.
Robin has been in mental health practice 21 years — and counting!

Adapted for SEALS III from LMS VI by Sandra Negley, MTRS, CTRS, Salt Lake City, UT,
author of *Crossing the Bridge, A Journey in Self-Esteem, Relationships and Life Balance.*

Ways to Relieve STRESS

blow bubbles	watch a sunrise or sunset	
meditate	do deep breathing exercises	use visual imagery
go bowling	luxuriate in a bath or shower	lie back and watch clouds
take pleasure in quiet-time	listen to a relaxation tape	give of yourself
read a book	prioritize	reflect on the positives in your life
fix yourself hot chocolate	play an instrument	enjoy the weather
make an edible treat	sing or whistle a song	attend a free concert
visit the library	go for a jog	listen to music
	work on a jigsaw puzzle	play your favorite game
write a letter to a friend	write creatively	tear up an old newspaper
see a movie		roller-blade
join a club or group	draw or paint a picture	have a good laugh
window shop	take a walk in the rain	swim or splash in the water
have fun with a pet	talk with a friend	delight in your spirituality
go to the park	take a long ride	light a candle
nap for ten minutes	play a game	finish something
plan your dream trip	catch-up with a family member	reach out to a support
sit under a shady tree	begin a new hobby or craft	count your blessings

Ways to Relieve STRESS

I. PURPOSE:

To explore multiple techniques to maintain wellness through stress management.

II. GENERAL COMMENTS:

Stress is inevitable in our lives. Coping positively and effectively with that stress can be challenging at times. Reviewing choices, expanding options and having a ready-made list of stress-reducing ideas may prove to be helpful in managing stress.

III. POSSIBLE ACTIVITIES:

A. 1. Introduce the topic of stress management as a lifelong skill, one that needs constant re-evaluating and updating.

   2. Distribute handouts, pencils and highlighters.

   3. Review the list of stress relievers on the handout, as a class.

   4. Ask each member to highlight two or three they might find helpful.

   5. Instruct students to add additional techniques to the list by writing ideas in margins.

   6. As a class, share techniques each student selected.

   7. Process by sharing benefits to overall health of effective stress management.

B. 1. Divide class into pairs or triads. Distribute one piece of blank paper and pencil to each sub-group.

   2. Give sub-groups five minutes to identify any stress management techniques of which they are aware. Discuss each sub-group identified and how effective members feel these techniques may be for them in relieving stress

   3. Distribute handouts.

   4. Give one point for each stress management technique they identified that is NOT listed on handout. Token gift could be awarded to winning sub-group.

   5. Prepare ahead of time by copying one handout, cutting each stress management idea apart and then gluing each one to a separate index card to create a 51-card deck. Place deck in a basket in center of table.

   6. Instruct group members to choose a card and answer… "Have you ever done this?
      If so, how did or does it work for you?
      If not, why not?
      Could you use this in the future?
      Would it be helpful?"

   7. Once the card has been discussed, leave card face up on table.

   8. After all cards have been discussed, ask students to identify at least one technique they will try the following week.

Activity handout and facilitator's information submitted by Marla Yoder-Tiedt, MSW, LISW and Sandi MIller, RRT, both employed at a psychiatric hospital in Columbus, OH, with 15 years and 22 years in the mental health field respectively. Assistance with facilitator's sheet - Lucy Ritzic, OTR/L, Product Administrator of Wellness Reproductions & Publishing, Inc.

Adapted for SEALS III from LMS VI by Sandra Negley, MTRS, CTRS, Salt Lake City, UT,
author of *Crossing the Bridge, A Journey in Self-Esteem, Relationships and Life Balance.*

HELP:

IT IS VERY IMPORTANT TO KNOW THAT WE ARE NOT ALONE AND THAT THERE IS HELP OUT THERE IF WE NEED IT.

Below are some ideas on people to call or go to for help. Look in your local telephone directory and find the numbers of the people or services listed below:

1. Parents or guardians work:
Name: _____
(_____) _____ - _____ ext._____
Name: _____
(_____) _____ - _____ ext._____

2. Grandparents:
Name: _____
(_____) _____ - _____ ext._____
Name: _____
(_____) _____ - _____ ext._____

3. Emergency Fire or EMS
(_____) _____ - _____ ext._____
Non-Emergency Fire or EMS
(_____) _____ - _____ ext._____

4. Police/Sheriff
(_____) _____ - _____ ext._____

5. Poison control
(_____) _____ - _____ ext._____

6. Juvenile Protective Services Agency
(_____) _____ - _____ ext._____

7. Local Crisis Center
(_____) _____ - _____ ext._____

8. Suicide Prevention
(_____) _____ - _____ ext._____

9. Your Doctor
(_____) _____ - _____ ext._____

10. Your Dentist
(_____) _____ - _____ ext._____

11. Free Clinic
(_____) _____ - _____ ext._____

12. Your Counselor, Therapist, Case Worker, Mentor, "Big Brother or Big Sister"
Name: _____
(_____) _____ - _____ ext._____
Name: _____
(_____) _____ - _____ ext._____

13. Two friends or relatives
Name: _____
(_____) _____ - _____ ext._____
Name: _____
(_____) _____ - _____ ext._____

14. Clergy, Pastor, Youth Leader
(_____) _____ - _____ ext._____

15. Local Domestic Violence Shelter
(_____) _____ - _____ ext._____

16. Local support group
(_____) _____ - _____ ext._____

17. Legal Aid
(_____) _____ - _____ ext._____

18. To stop harassing or obscene phone calls
(_____) _____ - _____ ext._____

19. Gas, electric or/and phone companies
(_____) _____ - _____ ext._____
(_____) _____ - _____ ext._____
(_____) _____ - _____ ext._____

20. Time and weather
(_____) _____ - _____ ext._____

21. Hearing Impaired TTY
(EMS, Fire, Police or Sheriff)
(_____) _____ - _____ ext._____

22. Juvenile Justice contact person
(_____) _____ - _____ ext._____

23. School
Name: _____
(_____) _____ - _____ ext._____

24. Other
Name: _____
(_____) _____ - _____ ext._____
Name: _____
(_____) _____ - _____ ext._____

HELP:

I. PURPOSE:

To develop a directory of supports and resources for those who may need help.

II. GENERAL COMMENTS:

When feeling down and out, it is often difficult to reach out to others and give others an opportunity to help. During a perceived emergency, panic, anxiety, fear and confusion may impair one's capacity to think clearly. A visual list of available supports can be a handy resource and source of comfort when confronted with a problem where immediate assistance might be required.

III. POSSIBLE ACTIVITIES:

A. NOTE: It is suggested to confer with librarian/information specialist to reserve library time or assistance in collecting directories required to complete this activity.

   1. Distribute handouts and local phone books.

   2. Explain concept to class, instruct students to divide themselves into pairs. Encourage each pair to look up and record all of the numbers of the agencies listed on handout, skipping any personal or confidential information. Those spaces can be completed in privacy with their parents/guardians.

   3. Go around the room asking one student from each pair to state the telephone number found (to make sure that everyone found the correct number). If students are from different communities, allow extra time to list everyone's correct number.

   4. Distribute an additional copy of the handout to each student, instructing class to recopy information neatly and accurately. Request that students complete any confidential sections of the handout with information provided by their parents/guardians.

   5. Review the purpose or function for each person/agency listed.

   6. Problem solve where students can place the completed handouts in home situations.

B. 1. Provide a 5" x 8" index card for each member of the class. Write the following words on a flip chart or board: depressed, isolated, withdrawn, lonely, hopeless, panicked, frustrated, defenseless, powerless and helpless.

   2. Open a discussion of what it feels like to experience these strong emotions. Encourage a further discussion of awareness of possible community resources available, which can assist in times of panic or crisis.

   3. Distribute handouts and index cards. Instruct students to write the following on each card:
Name of agency_____
Address _____
Phone (_____) _____-_____
Contact person _____
General resources available _____
_____
Steps to follow if you need resources personally: _____
Steps to follow if the resources are needed for a family member or friend:_____

   4. Assign one community resource listed on the handout to each student to research by the next session. To avoid confusion, divide class geographically if students are from different communities, or provide the names of additional local agencies, which might be beneficial. Provide instructuction to students on how to use local phone directories, the Internet or other community directories to locate information. Tell the students that in order to complete each index card, it is possible that they will be required to call the agency on their own and interview support personnel. Provide address of school. Instruct students to request that any additional information or literature from agency is sent to the class as part of a resource file for future reference if needed. Ask class to be prepared to present a one-minute presentation to the class describing assigned agency.

   5. Reconvene as a class during next session. Ask students to provide descriptions and details about these services and the benefits one might derive from them. Class should complete appropriate sections on handout using information from presentations.

   6. Ask students, "What is the best place in your home to post the handout where the information can be easily found in a time of need?"

   7. As a follow-up activity, collect index cards and create a classroom resource file along with any additional literature provided by community agencies.

Activity handout and facilitator's information originally submitted for Life Management Skills V by Trish Breedlove, OTR/L, Canton, OH. Trish graduated with her OT degree in 1984 and presently works full time as an occupational therapist. She's a single mother of Bryan and truly enjoys creating and finding solutions that work!

Adapted for SEALS III from LMS V by Elaine Hyla Slea, M.Ed., Euclid, OH,
adaptor of *SEALS+PLUS (Self-Esteem and Life Skills)* and *SEALS II.*

PERSONAL NETWORK PROFILE

Fill in the names of support people in all appropriate roles.
The same name may appear several times.
Then rate how helpful they are on a scale from 0 to 5 with 5 being high.
If a name does not come to mind, leave that category blank.

Support Roles	The person I turn to: (list the names)	How helpful is each person? (scale of 0 to 5)
1. For close friendship		
2. To share problems		
3. To play with		
4. For expert advice		
5. To energize me		
6. As a teacher		
7. When I just need to "chill out"		
8. As a mentor		
9. For acceptance or approval		
10. To help me try new things		
11. When I need a safe haven		
12. For a good social time		
13. When I am hurting		
14. When I need good advice with a problem		
15. When I want to be with someone who knows me well		

A-B-C D-E-F G-H-I J-K-L M-N-O P-Q-R S-T-U V-W-X Y-Z

Look over each of the categories and circle the areas where you feel you need, or would like, more support. Which members of your network do you rely on too much, and which people might you rely on more often?_____

_____

PERSONAL NETWORK PROFILE

I. PURPOSE:

To assess personal support networks.

To develop support systems as a method for coping with stress.

II. GENERAL COMMENTS:

Most of us, at one time or another, will have to deal with some type of crisis in our lives (e.g., personal illness, loss of a friend/family member, relationship difficulty, etc.). Both physical and mental health are connected to the presence of helpful and supportive people in our lives, family, community, and work environment. By developing support systems day-to-day, we will have the support and friendship we need in times of personal crisis or upheaval.

III. POSSIBLE ACTIVITIES:

A. NOTE: This activity can be used as an icebreaker at the beginning of a new term or grading period.

1. Divide class into sub-groups that allow for a small group experience. Distribute handouts. Ask students to write their names on top of handout. Assign questions equally among each small group. For example, if there were five students in each group, each student would then be responsible for three questions, and so on. Students should pair up within the sub-group, switch papers and interview each other, recording responses on each other's handout. Instruct students to ask <u>only</u> their assigned questions from the handout. Remind students that each question has three parts to be completed. Return papers to owner and switch partners. Repeat process until all handouts are completed. (Note: Interviewers will ask the <u>same questions to every member of the sub-group</u>.)

2. Reconvene. Collect handouts. Redistribute them at random. Instruct students to read the handout carefully and then introduce fellow-student to the rest of the class. Once everyone has been introduced, ask students to return handouts to original owner.

3. Process activity by asking students if they discovered that they had 'gaps' in their own personal network profile. If so, encourage students to use new information learned from activity to fulfill search for supports/friends in these areas.

B. 1. Explain the importance of support people as a method for coping with the stress of life as well as crisis situations. Share and facilitate sharing of personal stories to highlight the power of supports/friends during crisis times as well as non-crisis times.

2. Distribute handouts. To assist class in thinking beyond their own personal situation, explain that successful people oftentimes have powerful personal networks. As a class, choose a well-known character, political figure, celebrity, etc., and discuss how that person might fill out this handout (as well as the class can, with the knowledge that is available).

3. Instruct class to complete handout about themselves.

4. Share and discuss. Ask class which items were easiest to complete? Most difficult? Are there commonalities in the class or is every person completely different?

5. Problem solve as a class how to improve the circled areas.

6. Discuss methods of developing support networks.

Activity handout and facilitator's information originally submitted for Life Management Skills V by
Nina Beth Sellner, M.Ed., Owatonna, MN.
Nina is a Certified Personal Trainer and specializes in stress management and worksite wellness.

**Adapted for SEALS III from LMS V by Elaine Hyla Slea, M.Ed., Euclid, OH,
adaptor of *SEALS+PLUS (Self-Esteem and Life Skills)* and *SEALS II.***

APARTMENT HUNTING Crossword Puzzle

ACROSS

1. Straighten up your apartment.
2. The theme of this puzzle.
6. People in charge of apartment maintenance.
11. Room where you cook.
14. Rent is usually due on the _____ of the month.
16. Services such as electricity, heat and hot water.
17. Smaller than one bedroom, also called efficiency.
20. _____ Estate Agents usually charge hefty fees.
24. If you have a car, a _____ space may be extra.
27. _____ sweet home.
28. A person who lives in a rented apartment.
29. Where it is (_____, location, location).
31. One utility almost never included in rent.
32. Utility you need to turn your lights on.

DOWN

1. Some landlords want young people to have an older adult ___-_____ the lease.
3. No _____ allowed.
4. Monthly payment to landlord.
5. Your stove can be_____ or electric.
7. Person you live with.
8. In ad: Kitchen big enough for table/chairs.
9. _____ deposit.
10. In ad: W/D = _____ and dryer.
12. The owner of the apartment.
13. In ad: HHW stands for this.
15. Bath ___.
16. In an ad: This is short for bathroom.
18. People who can vouch for you.
19. _____ ad (where you look for apartments).
21. Agreement signed by tenant and landlord.
22. In ad: this is short for bedroom.
23. Extra features in luxury apartment buildings.
25. You might need pay stubs as proof of _____.
26. An indoor parking structure.
30. In ad: w/ is an abbreviation for this word.

APARTMENT HUNTING Crossword Puzzle

I. PURPOSE:

To provide terms associated with apartment hunting and apartment living.

Answers:

ACROSS:
1. CLEAN
2. APARTMENT HUNTING
6. SUPERINTENDENTS
11. KITCHEN
14. FIRST
16. UTILITIES
17. STUDIO
20. REAL
24. PARKING
27. HOME
28. TENANT
29. LOCATION
31. PHONE
32. ELECTRICITY

DOWN:
1. CO-SIGN
3. PETS
4. RENT
5. GAS
7. ROOMMATE
8. EIK
9. SECURITY
10. WASHER
12. LANDLORD
13. HEAT AND HOT WATER
15. TUB
18. REFERENCES
19. CLASSIFIED
21. LEASE
22. BR
23. AMENITIES
25. INCOME
26. GARAGE
30. WITH

Supplemental activity handout originally submitted for Life Management Skills VI by Sherikaa Swift, Rosarlo Mendez, Weschester, NY and Kerry Moles, CSW, Bronx, NY. Sherikaa and Rosario are members of a youth leadership program of which Kerry is a former advisor. Kerry is a social worker and an Independent Consultant specializing in educating youth and youth workers on issues of domestic violence, sexual assault and independent living skills.

A

Role-Plays

You overhear a friend talking to another friend about the fact that she might be pregnant. An hour later a friend asks you if you heard anything about it. Role-play what you would say.

You find a CD player and decide to keep it. It had no name on it. One week later a friend tells you s/he lost his/her CD player. Role-play the situation.

A schoolmate teases you repeatedly until it begins to make you upset. Role-play what you would do.

You go to a party. The kids there are smoking and drinking. You do not partake. Your parents would not approve of you being at a party with substances. Later that evening, your parents ask you if anyone was smoking or drinking at the party. Role-play what you would say.

A friend confides a serious issue in you. For his or her safety, an adult needs to be informed. How do you approach this friend and make this happen?

You are struggling in school. A friend is trying to coax you into playing or going out. Role-play what you would say.

Your best friend asks to be your roommate after high school. She or he is a slob! Role-play the situation.

You want to go to the dance with your crush but you never find the right moment. She or he is always with another crowd of people. What should you do?

You get into a fight with a friend but no matter what you try to say or do, they always 'bash' you down. Your goal is to keep this person as a friend. What is your next step in regaining this friendship? Role-play the interaction.

You are at a party and someone makes a slur or comment about a race or minority. Role-play your response.

A guy makes a crude or sexual comment about a girl in the hall. Role-play what you would do or say?

A girl makes a crude or sexual comment about a guy in the hall. Role-play what you would do or say?

Your parents are divorced and your father or mother asks you to do something you know the other parent disapproves of. Role-play the interaction.

All your friends are watching a movie at a party that you know your parents don't approve of. Role-play what you would say to your friends.

You like music your parents hate. You feel this music expresses the 'real you.' Role-play how you would deal with them.

Someone on the internet who you do not know asks you to call him or her, give them your phone number or meet them. You are flattered. What do you do?

over

Role-Plays

You get an A+ on a sewing or woodworking project and a friend of yours is not as good at this type of thing. They ask to borrow or even pay for your project. Role-play the interaction.

You witness a friend, who is an average student, cheating on a test. Later that day you see you teacher in the hall and she or he mentions to you that your friend got a perfect score. You feel the stress rising! Role-play what you would say.

You work in the computer lab as a tutor. You stumble upon the school computer password and tell a friend. Something goes wrong with the whole computer system. You are brought to the principal's and asked if you are responsible. Role-play the situation.

You win an award for a sports event. Someone comments to you on how nice the award is. The next day mysteriously the trophy is missing from the school showcase; the school officials ask you if you might know who took it. Role-play what you would say or do.

There is a bomb threat at your school; you and a friend were joking just the day before about how nice it would be if the school did blow up. You are called to the principal's office and told that your name was given anonymously. Role-play what you would say.

Your brother or sister is always borrowing clothes and doesn't return them timely or in good shape. He or she wants to borrow a really nice sweater for a special day. Role-play what you would say.

Your best friend has a habit of borrowing money and 'forgets' to return it. You suspect a drug problem. What do you say to him or her the next time he or she asks to borrow $20?

You want to buy a new computer game. You are short by $25.- and it's on sale now. Role-play how you would approach your folks or guardians to get the money.

Someone at work vandalized something of yours. You think you know who did it. How do you approach that person?

You are driving with a full load of kids in the car. A seventeen-year-old allows a fifteen-year-old, without a license, to get behind the wheel to have fun. You are afraid. Role-play what you would do!

You know that a friend has a drinking problem. She or he asks you if you would like a ride home. What do you say?

You have a friend that you feel dresses inappropriately for school. She or he asks you what you think of the outfit. Role-play what you would say.

Your friend of the opposite sex flirts a lot. She or he invites you to go to a dance. Role-play what you would say.

A friend is driving you home. There are 4 other kids who are also being driven. You need to be dropped off first and at home in 10 minutes. Your parents are expecting you. Role-play what you say to the driver and to the other kids.

You confide a harmless secret to one friend. The next day, the 'whole school' knows. Role-play what you say to the gossiper.

You and your girl/boyfriend disagree on a significant spiritual issue. Role-play the discussion.

B

GLOSSARY

abrasive PAGE: 32
causing irritation

acceptance PAGE: 23
acknowledging as true or as a reality

affirmation PAGE: 64
a positive assertion, declaration or oath; may be said silently or aloud repetitiously for emphasis and learning

anxiety PAGE: 13
an abnormal and overwhelming sense of fear or apprehension resulting in an uneasiness, often accompanied with physiological signs such as increased pulse and sweating

apprentice PAGE: 26
a beginning student; one who is learning by practical experience under a skilled worker

body image PAGE: 39
how one views or perceives his/her own body

brainstorm PAGE: 37
a group problem-solving strategy that involves the spontaneous contribution of ideas from all members of the group

broken record PAGE: 31
a communication technique that involves repeating the same statements for clarification and understanding

camaraderie PAGE: 55
a spirit of friendly good fellowship

denial PAGE: 23
refusal, inability or avoidance to see the truth or reality

diplomatic PAGE: 71
employing tact in a situation of stress

disability PAGE: 26
a restriction or disadvantage; inability to pursue an occupation because of physical or mental impairment

disclose PAGE: 44
to reveal, open up; to expose to view

discreet PAGE: 54
being careful or cautious; showing good judgement in relations to modesty, conversation, conduct, etc.

drawbacks PAGE: 60
objectionable features

eavesdrop PAGE: 31
to listen secretly to what is said in private

emotional abuse PAGE: 53
systematic tearing down of another human being resulting in low self-concept whereby the victim comes to see him or herself as unworthy of love and affection

empathy PAGE: 31
the action or understanding of being sensitive to the experiences and feelings of another

expense PAGE: 28
cost, financial loss

foundation PAGE: 24
a basis upon which something stands or is supported

GED PAGE: 26
General Educational Development - a high school equivalency test and diploma which documents that one has achieved high school skills

gratitude PAGE: 44
the state of being thankful

grief PAGE: 21
deep distress associated with loss

icebreaker PAGE: 31
a beginning of an interaction to break down reserves; may be in conversation or in activity

lease PAGE: 27
a contract by which one handles real estate or equipment for a specified term and dollar amount

(over)

GLOSSARY

lethargic PAGE: 10
abnormal drowsiness, or sluggish, lazy

manipulative PAGE: 32
to play on or control by artful, unfair means especially to one's own advantage

mind-set PAGE: 43
a mental attitude

mission PAGE: 19
a specific task or job with which an individual or group is charged

moderation PAGE: 57
within reasonable limits or boundaries, not in extremes

network PAGE: 80
an interconnected or interrelated chain, group or system; allows for exchange of information and services among individuals or groups

numbness PAGE: 23
void of sensation or emotions

obscene PAGE: 41
repulsive, coarse; offensive

overindulge PAGE: 5
excessive care or attention to satisfy one's desires

pamper PAGE: 68
to treat with extreme attention and care

paraprofessional PAGE: 26
a trained aide who assists a professional person

personal space PAGE: 31
the invisible boundary individuals have relating to their own comfort level of physical closeness

procrastinate PAGE: 59
to intentionally put off doing something

profile PAGE: 80
outline

recovery PAGE: 40
to regain a normal condition (of health)

relapse PAGE: 40
the act or an instance of backsliding or worsening; a recurrence of symptoms of a disease after a substantial time of improvement

resume PAGE: 26
a written summary of skills and experiences typically designed to get a job

retaliating PAGE: 32
to repay as in get revenge

role-play PAGE: 31
a learning technique involving acting out the thoughts, feelings and behaviors of characters and situations

self-awareness PAGE: 48
having or showing a realization, perception or knowledge of oneself

self-defeating terms PAGE: 21
negative or destructive words towards oneself

self-defeating thoughts PAGE: 21
regarding oneself with negative or destructive thoughts

simile PAGE: 61
a figure of speech comparing two unlike things that is often introduced by 'like' or 'as'

spiritual PAGE: 73
a sense or feeling of connectedness one has with the universe, life; part of a person that is conscious, perceptive or aware

technician PAGE: 26
a specialist who has technical knowledge or skill in a specific area

unconditional love PAGE: 55
absolute and unqualified giving of love and acceptance

This is a list of topics covered in the SEALS series! (The Bold Topics are new to SEALS III)

(See the reverse side of the next page for ordering information.)

SEALS+PLUS, II & III Topics	SEALS+	SEALS II	SEALS III	Total Handouts
• Anger Management	6			6
• Assertion	7			7
• Body Image		2		2
• Communication Skills	4	6		10
• Conflict Resolution		2		2
• Coping Skills	6	5	7	18
• Creative Expressions		5		5
• Emotion Identification	5			5
• **Expressive Therapy**			5	5
• **Fear**			3	3
• Goal Setting	5		5	10
• **Grief**			3	3
• Health Awareness	6			6
• Humor		2	2	4
• **Independent Living/Transition Skills**			3	3
• **Interpersonal Skills**			5	5
• Job Readiness		4		4
• Leisure Skills		2	5	7
• **Making Changes**			3	3
• Money Management	3			3
• Nurturance		4		4
• **Positive Outlook**			4	4
• Problem Solving	3			3
• **Recovery**			3	3
• Relapse Prevention		2		2
• Relationships		9	7	16
• Responsibility		5		5
• Risk Taking	3			3
• Roles		2		2
• Self-Esteem/Self-Awareness	9	11	17	37
• Sexual Health		2		2
• Social Skills		5		5
• **Spirituality**			3	3
• Stress Management	4	7	3	14
• Suicide Issues		2		2
• Support Systems	3		2	5
• Time Management	6			6
• Values Clarification	5	3		8
TOTAL ACTIVITY HANDOUTS	**75**	**80**	**80**	**235**

WELLNESS REPRODUCTIONS & PUBLISHING, LLC
A Guidance Channel Company

P.O. Box 760
Plainview, New York 11803-0760
800 / 669-9208 • FAX: 800 / 501-8120
e-mail: info@wellness-resources.com
website: http://www.wellness-resources.com

SEALS Card Games Corresponding to the SEALS Book Series

Use these card games to facilitate development of life management skills with SEALS books! Each deck of cards covers the wide variety of topics in its corresponding book. Since there are more cards than required for a typical 50-minute group session, you can choose the specific topics and cards that would be most beneficial for your intended population and setting.

You can liven up groups with relevant topic cards. Teach by 'DOING'! Use these open-ended cards, integrating knowledge while playing a card game! Each deck of cards corresponds with one of the SEALS books. In the lower right corner of each card is the page number of its corresponding book. Can be used alone or with corresponding books.

FOR YOUTH - AGES 12-18

15 FOCUS TOPICS including: Anger Management, Assertion, Communication, Coping, Health Awareness, Problem Solving, Self-Esteem and more.

Here are some examples from 4 of the other topics:

MONEY MANAGEMENT: *Do you believe money can or cannot buy happiness? Why?*

RISK TAKING: *When was the last time you tried something new that you were hesitant about? How did it go?*

EMOTION IDENTIFICATION: *Describe a situation in which you feel one way inside and express an emotion differently on the outside.*

GOAL SETTING: *What is one of your long-term goals — and what steps are you taking towards it?*

75 cards (Corresponds with SEALS+PLUS)

| PRDW-71343 SEALS+PLUS cards | $15.95 |

FOR YOUTH - AGES 12-18

20 FOCUS TOPICS including: Body Image, Creative Expression, Humor, Leisure Skills, Relapse Prevention, Relationships, Self-Esteem and more.

Here are some examples from 4 of the other topics:

SEXUAL HEALTH: *Why can the decisions you make now about your sexual behavior affect you for the rest of your life?*

RESPONSIBILITY: *When was the last time you had to make up an excuse for your behavior? What was the immediate result? What could be the long term result?*

ROLES: *Who is your male role model in the area of leadership? Female role model?*

CONFLICT RESOLUTION: *Describe a situation from your own life where mediation might have been a helpful tool in resolving conflicts.*

75 cards (Corresponds with SEALS II)

| PRDW-71341 SEALS+PLUS cards | $15.95 |

FOR YOUTH - AGES 12-18

18 FOCUS TOPICS including: Fear, Making Changes, Positive Outlook, Recovery, Spirituality, Grief, Self-Awareness and more.

GOAL-SETTING: *Why do teachers and/or parents sometimes see your progress toward a goal different than you see your progress?*

STRESS MANAGEMENT: *What does this expression mean? "When life hands you a lemon, make lemonade." How can this meaning be used as a stress tool?*

INDEPENDENT LIVING / TRANSITION SKILLS: *Many jobs require you to bring a resume. Ask each group member to share one thing they would place on their resume.*

EXPRESSIVE THERAPY: *When feeling sad, what type of music do you listen to in order to brighten your spirits?*

75 cards (Corresponds with SEALS III)

| PRDW-71342 SEALS+PLUS cards | $15.95 |

WELLNESS REPRODUCTIONS & PUBLISHING, LLC
A Guidance Channel Company

Call for catalogue 800 / 669-9208
or Fax 800 / 501-8120
e-mail: info@wellness-resources.com
website: http://www.wellness-resources.com

FEEDBACK SEALS III

Check the topics that were of special interest in SEALS III:

☐ Coping Skills   ☐ Independent Living/ Transition Skills   ☐ Relationships

☐ Expressive Therapy   ☐ Interpersonal Skills   ☐ Self-Awareness

☐ Fear   ☐ Leisure   ☐ Self-Esteem

☐ Goal Setting   ☐ Making Changes   ☐ Spirituality

☐ Grief   ☐ Positive Outlook   ☐ Stress-Management

☐ Humor   ☐ Recovery   ☐ Supports

Comments on SEALS III: _____

_____

_____

Can this comment be published as an attestation? _____

_____
(Signature)

Name _____   Title_____

School/Facility _____   Dept._____

Address _____   Home Address_____

City _____   City_____

State _____   State_____

Phone (work) _____   Phone (home) _____

Fax _____   Email_____

FOR OFFICE USE ONLY: Order # _____ Date _____

SHIP TO:

First Name / Last Name / MI

Title or Initials / Department

Organization/Facility

Street Address / Suite or Apt. No.

City / State / Zip + four

Phone / Fax

E-mail Address

BILL TO:

First Name / Last Name / MI

Title or Initials / Department

Organization/Facility

Street Address / Suite or Apt. No.

City / State / Zip + four

Phone / Fax

E-mail Address

GUARANTEE: *Wellness Reproductions & Publishing, LLC stands behind its products 100%. We will refund, exchange or credit your account for the price of any materials returned **within 30 days** of receipt (excluding shipping).* **ALL MERCHANDISE NEEDS TO BE IN PERFECT, RESALE-ABLE CONDITION.** *Simply call us at 1-800-669-9208 for a return authorization number.*

Order Code	Quantity	Name of Product / Description		Page No.	Price Each	Total Price
PRDW-71353		SEALS+PLUS book			$ 49.95	
PRDW-71351		SEALS II book			$ 49.95	
PRDW-71352		SEALS III book			$ 49.95	
PRDW-71343		SEALS+PLUS cards			$ 15.95	
PRDW-71341		SEALS II cards			$ 15.95	
PRDW-71342		SEALS III cards			$ 15.95	
PRDW-71390		SEALS+PLUS book and cards			$ 59.95	
PRDW-71360		SEALS II book and cards			$ 59.95	
PRDW-71370		SEALS III book and cards			$ 59.95	
PRDW-71350		SEALS+PLUS, SEALS II, SEALS III books (value $149.85)			$ 135.95	
PRDW-71380		SEALS+PLUS, SEALS II, SEALS III books & cards (value $194.70)			$ 174.95	
PRDW-71340		SEALS+PLUS, SEALS II, SEALS III cards (value $44.85)			$ 39.95	
PRDW-71280		SEALS+, II and III books and cards, Bridge of Self-Confidence / EMOTIONS© (value $255.65)			$ 219.95	
PRDW-71276		WAYS TO RELIEVE STRESS	black & white laminated poster - 24" x 36"	(page 78)	$ 15.95	
PRDW-71218		GOAL FOR THE GOAL	black & white laminated poster - 24" x 36"	(page 17)	$ 15.95	
PRDW-71221		HELP	black & white laminated poster - 24" x 36"	(page 79)	$ 15.95	
PRDW-71223		I'M READY FOR THE WORLD WITH...	black & white laminated poster - 24" x 36"	(page 67)	$ 15.95	
PRDW-71245		INTERACTING & COPING WITH DIFFICULT PEOPLE	black & white laminated poster - 24" x 36"	(page 32)	$ 15.95	
PRDW-71251		PROCESS OF MAKING CHANGES	black & white laminated poster - 24" x 36"	(page 40)	$ 15.95	
PRDW-71284		UNDERSTANDING THE RIPPLE EFFECT	black & white laminated poster - 24" x 36"	(page 63)	$ 15.95	

Method of Payment:

☐ Check or money order in U.S. funds.

☐ Purchase Order (must be attached) P.O. # _____

☐ Visa   ☐ MasterCard   ☐ American Express

Account Number / Expiration Date / Signature _____

Subtotal	
Shipping and Handling	
Subtotal	
NY and OH Sales Tax	
Grand Total	

See below for Shipping/Handling information.

5 Easy Ways to Order:

To expedite all orders include order code above.

① **CALL us Toll-Free:**
1/800/669-9208

② **SEND us:**

Wellness Reproductions & Publishing, LLC
P.O. Box 760
Plainview, NY 11803-0760

③ **FAX us Toll-Free:**
1/800/501-8120

④ **ORDER ONLINE:**
http://www.wellness-resources.com
(with credit card - **secured!**)

⑤ **EMAIL:**
info@wellness-resources.com

SHIPPING/HANDLING

*REGULAR GROUND:

Add 8% (min. $5.95) in 48 contiguous states.

For Alaska, Hawaii, Puerto Rico, Canada and all other international locations; and for rush, express or overnight delivery, please call for rates and delivery information.

Shipments outside of the United States may be subject to additional handling charges and fees. Customers are responsible for any applicable taxes and duties.

*CANADA:

Orders may be sent to Wellness Reproductions and Publishing, LLC, or call for a distributor in your area.

Our Order Policies ensure fast, efficient service!

SALES TAX: New York and Ohio residents, add sales tax on total, including shipping and handling. Tax-exempt organizations, please provide exempt or resale number when ordering.

SHIPPING: Every order, including small orders, will receive our best service. However, a minimum charge of $5.95 shipping and handling must be added to offset the cost of processing the order. Please provide complete street address including suite or apartment number.

TERMS: Purchase orders, net 30 days F.O.B. NY. All international orders must be **prepaid in U.S. Funds.**

PRICING: Prices effective July 1, 2001. This order form supersedes all previous order forms. Prices subject to change without notice. If this form has expired, we will bill you any difference in price.

UNIVERSITY INSTRUCTOR? If you are considering using this book as a school text or supplemental resource, please call our office to discuss desk copies and quantity education discounts.

METHODS OF PAYMENT:

Check: Make your check payable to Wellness Reproductions & Publishing, LLC.

Purchase Order: Mail or fax a purchase order. Be sure to include name of person using products, title, and department. Include signature of person placing order.

Credit Card: Please include account number, expiration date and signature.

UPDATE OUR MAILING LIST: You are automatically added to our mailing list when you order your first product from us. If you want to change your address, remove your name, or eliminate duplicate names from our file, please contact us. Until we correct our duplicate mailing, please pass along an extra copy of this catalogue to one of your colleagues.

PROBLEMS? WE'LL TAKE CARE OF THEM! Call us immediately if you have any questions about your order.

OUR IRONCLAD GUARANTEE:

We guarantee your complete satisfaction. You may return any product within 30 days for immediate refund or credit.